GW00392410

Doomed Interventions

Between 2002 and 2013 bilateral donors spent over $64 billion on AIDS intervention in low- and middle-income countries. During the same period, nearly 25 million people died of AIDS and more than 32 million were newly infected with HIV. In this book for students of political economy and public policy in Africa, as well as global health, Kim Yi Dionne tries to understand why AIDS interventions in Africa often fail. The fight against AIDS requires the coordination of multiple actors across borders and levels of governance in highly affected countries, and these actors can be the primary sources of the problem. Dionne observes misaligned priorities along the global chain of actors, and argues that this misalignment can create multiple opportunities for failure. Analyzing foreign aid flows and public opinion polls, Dionne shows that while the international community prioritizes AIDS, ordinary Africans view AIDS as but one of the many problems they face daily.

KIM YI DIONNE is Assistant Professor of Government at Smith College. She collected much of the data for this book when she was a Fulbright Scholar in Malawi in 2008. She earned her PhD in political science from UCLA, where she was a Foreign Language and Area Studies (FLAS) fellow in Swahili. Her work has been published in *African Affairs*, *Comparative Political Studies*, *World Development*, and other academic journals. She has also written essays for *Foreign Affairs* and *Foreign Policy*, and is an editor for *The Monkey Cage*, a blog on politics and political science at *The Washington Post*.

Doomed Interventions

The Failure of Global Responses to AIDS in Africa

KIM YI DIONNE
Smith College, Massachusetts

CAMBRIDGE
UNIVERSITY PRESS

CAMBRIDGE
UNIVERSITY PRESS

University Printing House, Cambridge CB2 8BS, United Kingdom

One Liberty Plaza, 20th Floor, New York, NY 10006, USA

477 Williamstown Road, Port Melbourne, VIC 3207, Australia

314–321, 3rd Floor, Plot 3, Splendor Forum, Jasola District Centre,
New Delhi – 110025, India

79 Anson Road, #06-04/06, Singapore 079906

Cambridge University Press is part of the University of Cambridge.

It furthers the University's mission by disseminating knowledge in the pursuit of
education, learning, and research at the highest international levels of excellence.

www.cambridge.org
Information on this title: www.cambridge.org/9781107195592
DOI: 10.1017/9781108157797

© Kim Yi Dionne 2018

This publication is in copyright. Subject to statutory exception
and to the provisions of relevant collective licensing agreements,
no reproduction of any part may take place without the written
permission of Cambridge University Press.

First published 2018

Printed in the United Kingdom by Clays, St Ives plc

A catalogue record for this publication is available from the British Library.

ISBN 978-1-107-19559-2 Hardback
ISBN 978-1-316-64688-5 Paperback

Cambridge University Press has no responsibility for the persistence or accuracy of
URLs for external or third-party internet websites referred to in this publication
and does not guarantee that any content on such websites is, or will remain,
accurate or appropriate.

Dedicated to my mother, Chong Hui Kim Shimakawa

Contents

Figures

Tables

Acknowledgments

My debts are many.

None of this work would have been possible without the participation of rural Malawians who invited us into their homes, shared intimate details of their lives, and, in most cases, gave blood samples to test for HIV. The same is true for the survey respondents across Africa who have shared their experiences with Afrobarometer and the Demographic and Health Surveys, both of which I draw on in this book. I would have nothing to write were it not for the everyday people who gave survey interviewers their time, knowledge, and opinions. I thank them for their thoughtfulness.

When conducting research in Malawi, I benefited from the support of affiliation with the US Embassy, thanks to Ulemu Malindi and Pamela Kuwali. I also benefited from connection to the Political and Administrative Studies Department at Chancellor College, University of Malawi, thanks to faculty member Richard Tambulasi. My extended field research in 2008 was financially supported by a Fulbright IIE grant as well as funding from an NICHD grant awarded to Principal Investigator Hans-Peter Kohler (R01 Grant #RHD053781). The California Center for Population Research at UCLA, Sara's Wish Foundation, Invest in Knowledge Initiative-Malawi, and the Globalization Research Center-Africa at UCLA also funded various parts of my field research.

I am grateful to my Malawian research assistants and fieldwork colleagues for helping me collect – and later make sense of – the data used in this manuscript. Kondwani Chavula, Wyson Chimesya, Humphreys Chingaipe, Davie Chitenje, Augustine Harawa, Austine Jana, Francis Kudzula, Eric Lungu, Paul Mwera, Synab Njerenga, Memory Phiri, and the late Fanizo George encountered numerous challenges with me in the field and yet managed to make fieldwork not only successful but enjoyable. I am particularly grateful to Hastings Honde for listening to my ideas and being frank with me about what seemed on the right track and what seemed half-baked. I also appreciate the hard work by research assistants back in the United States: Amanda Edgell, Lynn Hancock, Juliana Mishkin, Jacob Olivo, Amy Polglase, Gretchen Walch, and Mindy White – three of whom went on to pursue doctorates in political science! For the friendship and insights they offered in the field and beyond, I thank jimi adams, Nicole Angotti, Crystal Biruk, Muhammad Chilungo, Pete Fleming, Lauren Gaydosh, Richard Kusseni, James Mwera, Michelle Poulin, Iddo Tavory, Sara Yeatman, and all the other "Let's Chat" alumni.

I am indebted to a number of people who helped shape how I translated what I learned when collecting data into something resembling an argument and evidence. This project started as a dissertation at UCLA and I thank the members of my dissertation committee, James Honaker, Evan Lieberman, Arthur Stein, Susan Watkins, and especially my chair Dan Posner, who pushed me to venture beyond the policy implications of a serious social problem to be a critical social scientist. I also thank Leo Arriola, Asiyati Chiweza, Blessings Chinsinga, Mark Daku, Boniface Dulani, Karen Grépin, Bob Harmel, Seth Hill, Marisa Kellam, Sylvia Manzano, John McCauley, Amy Patterson, Francisco Pedraza, Jemima Pierre, Rachel Beatty Riedl, Tyson Roberts, Laura Seay, Candis Watts Smith, Lahra Smith, Ann Swidler, Peter VonDoepp, and Rick Wilson for their feedback, support, and advice at various stages of this project.

Drafts from this work were presented at the Better Governance for Better Health Conference at Stanford University, the Princeton AIDS Initiative, a Working Group in African Political Economy Meeting, the 2009 meeting of the American Political Science Association, a 2011 conference at Mount Holyoke College on Corruption and the Pursuit of Accountability in Africa, the 2015 African Studies Association annual meeting, and invited talks at UNC-Charlotte, Middlebury College, and Johns Hopkins/SAIS. I thank participants – especially Beth Whitaker, Sarah Stroup, and Dan Konig – for useful feedback. I am also grateful to Zulema Valdez and Tanya Golash-Boza for inviting me to the Creative Connections Retreat in Yosemite National Park in 2016, when I made critical progress on this project.

Much of the writing for this book happened after I joined the faculty at Smith College. Luck would have it that another colleague was writing a book about principal–agent problems at the same time; Brent Durbin shared helpful insights about the book's arguments and his family has been a great reminder to me and mine about what's really important in life. Monday morning write-on-sites at the Lewis Global

Studies Center and Wednesday writing retreats in the Bechtel Environmental Classroom at the MacLeish Field Station gave me (regular) space to get 'er done. Fellow writers Carrie Baker, Holly Hanson, Liz Klarich, and Regine Spector helped me keep my eyes on the prize. College support via a Picker Fellowship and Connexions grant facilitated the time and attention needed to finish the book. Crucial feedback from Adia Benton and Jenny Trinitapoli who read entire drafts as the book neared completion greatly improved the manuscript. Adia Benton, Mlada Bukovansky, Brent Durbin, Elliot Fratkin, Howard Gold, Holly Hanson, Alice Hearst, Zaza Kabayadondo, and Greg White participated in a book workshop at Smith where they all helped me to sharpen the argument and tell the story I wanted people to learn. Also helpful was the feedback I received from students enrolled in my Spring 2016 course on AIDS in Africa.

My editor at Cambridge University Press, Maria Marsh, has always been a light of hope in the darkness only first-time book authors know. I thank her for her support of this project. I also thank the three anonymous referees who gave critical, thorough reviews of the manuscript. Of course, only I retain responsibility for the arguments and evidence presented in the book.

Finally, I would like to thank my family for their support in this endeavor. I met Josh during my first visit to Malawi in 2006 and because of his belief in my work, he took a leap of faith with me in bringing our young daughter Kezia to live for seven months in a country where many children don't see their fifth birthday. Both of them gave me something to look forward to at the end of a long day's work collecting data. Amayi Malaya took great care of the three of us and Kezia especially, allowing both Josh and I to get work done. Josh's mother Angela (aka "Oma") pitched in more times than I can count when we returned to the United States. Josh, Kezia, and later Asher gave me space to work on this project and good reason to set it aside from time to time. My sister from another mister, Noelia Ochoa, has always supported me and my work, and for all she has given me, I can never give enough thanks. Perhaps my greatest debt is to my mother, Chong Hui Kim Shimakawa, who was rather nervous about my decision to go and study a place she knew very little about. Her own ambitions to venture beyond her rural Korean village about four decades ago inspired me to seek more than that available in the small farming community where I grew up. It is to her and her dreams of my success that I dedicate this book.

1 | *Misaligned Priorities: How Disconnect between Donors and Citizens Doomed AIDS Intervention in Africa*

Even the group that is looking after sick people in this village do not really know everyone who has HIV ... I feel it is important that the village headman and other people should know because say if you want to marry someone, you have an idea of what is going on with them. If you get sick, other people will have an idea of how to address your sickness.

Headman Interview #155, Balaka District, August 27, 2009

He repeated his question, "Why won't you list the names of everyone who tests positive?" He went on, suggesting the list could be kept by a respected elder in the village who would advise others on how to avoid infection. Glory, my Tanzanian teaching partner, retranslated the question, trying even simpler English words the second time to convey what the *mzee* (elder) at this community meeting in a rural village in Arumeru District was asking. But I understood his question perfectly the first time he asked it. My silence was not because I did not understand the question. My silence was a manifestation of my not understanding how we had failed to convince the most powerful people in this community of the importance of confidentiality in human immunodeficiency virus (HIV) testing.

After completing my first year in graduate school in 2004, I volunteered with a small nongovernmental organization (NGO) that coordinated partnerships between American university students and recent graduates of Tanzanian secondary schools to provide HIV awareness education in schools, and at large community gatherings. The village meeting where this *mzee* asked his question was a culmination of our efforts in the area following weeks of working in the local schools teaching HIV epidemiology and the current best practices for avoiding HIV infection. Previous volunteers were positive about these village meetings, characterizing them as celebrations marked with community acceptance of the knowledge imparted by well-trained volunteers. Of course, it is easy today to see the warts of this NGO's approach to HIV/acquired immunodeficiency syndrome (AIDS) intervention and the naïvete of its volunteers, myself included.

The *mzee*'s question that day has stayed with me. For a long time, I regarded it as a failure: we had failed to change the minds of men and women in Arumeru to match our own ideas about how to respond to AIDS. Only after much learning and thinking did I take a new lesson from his question. In asking that the HIV status of villagers be publicized, he was offering a public health solution that could prevent the spread of HIV. This chapter's epigraph captures a similar sentiment from a village headman in Malawi. Our rejection of the *mzee*'s proposal in Arumeru, Tanzania, in 2004 is consistent with many AIDS interventions I have witnessed and studied over the last decade: interventions are often funded and designed from afar and rarely engage influential people at the grassroots in shaping the nature of the intervention. In short, the people navigating the AIDS epidemic are objects to whom interventions are targeted. What this *mzee* was trying to demonstrate to me was that people navigating the AIDS epidemic also had ideas for intervention design. More simply, they had opinions on AIDS interventions.

AIDS has hit hardest in the young democracies of East and Southern Africa and a significant chunk of the funding for AIDS interventions is spent there. Yet these interventions do not reflect the opinions or ideas of their "intended beneficiaries." As this book will show, citizens and key decision-makers in the global community diverge on how AIDS interventions should be prioritized vis-à-vis other pressing policy issues. The significant threat AIDS poses to public health requires a strong response. However, failing to consider the ideas and opinions of African citizens in AIDS response could also take its toll. By privileging donor priorities over citizen priorities, global elites cripple states' abilities to implement policies representing citizens' interests. It is no small irony that the West has called for democratization in Africa while at the same time failing to recognize its interventions – like those against AIDS – undermine the fundamental democratic principles of citizen participation and representation.

Readers should not see this book as a pessimistic, misanthropic take on AIDS response in Africa. Rather, looking at our failures to improve the human condition can help us formulate better strategies and approaches going forward. Whether one's goal is fighting AIDS in Africa or poverty in your neighborhood, we must ask what the failures were in previous attempts. As my experience with the *mzee* in 2004 should show and as this book will argue, we must also ask and listen to the opinions and priorities of the ordinary people to whom interventions are targeted.

* * *

AIDS is one of the leading causes of death in the world and is the top cause of death in Africa.[1] In 2016, UNAIDS estimated 1 million people died of AIDS.[2] In the same year, another 1.9 million people were newly infected with HIV. There are 36.7 million people with HIV in the world and more than two-thirds of them live in Africa. Only 54% of AIDS patients in Africa needing treatment have access to it.[3]

Billions of dollars have been spent to curb the AIDS epidemic. Donor governments spent $8.6 billion in 2014 alone on anti-AIDS initiatives (Kates, Wexler and Lief, 2015). While this outpouring has had a tremendous impact – particularly in increasing treatment access in resource-poor countries – many donor-supported AIDS interventions have shown little objective impact on stemming the spread of HIV and bettering the lives of those affected by AIDS. For example, between 1997 and 2006, only 18% of projects in the World Bank's African Multicountry AIDS Program had satisfactory outcomes according to internal evaluations (Independent Evaluation Group, 2009, 38). When a mobilized international community commits billions of dollars to fight a disease, what impedes its efforts to improve outcomes for intended beneficiaries?

In this book, I identify obstacles in AIDS interventions. Scholars, journalists, and activists have pointed to insufficient political will and financial resources.[4] But there is little variation in governments'

---

[1] HIV/AIDS was the cause of 11.7% of deaths in Africa in 2013; the next highest cause of death was lower respiratory infection, which accounted for 9.1% of deaths (Institute for Health Metrics and Evaluation, 2015).

[2] Statistics come from AIDSinfo, a data portal managed by UNAIDS at http://aidsinfo.unaids.org (UNAIDS, 2017).

[3] Author's calculations are based on UNAIDS data. It is important to note the significant variation across African countries. While 80% of HIV-positive Rwandans are reported to be accessing treatment, only 30% of HIV-positive Nigerians are on treatment.

[4] On the lack of political will, see Campbell (2003) and de Waal (2006). See Attaran and Sachs (2001) and Stover et al. (2002) for calls for greater financial resources.

"political will" to fight AIDS and the global response to AIDS is one of the most heavily financed interventions to improve the human condition. Surely, political will and resource constraints are insufficient explanations for why many AIDS interventions have so little impact on improving the lives of their intended beneficiaries. I argue the critical characteristic challenging the global intervention against AIDS is its reliance on many actors to deliver the response.

① Too many actors involved / long chain of connections

More specifically, I argue the global intervention against AIDS in Africa has faced two related challenges. First, the global intervention's many actors complicate response. Decision-makers in corridors of power design interventions and then delegate responsibilities to faraway agents who ultimately shape the intensity and efficacy of response. These global interventions require coordination of multiple actors, not just across borders, but also across levels of governance within target countries. I show that delegating implementation across multiple levels of governance is ineffective, and in the worst-case scenarios creates opportunities for corruption.

② misaligned priorities

Second, the many actors involved in the global AIDS intervention – from international organizations making record financial commitments for fighting AIDS to the ordinary people themselves navigating AIDS in Africa – have misaligned priorities. One might expect that because AIDS is so devastating, there would be a global alignment of preferences: everyone wants good public health and AIDS is a serious threat locally and globally to public health. However, using public opinion survey data I join a growing chorus of scholars who show that Africans do not prioritize HIV/AIDS intervention, even in the world's worst affected countries. Unlike Western donors who highly prioritize AIDS interventions in Africa, citizens in African countries view AIDS as one of many problems they face and give it relatively less priority.

Misaligned priorities across the global supply chain of AIDS intervention make space for resources to be used in ways they weren't intended. For example, elites near the top of the global hierarchy can mismanage funds with little concern that their stewardship is being monitored by intended beneficiaries because citizens are focusing on other pressing issues. Likewise, agents implementing AIDS interventions may reappropriate or redirect resources toward issues more salient to themselves and more salient to the interventions' intended beneficiaries. In both of these scenarios, we would expect the resources intended for HIV/AIDS programming not having any impact on stemming the tide of the epidemic.

This book examines the disconnect between actors in the global intervention against AIDS in Africa. It focuses on how agents implementing interventions are pulled in different directions by two competing principals: the external donors funding interventions and the ordinary citizens who are the "intended beneficiaries" from whom local agents derive their legitimacy. When these two important constituencies have misaligned priorities, whose policy preferences will prevail? In a field mostly concerned with national-level policymaking, my research expands earlier scholarship on HIV/AIDS policy intervention by shifting perspective from international agency headquarters or state houses in African capitals to villages and peri-urban trading centers where agents are actually implementing programs at the grassroots.

While this is a book about AIDS in Africa, it is at the same time a book highlighting the challenges faced by health and development interventions in poor countries more broadly. The framework used here could be applied, for example, to interventions against famine. Like famine, AIDS is often seen as a problem particularly endemic to Africa and triggers a "humanitarian" response from the global community that then involves multiple countries and multiple levels of government to assess needs, deliver aid, and measure impact. Often the local reality of a humanitarian intervention is disjointed from how it was imagined in global corridors of power. Likewise, there is often a disconnect between the aid given and the needs and desires of intended beneficiaries. Like with AIDS, critical examination of famine interventions is met with counterfactual critiques that doing something is surely better than doing nothing. Without critical study of global interventions and thoughtful analysis of the local realities of these interventions, we will continue to recycle ineffective policy. I argue in the book's conclusion that interventions that proceed despite misaligned priorities can have negative consequences in young democracies like those facing serious AIDS epidemics. One contribution this book makes is to join the growing body of scholarly literature examining failures to improve the human condition in Africa (de Waal, 1997; Campbell, 2003; Autesserre, 2010). Like these earlier works, this book studies closely an intervention seemingly rooted in a humanitarian purpose and in which there are multiple actors and levels of actors involved.

1.1 Global Hierarchy, Grassroots Opinions

Organizational charts of agencies and organizations involved in AIDS interventions are crowded and complicated with many actors and relationships between actors. Take for example the two graphics published in a UNAIDS document featured in Figure 1.1. These depictions of key organizations fighting AIDS in Tanzania and Mozambique seem like caricatures of the entangled web of "stakeholders" in AIDS intervention in Africa. The graphics make clear how complicated AIDS response is in two heavily affected countries. And yet, Figure 1.1 is missing at least one set of critical actors, namely, the people to whom interventions are targeted.

In Chapter 3, I present a stylized hierarchy of the many actors involved in AIDS response, from international donors to national governments and AIDS commissions to subnational middlemen and ultimately local agents and beneficiaries who, respectively, implement and receive AIDS interventions. Identifying the multiple levels of governance that are essential to AIDS interventions is an exercise in linking interventions as they are conceived in corridors of power to how they are ultimately implemented and received in African contexts.

International NGOs and national governments are essential to AIDS interventions in Africa because they furnish necessary resources; however, the provision and distribution of public health services must be done at the local level, thus the importance of local actors in implementation. One illustrative example is how the Malawian government rations care for AIDS patients. The Malawian government – as advised by the World Health Organization (WHO) and the Global Fund – created an AIDS drug distribution policy in 2005 that limited access to AIDS drugs to Malawians with advanced disease (Ministry of Health [Malawi], 2005). The Malawian government receives funding for its national antiretroviral (ARV) treatment program from a few donors, predominantly the U.S. President's Emergency Plan for AIDS Relief (PEPFAR). In addition to relying on external donors for financial support, the Malawian government would also rely on local clinicians to determine patient eligibility on the basis of clinical presentation.[5]

---

[5] When the aforementioned Malawian ARV policy was implemented, WHO guidelines recommended drug access for HIV-positive patients clinically presenting with symptoms of AIDS or HIV-positive patients with CD4 cell counts below $350/\mu L$ (World Health Organization, 2009, 10). Access to

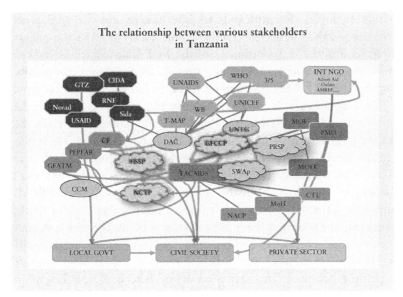

(a)

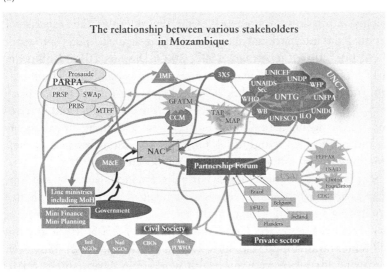

(b)

Figure 1.1 HIV/AIDS intervention stakeholders in Tanzania and Mozambique (a) Tanzania stakeholders, Figure 1 in UNAIDS (2005, 19) (b) Mozambique stakeholders, Figure 2 in UNAIDS (2005, 20)

In this example, the principals of intervention are the Malawian government, the WHO, the Global Fund, and PEPFAR; the agents implementing the intervention were the Malawian clinicians, tasked with determining who among their friends, relatives, and community neighbors would obtain the limited access to life-lengthening therapy.

This simple example shows the intervention's success relies on the actions taken by multiple actors, but especially those of PEPFAR, the Malawian government, clinicians, and ultimately, patients. The intervention would end if PEPFAR discontinued financial support. The intervention would serve fewer AIDS patients if employees of Malawi's Ministry of Health or Ministry of Finance misappropriate PEPFAR funds meant for ARV provision. If doctors did not show up for work, there would be no one to diagnose and treat patients. If patients default on their treatment, their condition could worsen, which increases the likelihood they will infect someone else and that their HIV will mutate to be drug-resistant. The major takeaway here is that intervention success depends on each link in the global hierarchy.

Much of the scholarship on HIV/AIDS politics and policy typically employs a top-down framework examining the roles and response of national and international actors intervening against AIDS (Patterson, 2006; Bor, 2007; Lieberman, 2007, 2009; Dionne, 2011; Robinson, 2017). This book offers instead a bottom-up perspective. The provision and distribution of public health services must inherently be done at the local level, which requires we study the constraints and motivations of the agents actually implementing interventions. Local agents are integral to health and development interventions because of their proximity to and influence over intended beneficiaries.

Scholarship examining local agents in international aid interventions often focuses on motivating agents to be engaged and effective by better monitoring agents (Björkman and Svensson, 2009) or through monetary incentives (Banerjee, Duflo and Glennerster, 2008; Muralidharan and Sundararaman, 2011; Duflo, Hanna and Ryan, 2012). However, a growing literature studying health workers in Africa shows financial incentives are insufficient in motivating them and this literature underscores the value of other motivating factors (Franco, Bennett and

---

technology necessary to count CD4 cells has improved in Malawi in recent years; however, most HIV-positive Malawians relied on clinical diagnoses to access ARVs because of the limited availability or nonoperation of laboratory equipment capable of counting CD4 cells.

Kanfer, 2002; Manongi, Marchant and Bygbjerg, 2006; Mathauer and Imhoff, 2006). My research suggests we should also consider nonmonetary motivations – such as agent policy preferences – and how those may constrain agent behavior. I argue that the disconnect we see between globally imagined HIV/AIDS interventions and the programs ultimately implemented is due to local agents actually implementing interventions on the ground acting in ways congruent with both their policy priorities and the policy priorities of ordinary citizens.

I focus on local implementation of HIV/AIDS interventions and citizens' prioritization of AIDS to address a set of general questions with implications for a wide range of foreign aid activities: do those who intervene against AIDS and the intended beneficiaries of AIDS interventions share common goals? Do they also have other, perhaps divergent, interests that they are simultaneously trying to maximize? If so, what are these interests, to what extent do actors diverge in prioritizing these interests, and will divergence lead to variation in the provision of interventions?

1.2 Data and Methods

To answer these questions, we must ask the opinions of agents implementing AIDS interventions in Africa as well as the opinions of the interventions' intended beneficiaries. Only recently through Afrobarometer – a Pan-African research network conducting public attitudes surveys in more than 30 African countries – have ordinary Africans been regularly polled about their opinions on politics and policies (Bratton, Mattes and Gyimah-Boadi, 2005). In young democracies in Southern Africa where AIDS is taking its toll, how aligned is AIDS response to citizens' priorities?

The data I marshal in this study were collected using a mixed-methods approach and include both original and secondary data sources. The original data draw entirely from fieldwork conducted in Malawi between 2006 and 2010 and includes survey interviews conducted with a random sample of rural Malawians, structured and open-ended interviews with village headmen and other key informants, archives of articles published on HIV/AIDS between 1998 and 2009 in Malawi's two major daily newspapers, and semi-ethnographic methods, like my field notes and diaries written by research assistants and a village headman living in a context of high HIV prevalence. I describe in more detail the data and methods used in this book in Chapter 4.

I complement the Malawi data with secondary data from the broader context of HIV-affected countries in Africa. The secondary data I analyze include time-series cross-sectional survey data collected by Afrobarometer and the Demographic and Health Surveys in more than 30 African countries. I also use data compiled by international agencies like UNAIDS, the World Bank, and the Organisation for Economic Co-operation and Development (OECD) for HIV/AIDS indicators, development measures, and flows of official development assistance (ODA). Beyond the quantitative data, I draw on news articles and policy documents written by government agencies, major donors, and influential international organizations. The scope of my analysis is also broadened by a review of scholarly literature on HIV/AIDS, including peer-reviewed articles documenting biomedical advances, operations research studying effectiveness of interventions, and social scientific analysis of how people and governments are responding to the ongoing AIDS epidemic in Africa.

1.3 Outline of the Book

The net product of the chapters that follow is a framework for understanding challenges inherent to global interventions to improve health and development in Africa.

Chapter 2 is an overview and introduction to the AIDS epidemic in Africa and the corresponding response. It brings readers up to speed on the current state of the epidemic in Africa and details grassroots, national, and global responses to AIDS in Africa. In it I share examples of how AIDS interventions implemented at the grassroots level are disconnected from how they were imagined in global capitals. I also draw on scholarship about HIV exceptionalism to develop the book's argument.

In Chapter 3, I detail my argument about two related challenges facing AIDS interventions in Africa: principal–agent problems and misaligned priorities. First, I give an overview of the principal–agent problem, or the act where a person or group, known as a principal, relies on another person or group, known as the agent, to perform a task on behalf of the principal and be accountable to the principal in carrying out the task. I use the principal–agent framework to name the principals and agents involved in AIDS interventions in Africa and illustrate the pitfalls associated with delegating responsibility across a global supply chain of intervention through the example of a Kenyan corruption scandal. I also show in Chapter 3 that if we consider the policy priorities of agents as motivation for implementing interventions, we should expect divergence from international protocols at the grassroots level because of a global misalignment of priorities.

Chapter 4 zeroes in on Malawi, describing the political and epidemiological context, the response to AIDS, and the original data collected and analyzed in this book. Malawi is an excellent place to study AIDS because it, unfortunately, is one of the countries hardest hit by the epidemic. Malawi has the ninth highest HIV prevalence in the world, estimated at 9.2% of adults in 2016 (UNAIDS, 2017). Malawi's high HIV prevalence has captured the attention of donors, who wield significant influence in shaping AIDS response in Malawi, especially when compared to the power of ordinary citizens.

In Chapter 5, I substantiate the misalignment of AIDS priorities across levels of intervention – the empirical reality upon which the book's argument depends. First, I show how the international community, especially powerful donors, have highly prioritized AIDS through analyzing data on ODA. Then, I shift perspective to the location of intervention and draw on public opinion data from more than 30 African countries and original survey data from rural Malawi. These data confirm that citizens give relatively weak priority to AIDS interventions, especially when compared to other pressing concerns.

The global mobilization against AIDS in Africa depends on the decisions of local agents implementing interventions on the ground. In Chapter 6, I describe one such agent – village headmen – and detail their priorities and the context in which they make decisions. Because many of Malawi's rural villages lack public services or infrastructure, the headman plays an important role in shaping organization and mobilization to meet the village's needs. My qualitative research shows village headmen engage in a variety of HIV/AIDS interventions. For example, they mediate marital disputes arising from the threat of infecting spouses, they help promote HIV testing to their villagers, and they assist donor organizations in identifying beneficiaries for AIDS orphan programs. In Chapter 6, I provide additional evidence of priority misalignment in the global hierarchy of AIDS intervention in Africa: while headmen's policy priorities are aligned with those of their villagers, their priorities are not aligned with international donors and activists supporting AIDS interventions. Qualitative data demonstrate that when headmen must navigate the competing preferences of external donors and local citizens, they favor outcomes beneficial to local people.

In the concluding chapter, I discuss the major findings of the book as well as the implications, not just for interventions against AIDS in Africa, but more generally for interventions to improve the human condition. I conclude the book by raising normative questions about whose priorities should take precedence in democratizing countries in East and Southern Africa, where AIDS has hit hardest.

2 | AIDS in Africa: A Significant Challenge and a Disconnected Response

AIDS is everywhere, either in rich or poor countries. Young or old people ... people are dying with AIDS everyday.
                    Malawian Journals Project, Graciano Magwira, August 11, 2005

AIDS took the lives of 1 million people in 2016, more than two-thirds of whom lived in Africa.[1] Although Africa has only 16% of the world's population, it is home to 65% of all new HIV infections.[2] This chapter describes both the challenge AIDS has been in Africa as well as the responses to AIDS by ordinary Africans, their governments, and the greater international community. Because evaluating HIV/AIDS interventions requires a general understanding of HIV prevalence and transmission patterns, I start with a brief overview of the AIDS epidemic in Africa. I then describe responses to AIDS, including local community responses and large global initiatives. The next section highlights the disconnect between interventions as imagined in global capitals and as actually implemented at the grassroots level. The final section examines why there is a disconnect and proposes how to explain it.

2.1 HIV/AIDS in Africa: A Brief Overview

HIV is the acronym for human immunodeficiency virus, a virus that causes acquired immunodeficiency syndrome, or AIDS. Progression from HIV infection to AIDS disease is long, usually taking 8 to 12 years

---

[1] While I do not bifurcate Africa according to the Sahara desert, most agencies measuring HIV and AIDS indicators do. Their delineation is imperfect, however, as Mauritania is almost entirely in the Saharan desert but is often listed in global AIDS reports under "sub-Saharan Africa." When I refer to sub-Saharan Africa in this book, it is only because the data cited in such a reference were originally collected by those who bifurcate the continent and do not provide sufficient data transparency for me to repair their separation.

[2] All HIV and AIDS estimates come from UNAIDS (2017); population estimate comes from Population Reference Bureau (2016).

in the absence of treatment. Although people may experience mild symptoms immediately after infection, there is a long latent phase before AIDS weakens the immune system. AIDS makes the body less capable of fighting infections and ultimately leads to death from opportunistic infections. There is no vaccine for HIV and there is no cure for AIDS.

HIV is a global pathogen with African roots. The original discovery of the virus in the 1980s is credited to laboratories in the United States and France (Epstein, 1996; Crane, 2013), but the most detailed analysis suggests the virus' origins lie somewhere in Central Africa (Vidal et al., 2000; Iliffe, 2006; Pepin, 2011), where some of the earliest evidence of HIV has been found (Nahmias et al., 1986; Worobey et al., 2008). Scientists estimate HIV was "circulating in the African population near the beginning of the 20th century" (Worobey et al., 2008, 663).

HIV transmission requires intimate contact and the primary mode of transmission in contemporary Africa is the same as in the rest of the world: through sexual intercourse. There are two other classes of transmission. Parenteral – also called blood-to-blood – refers to transmission via contaminated blood or medical instruments, including sharing needles associated with recreational drug use.[3] Mother-to-child transmission of HIV occurs during pregnancy, labor, or breastfeeding. Mother-to-child transmission has nearly vanished in industrialized countries, and HIV infections among children globally has fallen by 59% from 2001 to an estimated 220,000 in 2014 (UNAIDS, 2015). New HIV infections overall have declined by 35% globally between 2000 and 2014, with one of the sharpest declines (41%) occurring in sub-Saharan Africa (UNAIDS, 2015).

The introduction in the mid-1990s of antiretroviral (ARV) therapy[4] generated a remarkable decline in AIDS death rates in resource-rich countries (Mocroft et al., 1998, 2003). ARV had similar success in low-income countries, though patients starting ARV in resource-poor settings have increased mortality in the first months of therapy when

---

[3] Although injection drug users are a major risk population, the rate of HIV infection in Africa through blood contact is sufficiently low to not be reported in UNAIDS estimates.

[4] Antiretroviral therapy – referred to in this book as ARV – is a combination of at least three anti-AIDS drugs. It has also been abbreviated as ART and sometimes referred to by the longer acronym HAART, or highly active antiretroviral therapy. Unthinking folks may have also referred to the generally toxic and decidedly not-fun drug combination as a "cocktail."

compared to their counterparts in resource-rich settings (Braitstein et al., 2006). Life-lengthening treatment is not yet universally available, with access rationed in particular in resource-poor settings. Treatment access in Africa increased after a commitment from the international community at the turn of the millennium to support treatment and prevention interventions in resource-poor countries. Treatment had been more widely available in industrialized countries a decade before access was scaled up in Africa. Some in the international community – including head of USAID Andrew Natsios in an infamous *Boston Globe* interview[5] – asserted AIDS treatment was too complicated and too costly to provide treatment to the millions of people living with HIV (PLHIV) living in poor countries (Boyd, 2015, 36). Expansion of treatment access to poorer countries took a transnational social movement that brought together AIDS treatment activists, sympathetic policy entrepreneurs, and corporate executives (Kapstein and Busby, 2013).

Geography determined the different understandings of HIV transmission during the early days of AIDS. When what would later be known as HIV/AIDS was first discovered in the West, it primarily afflicted men who have sex with men (MSM), injection drug users (IDU), and patients using blood products (i.e., hemophilia patients receiving clotting factor and patients who had received blood transfusions). Thus, the initial response in the West identified MSM and IDU as high-risk groups and blood safety as a primary policy response. Early on in Africa, however, most scholars identified heterosexual intercourse as the primary mode of transmission (Piot et al., 1987; Caldwell and Caldwell, 1996) and mother-to-child transmission as another prominent mode of infection (Ryder et al., 1989). Thus, most research and policy efforts in Africa were focused on heterosexual transmission of HIV and prevention of mother-to-child transmission (PMTCT) and neglected same-sex transmission (Smith et al., 2009).

More than two-thirds of the global population infected with HIV live in Africa, where the virus originated. Why has HIV hit Africa hardest? Historian John Iliffe (2006, 58) asserts the fundamental reason why Africa has had the worst AIDS epidemic is because it had the

---

[5] Natsios claimed that if they were given access to treatment, Africans would have trouble knowing when to take it, as "Many people in Africa have never seen a clock or a watch their entire lives. And if you say, one o'clock in the afternoon, they do not know what you are talking about. They know morning, they know noon, they know evening, they know the darkness at night."

first AIDS epidemic. Pushing the historical angle further, journalist Craig Timberg and epidemiologist Daniel Halperin (2012) point to the legacy of colonial commerce in creating "massive new networks of sexual interactions – and massive new transmission of infections" (50). Colonial policies requiring male migration for labor manifested in significant gender imbalances in commercial centers and mining towns that in the late 1980s led to rapid HIV transmission (Pepin, 2011, 213). Norms regarding concurrent sexual partnerships in contemporary Africa are also advanced as an explanation for why Africa's epidemic is so severe (Morris and Kretzschmar, 1997; Epstein, 2007). Following a suite of clinical trials showing male circumcision to have some protective effect against HIV infection (Auvert et al., 2005; Bailey et al., 2007; Gray et al., 2007), there is a growing consensus among scholars and practitioners that low rates of male circumcision in African societies also accounts for high HIV prevalence in Africa.

To say AIDS has hit Africa hardest is correct if imprecise, as the epidemic has had an uneven impact across the continent. For example, fewer than 1 in 100 adults in Senegal are HIV-positive, compared to more than 1 in 4 adults who are HIV-positive in Swaziland. A map illustrating the varying rates (Figure 2.1) shows North Africa has not had to contend with generalized epidemics[6] and that Southern Africa is most deeply affected. Hargrove (2008) argues Southern Africa's epidemic is due at least in part to the structure of migration and the breakdown of family life resulting from the nature of earlier British colonial rule. Even within Southern African nations, there is variation in HIV rates. For example, South Africa has wide variation by region with its Western Cape province only registering 5% HIV prevalence while KwaZulu Natal province is at 16.9% (Human Sciences Research Council, 2014). Variation is not just geographic, either. In Malawi, only 7.5% of people in the poorest fifth of the population were HIV-positive, compared to 15.3% of the richest fifth of Malawians (National Statistical Office [Malawi] and ICF Macro, 2011).

* * *

This overview of the epidemic provides some context for understanding the world's response to AIDS in Africa. Although HIV is a

---

[6] A generalized HIV epidemic is one which goes beyond most-at-risk populations and affects the general population. The World Health Organization denotes countries with greater than 1% adult HIV prevalence as having generalized epidemics.

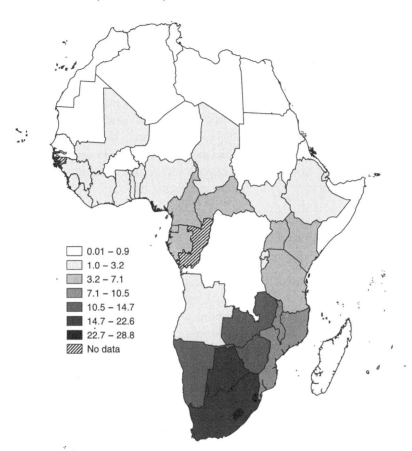

Figure 2.1 Adult HIV prevalence in Africa, 2015
Source: UNAIDS (2016). Missing data substituted with the most recent estimates, i.e., for Libya, 2005; for São Tomé and Principe, 2009; for Ethiopia, 2011; for Seychelles, 2013.

global disease, AIDS has hit Africa hardest. There has been a dominant narrative associating AIDS with Africa, unbothered by the nuances of geographic variation. Such a generic understanding of Africa as a place suffering from AIDS made space for interventions imagined in faraway corridors of power that could seemingly be implemented in any country where AIDS had reached the general population.

Likewise, the conventional wisdom that HIV transmission was different in Africa – that it was primarily through heterosexual intercourse or from mother-to-child – yielded responses that focused on preventing these modes of HIV transmission, and not, for example, prevention among men who have sex with men (van Griensven, 2007; Smith et al., 2009). Finally, AIDS treatment availability in Africa lagged far behind the industrialized world.

These distinctions are important because they demonstrate a disconnect: powerful global actors funded and designed interventions with poor understandings of the epidemic in Africa and gave less value to the lives of those suffering from AIDS in Africa than in the West. Without meaningful connection to Africans navigating the AIDS epidemic, it is hard to imagine how an intervention could be successful in stemming HIV transmission or caring for those affected by AIDS.

2.2 Responding to AIDS

In this book, I use "HIV/AIDS interventions" to refer broadly to actions taken against AIDS. I distinguish interventions and responses by level of governance: international, national, and grassroots. International response refers to interventions designed by international organizations or agencies of bilateral donors and implemented across many countries, e.g., the WHO issuing guidelines for PMTCT interventions in resource-poor countries. National interventions are responses by a country's government to the national epidemic. Falling in this category would be President Yoweri Museveni's "Zero Grazing" campaign in Uganda, when he toured the country to implore Ugandans to abstain from sex or be monogamous. Finally, local or grassroots interventions are those initiated at the community level. One example is a community health worker partnering with a village headman to hold an informational meeting at the village center to inform villagers of free HIV tests newly available at the local health center. These distinctions are useful in understanding the potential of interventions dreamed up in global corridors of power and the reality of implementation at the grassroots level. The following sections describe the responses to AIDS by people and organizations at the grassroots, national, and international levels of governance.

Grassroots Responses to AIDS

Before AIDS became the global priority it is today, communities experiencing the AIDS pandemic firsthand responded in diverse ways. Important social institutions like local healers, family, and religious organizations were critical early in the AIDS epidemic, as Africans formed their understandings of AIDS.

African understandings of HIV/AIDS early in the epidemic were much more sophisticated than one might interpret from Western media coverage or even from scholars studying AIDS during the early years. Even before being called AIDS or HIV, the disease had taken the name of other diseases, or named according to its affliction. For example, in rural Tanzania, scholars recorded people referring to some AIDS cases as "*lusumbo*, a witchcraft-induced illness that reportedly preceded the AIDS epidemic" (Mshana et al., 2006, 54). Likewise, in Mozambique, a few traditional healers claimed AIDS was not really a new disease but an old familiar disease for which there was already a variety of familiar medicines to cure or prevent it (Green, Jurg and Dgedge, 1993, 269). In Uganda in the early part of the AIDS epidemic, it was called "slim" (Serwadda et al., 1985), as sufferers wasted from the disease.[7] Before treatment was widely available and discussion around AIDS was more hushed – perhaps due to stigma or shame – people referred to it as the "new disease" or "the disease with no cure" or "radio disease" (because it was talked about on the radio),[8] rather than referring to it directly by name (Dow and Essex, 2010, 61). This range of names for AIDS early on illustrate that citizens navigating the epidemic knew about the disease long before internationally funded awareness-raising campaigns reached them.

Even in rural areas, by the late 1990s, the majority of people had heard of AIDS from the radio, public meetings, fellow villagers, or school (Mshana et al., 2006, 51).[9] Many Africans knew the disease was sexually transmitted and could perform "social autopsies," or create narratives of how the disease passed from one person to the next using facts and gossip about people's health and sexual histories (Chimwaza and Watkins, 2004; Watkins, 2004). Malawians navigating the AIDS epidemic relied on these social autopsies and "sexual biographies" of

[7] Research from rural Tanzania near Uganda also reports individuals referring to AIDS as "slim," among other names (Mshana et al., 2006, 50–1).

[8] Even in Sierra Leone, where HIV prevalence is relatively low (1.5%) in comparison to elsewhere in Africa, Benton (2015) reported hearing radio spots for HIV/AIDS prevention and testing three or four times per week during her fieldwork from 2003 to 2007 (35).

[9] In 1987, research in a rural village in then-Zaire showed many people had heard of AIDS and knew it was sexually transmitted (Timberg and Halperin, 2012, 97–8).

current and potential partners from trusted sources in their social networks to avoid HIV infection (Watkins, 2004; Smith and Watkins, 2005). Ugandans changed their behavior in ways that helped reduce HIV long before "behavior change" emerged as a popular phrase among AIDS interventionists (Boyd, 2015, 41).

Before the discovery and distribution of life-lengthening treatment for those suffering from AIDS, many sought AIDS treatment from local healers (Dow and Essex, 2010, 60–1).[10] Western attention on healing in Africa often focuses on prominent quacks who claim to have an AIDS cure – e.g., former Gambian President Yaya Jammeh (Cassidy and Leach, 2009b). However, local healers have provided useful advice for avoiding HIV infection[11] as well as great relief for people suffering from AIDS, especially early in the epidemic. In 2002, the WHO estimated 80% of people living in Africa depend on traditional medicine for their health-care needs, with varying uptake across countries; for example, 60% of the population in Uganda use traditional medicine compared to 90% of Ethiopians (Chatora, 2003, 4–5).

Sociologists Jenny Trinitapoli and Alexander Weinreb (2012, 146) list compelling reasons why many Africans sought and continue to seek traditional and/or religious approaches to healing: Traditional healing approaches "match culturally embedded distinctions between proximate and ultimate causes of illnesses"[12]; traditional healing approaches have more flexible demands on patients than, for example, a rigid ARV regimen; and traditional approaches are more financially accessible.[13] There are simply more traditional medicine practitioners than doctors available to the population. In Ghana, for example, it was estimated in 2002 that there is one traditional health practitioner for every 200 people compared to only one doctor for every 20,000 people (Chatora, 2003, 5).

---

[10] Local healers is a broad term that encompasses what others may have referred to as herbalists, traditional healers, or, pejoratively, witch doctors.

[11] On prevention strategies, traditional healers drew largely from their experience with other sexually transmitted diseases (STDs). In their study of healers in Mozambique, Green, Jurg and Dgedge (1993) characterized "virtually all of the preventive advice given by traditional healers" as "biomedically sound" (271). See also Schoepf (1992) on how healers can reinvent traditions to help people navigate the AIDS epidemic.

[12] People who believe an AIDS-like illness is not necessarily AIDS but rather a similar illness caused by witchcraft will seek traditional medicine (Mshana et al., 2006, 52–4).

[13] See also Green, Jurg and Dgedge (1993), 263.

Like in developed countries in the early period before anti-AIDS drugs were discovered, people with AIDS in African countries could only seek treatment of opportunistic infections, and they often sought this treatment from local healers. Before ARVs were available in Africa, local healers provided successful treatments for opportunistic infections associated with AIDS, including skin diseases (e.g., herpes zoster), cough, intestinal problems (e.g., diarrhea), wasting and weight loss, and oral thrush (UNAIDS, 2002, 13, 23, 25, 31).

While Americans were being stigmatized and even shunned for being HIV-positive, many Africans were being cared for by their families as they died of AIDS.[14] Care for AIDS patients – especially before ARVs were available – relied almost exclusively on relatives (Chimwaza and Watkins, 2004), supplemented by the psychosocial support offered by religious organizations (Dow and Essex, 2010; Trinitapoli and Weinreb, 2012). Most of the day-to-day help people receive as they face the challenges of AIDS they get from their friends, family, and neighbors (Swidler and Watkins, 2017). Local communities, whether as villages or as churches, or even sometimes as organic, newly formed community organizations, came together to respond to AIDS.

Local religious organizations responded to AIDS by caring for the sick and promoting HIV prevention strategies. In Malawi, local religious leaders advocated for behavior change to reduce the risk of HIV infection, and religious congregations – especially Christian ones – were central in providing for the sick and for AIDS orphans (Trinitapoli, 2006; Trinitapoli and Weinreb, 2012, 173). A study in southern Mozambique in 2003 found churches provided support to both members and nonmembers with HIV, though this predominantly consisted of psychosocial support (e.g., prayer, advice, encouragement) rather than tangible support (e.g., physical care, funds for transport to hospital), and support was infrequent (Agadjanian and Sen, 2007). Another scholar studying HIV/AIDS in Mozambique observed daily material support from a pastor to families of church members believed to be sick with AIDS (Pfeiffer, 2004*a*, 368). In her book on the church and AIDS in Africa, political scientist Amy Patterson (2011) lists 34 different AIDS activities churches engaged in that she drew from her research in Ghana and Zambia. These included abstinence and faithfulness

---

[14] This is not to say there has not been any AIDS stigma in Africa – there has (see, e.g., Kaleeba, 2004). As I show in Chapter 5, however, there is considerably less stigma in high-prevalence countries.

campaigns as well as palliative care, helping people adhere to treatment, making public statements against AIDS stigma, and advocating to governments and donors on AIDS-related issues (Patterson, 2011, 41–2). Of course, the nature and intensity of local religious response has varied over time and space.

* * *

The grassroots response to AIDS demonstrates significant knowledge about HIV and AIDS care-seeking behavior prior to the response by the larger global community. One important discontinuity in the global response to AIDS was how international actors often overlooked the already existing grassroots response. Take for example the many internationally funded AIDS awareness campaigns occurring *after* researchers had already learned in the late 1990s that adults living in African countries with mature epidemics were "acutely aware of the high levels of AIDS-related illness and death" and recommended anti-AIDS efforts focus on implementing control measures over awareness-raising (Kengeya-Kayondo et al., 1999, 2299–301). I turn now to the responses by those actors mediating between grassroots and international anti-AIDS efforts: the national governments of African countries most heavily affected by the AIDS epidemic.

Government Response in Heavily Affected African Countries

In my analysis of the challenges in HIV response, I depart from the perspective of many scholars – especially political scientists – who compare government response across countries and instead I examine the connections – and more importantly, the misalignments – between actors in the global supply chain of AIDS interventions. Examining these misalignments, however, requires an understanding of how governments and state leaders responded to AIDS and what – if any – patterns were there in government response.

Unsurprisingly, many political leaders in countries heavily affected by AIDS responded initially with fear, denial, and silence. For example, Zairean dictator Mobutu Sese Seko banned public discussion of AIDS and threatened scientists and public health officials who acknowledged its existence (Iliffe 2006, 67; Timberg and Halperin 2012, 92). One Congolese doctor was threatened with prison by a Ministry of Health official after addressing a plenary session of the Second International AIDS Conference in Paris in 1986 (Cohen, 1997). After losing a son to AIDS in 1996, Zimbabwean Vice President Joshua Nkomo, with President Robert Mugabe at his side, proclaimed in a graveside speech that AIDS was "harvested by whites to obliterate blacks."[15] But not all political leaders responded in this way. Also having lost a son to AIDS, Zambian President Kenneth Kaunda devoted his post-presidency efforts to raising awareness about HIV/AIDS.

The typical contrast of African political leaders' responses is between Uganda's President Yoweri Museveni and former South African President Thabo Mbeki (Parkhurst and Lush, 2004; Youde, 2007). Museveni's work against HIV is often hailed as a successful response to the HIV epidemic. Museveni responded early with making AIDS a national political issue and declaring that it was the political duty of all Ugandans to prevent HIV transmission (Parkhurst and Lush, 2004; Youde, 2007). Conversely, Mbeki's inaction against HIV is often chastised and sometimes blamed for a rise in HIV rates in South Africa. Mbeki stirred controversy by questioning the link between HIV and AIDS and through his government's resistance to providing ARVs to HIV-positive pregnant women to prevent transmission to their unborn babies (Parkhurst and Lush, 2004; Youde, 2007). But these examples are "at opposite ends of the spectrum" (Youde, 2007, 1).

Most leaders were focused on other pressing issues facing their countries, and only periodically addressed HIV/AIDS or interventions against HIV/AIDS publicly.[16] In some cases government interventions were helpful actions, like when the Swazi King endorsed male circumcision for HIV prevention in 2011 (Timberg and Halperin, 2012, 381). In other cases, leaders made matters worse, like when former Gambian President Yaya Jammeh proclaimed to have a cure for AIDS. Often, leaders' efforts were symbolic acts rather than profound policy changes. Political leaders have made public acts of being HIV tested and or sharing their experiences of being affected by HIV. Malawi's President Bakili Muluzi reported he tested negative for HIV but that his younger brother had died of AIDS; Zambian President Kenneth

---

[15] "Official Breaks with Tradition in Announcing AIDS Death, Blames West," *Associated Press*, April 6, 1996.
[16] For richer detail on the lack of political salience of AIDS, see de Waal (2006) and Patterson (2006).

Kaunda and South African Deputy President Gatsha Mangosuthu made similar public disclosures of family members who died of AIDS (Muula and Mfutso-Bengo, 2005).

What influences leaders taking action against HIV/AIDS? Using data from the AIDS Program Effort Index (API),[17] a cross-national measure of government response to AIDS, scholars find institutions constraining the leader predict a government's response to AIDS (Bor, 2007; Dionne, 2011). In epidemiologist Jacob Bor's (2007) study of the API in 54 developing countries, he finds a free and independent media and high HIV prevalence predicted greater government response to HIV and that greater income inequality made a vigorous governmental response less likely. Limiting scope to East and Southern African countries, I found presidents who expect to be in office longer will devote more of their budget to health spending than their counterparts with shorter time horizons (Dionne, 2011). Political scientist Evan Lieberman debates the power of the API in capturing country-level response, and so examined alternative measures of AIDS policy aggressiveness: AIDS expenditure, number of people on ARV, and coverage of PMTCT programs. In his analysis, Lieberman finds "that when countries have strong internal boundaries dividing societies into substantial and recognizable ethnic groups, the [AIDS] epidemic is also likely to be understood in these terms" (2009, 3); in these countries, what Lieberman calls "boundary institutions" slow and weaken AIDS response.

What we can take away from the results in these earlier studies is not just that political institutions shaped government response, but also that domestic pressure – whether high HIV prevalence in the population or the looming threat of being thrown out of office – can have some impact on how and whether leaders respond to AIDS. In other words, governments do not govern without thought to what citizens may want or need, even when faced with an epidemic.

In addition to managing pressure from below, governments must also manage the interests and demands of donors in their AIDS response. Sociologist Rachel Sullivan Robinson (2017) shows in her

---

[17] The API was a collaborative data collection effort developed by UNAIDS, USAID, and the POLICY Project, the latter of which was part of Futures Group, which was a global health consulting firm headquartered in Washington, DC. See Dionne (2011) and USAID et al. (2003) for further details on the API measure.

analysis that countries' transnational relationships to Western donors shaped their experiences of importing from the global community prevention programs for both pregnancy and HIV. These transnational relationships pushed governments to make "intimate interventions" and then local technocratic leadership and civil society shaped those efforts.

What exactly are the tangible HIV/AIDS interventions that make up government response? The most obvious government interventions against AIDS are the policies and national guidelines crafted by government agencies such as the Ministry of Health or National AIDS Commission. Public statements by official leaders, for example, anti-stigma messages, would also be included. But my research on the role of time horizons in government response suggests that political leaders may engage in "cheap talk" by making policies and statements about AIDS to draw donor support when they feel their tenure is vulnerable; on the flip side, leaders who foresaw themselves being in power long enough to bear the burdens of a high-prevalence epidemic would increase spending on health initiatives (Dionne, 2011). It is for these reasons that I choose to study response as measured in governments' AIDS spending.

For example, in Malawi, most of the spending on HIV/AIDS (47%) goes toward treatment programs, which are implemented in government-sanctioned health facilities (Government of Malawi, 2015, 52). Only 5% of Malawi's HIV/AIDS budget supports PMTCT programs, which provide HIV testing and counselling to pregnant mothers, guidance for infected mothers on how to reduce risk of HIV transmission to their unborn children, and increasingly, specialized care to reduce HIV transmission risk. Government HIV spending also supports HIV prevention more broadly, which in Malawi accounted for 23% of HIV expenditure. Supported HIV prevention interventions include behavior change campaigns geared toward youths, free condom distribution, and broadcasting HIV prevention messages on radio and TV (Government of Malawi, 2015, 25–30). Other categories of government "investment" in HIV/AIDS interventions include "governance and sustainability" (13%), "critical enablers" (5%), and "other" (3%) (Government of Malawi, 2015, 53). While I characterize all of these actions as part of a government response to AIDS, it is important to note that most of the funding for these government activities comes from international donors. In the case of Malawi, 99% of

HIV expenditure came from donors (Clinton Health Access Initiative, 2015).[18]

* * *

Earlier work established that key characteristics shaped government AIDS response, including: contextual constraints (e.g., high prevalence epidemics), institutional constraints of leaders (e.g., independent media, time horizons, and ethnic boundaries), and connections to the greater global response (e.g., transnational relationships to donors). Having characterized response to AIDS by the first two levels of governance – grassroots and national governments – I now turn to the international community's response.

International Response to AIDS in Africa

Whether framing AIDS as a public health problem (Kim and Farmer, 2006), a development crisis (Mukherjee et al., 2003), a humanitarian issue (Piot and Coll Seck, 2001), or a threat to US national security (Elbe, 2002; Ostergard, 2002; Feldbaum, Lee and Patel, 2006), advocates and activists called for a greater response to AIDS in Africa, particularly by Western donors and international NGOs. The international response has not been a uniform or coordinated effort, but rather a melange of activities taken on by often disconnected actors and organizations, some more powerful than others. In this section, I paint with broad strokes a picture of how the significant financial resources committed by the donor community has vested power with donors in the global-to-local hierarchy of AIDS response.

The international financial commitment to AIDS response in Africa has been tremendous. Chapter 5 shows how the international community has treated AIDS as exceptional using ODA commitments for HIV/AIDS from OECD member countries.[19] In 2007, these commitments totaled $7.4 billion – nearly half of all ODA committed to health and four times more than the next highest funded health area

---

[18] The government reports a lower, but still substantial, figure: 83.6% of financial resources for implementing national response to HIV (Government of Malawi, 2015, 61).

[19] The 22 OECD member countries are Australia, Austria, Belgium, Canada, Denmark, Finland, France, Germany, Greece, Ireland, Italy, Japan, Luxembourg, the Netherlands, New Zealand, Norway, Portugal, Spain, Sweden, Switzerland, the United Kingdom, and the United States.

(Kates, Lief and Pearson, 2009). In comparison, ODA commitments for improving water quality and expanding access to water totaled only $0.92 billion, even though deaths from diarrheal disease in sub-Saharan Africa (8%) accounted for about half as many deaths from AIDS (15%).

Two international actors dominate the global response to AIDS in Africa: The Global Fund to Fight AIDS, Tuberculosis and Malaria (Global Fund); and the US President's Emergency Plan for AIDS Relief (PEPFAR). Both were created in the early 2000s to increase resources for AIDS response in heavily affected African countries. Initial discussions on the creation of a global fund to fight AIDS, tuberculosis, and malaria occurred during a G-8 summit in Okinawa, Japan, in 2000 (Schocken, 2006; Garmaise, 2009). During an African summit on AIDS in Abuja, Nigeria, in April 2001, then UN Secretary General Kofi Annan called for support for such a fund and in June 2001 a United Nations General Assembly Special Session dedicated to HIV/AIDS ended with a commitment to create one. The Global Fund was established the following year to mobilize and coordinate donor funding. As of 2016, the Global Fund had disbursed $30.2 billion in aid (The Global Fund to Fight AIDS, Tuberculosis and Malaria, 2016). The Global fund solicits and vets proposals, which usually fund multiyear projects in specific countries, though there are also multi-country regional awards.[20] Funds are disbursed to a Principal Recipient in the country, usually the Ministry of Health or National AIDS Commission, but these Principal Recipients are only the initial recipients through whom funds are transferred to subrecipients who implement portions of the grant and report to the Principal Recipient (Garmaise, 2009).

One of the major principles of the Global Fund is that supported programs would be "country-led, with broad, cross-sectoral participation" (Schocken, 2006). Though the funding was global, the intention was that programming would be country-driven (Garmaise, 2009). The Global Fund was designed with some interest in creating a response not wholly dictated by international donors. Applying for a Global Fund grant required that countries first set up a country coordinating mechanism, which is a decision-making body representative of the diverse actors involved in AIDS interventions: government,

[20] In the first eight rounds, 1,508 proposals were submitted, of which 611 (41%) were recommended for funding (Garmaise, 2009, 36).

lack of civil society role.

dom of gov't actors

donors, NGOs, faith-based organizations, businesses, and PLHIV (Patterson, 2006, 44). While nongovernmental actors have a seat at the table, civil society groups – including PLHIV – have been underrepresented on country coordinating mechanisms (Patterson, 2006, 73), with democratic countries slightly more likely to include civil society representatives (Patterson, 2006, 77). While the Global Fund has been participatory and inclusive through its representation requirements (Patterson, 2006, 169), government actors dominate country coordinating mechanisms.

The largest bilateral effort against HIV/AIDS began just a couple of years after the creation of the Global Fund. President George W. Bush in his 2003 State of the Union address asked Congress to commit $15 billion over the next five years for his PEPFAR initiative. The eventual bill introduced in the House of Representatives – HR 1298 (108th): United States Leadership Against HIV/AIDS, Tuberculosis, and Malaria Act of 2003 – received wide bipartisan support and was signed into law May 27, 2003. President Bush reauthorized PEPFAR in 2008 when he signed into law HR 5501 (110th), the Tom Lantos and Henry J. Hyde United States Global Leadership Against HIV/AIDS, Tuberculosis, and Malaria Reauthorization Act of 2008, committing another $48 billion toward HIV/AIDS interventions.

PEPFAR is not a unitary actor but a federation of multiple government departments led by the US Global AIDS Coordinator. PEPFAR's implementing agencies include: the Department of State, the United States Agency for International Development (USAID), the Department of Defense, the Department of Commerce, the Department of Labor, the Department of Health and Human Services, and the Peace Corps. These agencies support HIV/AIDS programs in 65 countries, 27 of which are in Africa.[21]

In 2013, PEPFAR planned to spend just under $1 billion (30% of its budget) on AIDS treatment. The next largest category of PEPFAR spending was HIV prevention (28%), followed by care (20%), "governance and systems" (17%), and "management and operations" (5%). The latter two funding categories – governance and systems

---

[21] As of 2013, PEPFAR funds support programs in the following 27 African countries: Angola, Botswana, Burundi, Cameroon, Côte d'Ivoire, Democratic Republic of the Congo, Djibouti, Ethiopia, Ghana, Kenya, Lesotho, Liberia, Malawi, Mali, Mozambique, Namibia, Nigeria, Rwanda, Senegal, Sierra Leone, South Africa, South Sudan, Swaziland, Tanzania, Uganda, Zambia, and Zimbabwe.

and management and operations – account for about $724 million and support projects like the CDC Information Management Services initiative in Malawi. Estimated to cost $100,000, this CDC initiative paid US-based contractor Northrup Grumman to install and customize the PEPFAR information system platform in Malawi (PEPFAR, 2013). This Northrup Grumman contract highlights that some PEPFAR funding is actually spent on expatriate consultancies, not on goods or services in Malawi. It also demonstrates that while this kind of activity may reduce the potential negative consequences of delegating to faraway agents by choosing to fund agents who are compatriots, it also removes from the global hierarchy local agents who could provide useful knowledge about the context in which the intervention is implemented.

The United States and the Global Fund dominate global HIV/AIDS assistance, providing 80% of the financial resources for response. The United States is the largest donor in the world, providing 61% of HIV/AIDS foreign aid; the Global Fund is the next largest, providing 19% of HIV/AIDS foreign aid (Kates et al., 2013). Though these two are the largest international funding efforts, there are many other bilateral and multilateral donors supporting AIDS response. Worldwide, 37 different donors reported providing assistance in 143 countries between 2009 and 2011. Sub-Saharan Africa received funding from the greatest number of donors (34) and received the greatest share of assistance of any region: 57% of HIV/AIDS donor funding in 2009–11 went to sub-Saharan Africa (Kates et al., 2013).[22]

---

[22] The number of donors is potentially an undercount as the study only examines OECD DAC members, two non-DAC members, and 30 multilateral organizations. OECD DAC members include: Australia, Austria, Belgium, Canada, Czech Republic, Denmark, European Union, Finland, France, Germany, Greece, Iceland, Ireland, Italy, Japan, Korea, Luxembourg, New Zealand, Norway, Portugal, Spain, Sweden, Switzerland, the Netherlands, the United Kingdom, and the United States. The non-DAC members were Kuwait and the United Arab Emirates. Multilateral donors reporting to the DAC include: African Development Bank, African Development Fund, Arab Fund for Economic and Social Development, Asian Development Bank, ASDB Special Funds, Arab Bank for Economic Development in Africa, European Bank for Reconstruction and Development, Global Alliance for Vaccines and Immunization, Global Environment Facility, Global Fund, International Bank for Reconstruction and Development, International Development Association, Inter-American Development Bank, Inter-American Development Bank Special Fund, International Fund for Agricultural Development, International Monetary Fund, Islamic Development Bank, Nordic Development Bank, OPEC

Complicating the coordination of HIV/AIDS initiatives, African countries often have many donors. On average, sub-Saharan African countries had the highest concentration of donors of any region (15 donors per country) and the six countries with the most donors are all in sub-Saharan Africa: Ethiopia (27), Kenya (26), and Malawi, Mozambique, Tanzania, and Zimbabwe (all with 25 donors; Kates et al., 2013, 3).

Philanthropic organizations like the Bill and Melinda Gates Foundation also fund and support AIDS response. Other large funders include the Conrad N. Hilton Foundation, the M.A.C. AIDS Fund, the Ford Foundation, and philanthropic arms of major health-care corporations such as Gilead Sciences, Johnson & Johnson, and the Bristol-Myers Squibb Foundation. Philanthropy makes up a small share (roughly 3%) of the global response to HIV/AIDS and in 2013 it was at its lowest level since 2007 (Funders Concerned about AIDS, 2014). Still, current estimates put philanthropic funding of HIV/AIDS response at more than $600 million per year. About two-thirds of the international funding from philanthropic organizations goes to Africa (Funders Concerned about AIDS, 2014, 43); the greatest proportion (27%) of international philanthropic funding goes to prevention and the next largest amount (19%) supports research (Funders Concerned about AIDS, 2014, 45). This crowded donor landscape – comprised of bilateral and multilateral donors as well as philanthropists – complicates AIDS response in Africa as it creates multiple systems and structures for national governments and their citizens to navigate and interact with.

Beyond spending, the international community has also responded to the AIDS epidemic with advocacy. Scholars argue in leading medical journals for more to be done (Attaran and Sachs, 2001; Piot and Coll Seck, 2001; Schwartländer et al., 2001; Kim and Farmer, 2006; Stover et al., 2006). University students organize campus events to

---

Fund for International Development, Organization for Security and Co-operation in Europe (OSCE), UNAIDS, United Nations Development Programme (UNDP), United Nations Economic Commission for Europe (UNECE), United Nations Population Fund (UNFPA), Office of the United Nations High Commissioner for Refugees (UNHCR), United Nations Children's Fund (UNICEF), United Nations Peacebuilding Fund (UNPBF), United Nations Relief and Works Agency for Palestine Refugees in the Near East (UNRWA), World Food Programme (WFP), and WHO.

bring attention to AIDS in Africa.[23] Celebrities collaborate to hold benefits to raise awareness and money.[24] Even multinational corporations such as Apple, Nike, Motorola, and Starbucks (among others) have partnered with a brand, (PRODUCT)[RED] to create merchandise marketed to appeal to consumers who want to do something about AIDS in Africa.

The international community has also been active in research on HIV and AIDS in Africa. A simple search on Google Scholar of both the terms "HIV" and "Africa" yielded 1,230,000 results.[25] Biomedical research on AIDS in Africa has focused on HIV strains predominant in North America and Europe, which is problematic considering the same research is used to develop treatment and potential vaccines; these have different effects on different HIV strains, presumably privileging strains found in the global north (Crane, 2013). This disconnect between international research projects and the needs of Africans navigating the epidemic is important. A Congolese doctor who had assisted Projet SIDA – "one of the world's preeminent AIDS research centers in the 1980s" (Timberg and Halperin, 2012, 93) – highlighted how Projet SIDA focused on epidemiology and not on treatment or prevention. He said, "I'm sorry tell you that Projet SIDA had very little impact for infected people here. It would have been useful for them to ask us about what was the useful thing for us they could do here" (Cohen, 1997). Schoepf (1991) cautioned early in the AIDS epidemic in Africa that both biomedical and anthropological research paradigms could limit perspectives and even lead to counterproductive outcomes by defining what questions were asked and shaping which issues were legitimate. Researchers' responses exemplify responses to AIDS in Africa by the

[handwritten margin note: lack of research on treatment + prevention]

---

[23] Tiffany Pan, "Students Take Action to Fight against AIDS," *Daily Bruin*, December 1, 2005; James Fuller, "[Wheaton] College Embraces HIV/AIDS Fight," *Daily Herald*, December 2, 2005.

[24] Jill Yaffe, "Entertainment's Biggest Names Support Hasbro, Inc.'s PROJECT ZAMBI through Global Charity Auction," *Business Wire*, September 8, 2009; Adam Brandolf, "Pop Band Takes to the Streets to Raise Awareness of Issues Plaguing Africa," *Pittsburgh Tribune Review*, October 14, 2008; Sean Evans, "'Survivor' Star Raises AIDS Awareness with Celeb Soccer Match," *Daily News*, October 5, 2008; "Madonna Gala Raises $5.1M for Aid," *United Press International*, February 7, 2008.

[25] Malaria, discovered by scientists a century before AIDS, has yielded fewer publications; a search conducted the same day (August 2, 2017) for "malaria" and "Africa" yielded 962,000 results.

international community more generally in failing to meaningfully engage local knowledge and priorities.

* * *

International responses to AIDS center on resources, but also include advocacy and research. This brief look at responses by international donors, advocates, and even researchers highlights the crowded landscape of international responders and how their perspectives and goals shape their response. For all their good intentions, international actors are often disconnected from the grassroots contexts in which interventions occur, as I illustrate in the next section.

role of interests shaping response

2.3 Examples of Disconnected AIDS Interventions in Mozambique and Botswana

International actors rely on national governments and grassroots organizations to implement HIV/AIDS programs; such arrangements are often referred to as "partnerships," even if those involved are not equal partners. An illustrative example is the US-based NGO Population Services International (PSI) promoting a social marketing campaign to increase condom use in Mozambique.[26]

The Mozambique condom intervention's global-to-local hierarchy[27] involved actors across levels of governance: the donor, USAID, encouraged the Mozambican Ministry of Health to approve PSI's campaign; PSI managed the program and "collaborated" with NGOs and civil society, including a local song and dance troupe to promote the product (Pfeiffer, 2004a, 367). This song and dance troupe was employed

---

[26] Pfeiffer provides a helpful description of what a social marketing campaign is/does: "It borrows its methods from commercial advertising and marketing to develop promotional campaigns and create 'brands' that are focus group-tested in target communities. The products are then distributed primarily through private commercial networks using market forces, while the product pricing is normally set to be 'affordable' for target groups but cost enough to make a profit. PSI normally subsidizes the campaigns so products can be sold at below the manufacturing cost. In theory, the campaigns not only make health products available but also promote behavior change" (2004, 367).

[27] Another way to think of the relationships between global and grassroots actors is a web of interlinked relationships, rather than a hierarchy (Gibson et al., 2005). For ease of illustration, I adopt a hierarchical perspective that fits with how funding flows (from global to grassroots), without at the same time promoting a view that interventions could or should only be imagined as a hierarchy privileging the position of international actors.

to entertain and inform citizens such that citizens would be compelled to purchase condoms for HIV prevention, as the social marketing framework expects people only value condoms if they pay for them.

While external actors funded, designed, and led this condom campaign in Mozambique, implementation required ministry approval and engaging local agents to implement the intervention. There is no evidence that PSI amended its design to reflect feedback from its "collaborators." Ultimately, the intervention's success depended on whether citizens – the targeted beneficiaries of the condom campaign – positively accepted the intervention. A critical appraisal reported a hostile response to the program and attributed the backlash to a lack of genuine inclusion of local communities in developing the campaign (Pfeiffer, 2004*b*). In other words, the failure of this intervention is rooted in the disconnect between global and grassroots actors. The PSI condom campaign in Mozambique is but one example of many arrangements billed as partnerships but falling short in achieving equal power in intervention design and decision-making. We see similar – if less contentious – dynamics in a Botswana initiative.

The African Comprehensive HIV/AIDS Partnership (ACHAP) was established in July 2000 as a public–private partnership between the Government of Botswana, the Bill and Melinda Gates Foundation, and The Merck Foundation (Ramiah and Reich, 2006; ACHAP, 2014). The foundations brought financial support while the government's role was of chief implementer. Even in this role, the government was not an equal partner. Merck and ACHAP's Board of Directors – made up of representatives from Merck, Gates, and the Harvard AIDS Institute, but not from the Botswana government – held significant decision-making power early on in the partnership, and even bypassed government in implementation by reaching out to NGOs (Ramiah and Reich, 2006, 401).

ACHAP financially supported universal treatment access in Botswana and other prevention and care programs, including an AIDS orphanage, condom marketing and distribution, and a teacher capacity building program (Ramiah and Reich, 2006, 403). During the first year of the partnership, however, ACHAP attempted to establish HIV prevention programs by writing program proposals and expecting government officials to simply implement their programs without consulting them in program design (Ramiah and Reich, 2006, 404). ACHAP demonstrates that even the best funded good intentions fail to have authentic partnership and local buy-in.

These "partnerships" in HIV/AIDS interventions are a performance of participatory development – a way for donors to claim their response has local buy-in and is not a top-down imposition. Even if these performances of participation are successful, the actual implementation of interventions suffer when local partners lack decision-making power or a seat at the table when interventions are designed. Their absence and the absence of their specialized knowledge is an important disconnect in the response to AIDS.

2.4 Why the Disconnect in Global AIDS Response?

Coordinating actors across multiple levels of governance is a herculean task. However, a global health or development intervention is not necessarily doomed from the start. What, then, explains why the global response to AIDS in Africa has been disconnected? In this section, I build on the scholarship of HIV exceptionalism to offer an argument about what has challenged AIDS interventions in Africa: the global-to-local hierarchy of AIDS interventions favors powerful donors, whose priorities are misaligned with ordinary Africans, their intended beneficiaries.

HIV/AIDS as Exceptional

Anthropologist Adia Benton (2015) defines HIV exceptionalism as "the idea that HIV/AIDS is always a biologically, socially, culturally, and politically unique disease requiring an exceptional response" (8). One way of understanding the disconnect between the interventions supported and designed by powerful international actors and how those interventions are received by people facing AIDS is recognizing that the international community sees HIV as inherently special. However, this exceptionalism has negative consequences.

HIV exceptionalism creates what Benton (2015) calls an "economy of suffering," in which PLHIV can claim unique hardship even in a place where hardship is the norm (xi). Workshops and support groups for PLHIV sometimes offered per diems, meals, and other resources, which provided many poor PLHIV the opportunity to leverage their status in a resource-poor setting (Benton, 2015, 94, 106). Worse yet, HIV exceptionalism produces more HIV exceptionalism. Benton (2015) shows that the collection of HIV interventions implemented "entrench and reinforce HIV's exceptional status" – including a reproduction of the global hierarchical relationships between donors, NGOs, and government agencies and community-based organizations (CBOs) comprising the AIDS industry (9).

Global health analyst Roger England (2007) asserts HIV funding is used inefficiently and sometimes counterproductively; he argues the exceptional status accorded to HIV adversely affects the organization of health services by producing separate structures for care rather than strengthening general health services. England is only one of a handful of scholars questioning the international policy community's exceptionalism of HIV, calling attention to the implications for other global health priorities (MacKellar, 2005; Grépin, 2012; Dionne, Gerland and Watkins, 2013) and the negative consequences more broadly to public health systems in countries where HIV-specific aid can be damaging (Shiffman, 2008; Lee and Platas Izama, 2015).

These scholarly debates on exceptionalism notwithstanding, it may be hard to imagine HIV/AIDS interventions having a negative impact on local populations. But an article in the *Los Angeles Times* reporting on work in Lesotho supported by the Gates Foundation illustrates a negative consequence of HIV exceptionalism:

There was no oxygen tube for Mankuebe [a Lesotho newborn]. She asphyxiated for lack of a second valve. It would have cost $35 ... The Gates Foundation ... has given $650 million to the Global Fund. But the oxygen valve fell outside the priorities of the fund's grants to Lesotho. Every day, nurses say, one or two babies at the hospital die as Mankuebe did – bypassed in a place where AIDS overshadows other concerns.[28]

The *Los Angeles Times* investigation found that, because the programs funded by the Gates Foundation focused contributions into the fight against high-profile diseases like AIDS, Gates grantees had increased the demand for specially trained, higher paid clinicians, diverting staff from basic care:

Florence Mukakabano, head nurse at the Central Hospital of Kigali, the capital of Rwanda, said she loses many of her staff nurses to UN agencies, NGOs, and the hospital's own Global Fund-supported AIDS program.[29]

---

[28] Piller and Smith, "Unintended Victims: The Gates Foundation's Generous Gifts to Fight AIDS, TB and Malaria in Africa Have Inadvertently Put Many of Those with Other Healthcare Needs at Risk," *Los Angeles Times*, December 16, 2007.

[29] Ibid.

A study by the Center for Global Development, a Washington DC-based think tank, reported these trends more broadly and showed the negative consequences of HIV exceptionalism not just through recruitment of health-care workers to specialized jobs, but also through a diversion of their focus. For example, PEPFAR provided salary top-ups to public health workers in Zambia who provided ARV, which focused clinical staffs' attention on HIV/AIDS, reducing the time they devoted to other health services (Oomman, Bernstein and Rosenzweig, 2008, 6).

HIV exceptionalism in the international community has profoundly shaped the response to AIDS in Africa. Exceptionalism alone, however, does not account for the disconnect in HIV/AIDS interventions in Africa. It is possible to imagine, for example, that African citizens and communities experiencing the epidemic firsthand would also find HIV an exceptional problem requiring an exceptional response. Thus, while HIV exceptionalism characterizes very well the international response to AIDS, it does not explain the disconnect between mobilized international actors and the people navigating the AIDS epidemic.

Misaligned Priorities, the Power of Donors, and the Weakness of Citizens

Building on the scholarship on HIV exceptionalism, I argue that a serious challenge confronting AIDS interventions in Africa is the misalignment of priorities. In the coming chapters, I show that while the international community treats HIV as exceptional, the intended beneficiaries of AIDS interventions see AIDS as a relatively low priority. In Malawi, AIDS interventions are substantially better funded by international donors than any other health and development intervention. At the same time, villagers I surveyed across Malawi ranked HIV/AIDS as the lowest of five development priorities; AIDS fell behind access to clean water, agricultural development, education, and general health services.

What determines health priorities if not the public opinion of those to whom health interventions are targeted? One might guess the severity of disease threat. However, work by political scientist Jeremy Shiffman (2006a; 2009) shows disease burden also fails to predict global health priorities; he found that while acute respiratory infections accounted for more than a quarter of disease burden in the developing world, it received less than 3% of health aid from 42 major donors

(Shiffman, 2006*a*, 415). In his research, Shiffman (2009) argues that the prominence of a global health issue is determined by how effectively its policy community[30] can build institutions that can sustain a portrayal of their issue as important in a way that resonates with elites.

HIV prevalence estimates are lower today in most of the world than they were 15 years ago, yet advocacy for AIDS response remains constant. UNAIDS handled the less-bleak estimates delicately, shifting the message about AIDS response from an "emergency" to a call for "universal human rights." UNAIDS also shifted the goal posts, demonstrating greater ambition. Instead of highlighting declining HIV prevalence estimates among children, the benchmark is now "getting to zero" HIV infections. Even if there has been some success in AIDS response (or, at least, some better measurements of the problem), actors in the international community continue to frame AIDS as an exceptional problem requiring an equivalently exceptional response.

Misaligned priorities – where international donors give HIV/AIDS high priority and citizens don't – create a context in which internationally supported interventions will not match the needs and interests of intended beneficiaries. In resource-poor settings like the countries hard hit by AIDS, donors wield significant power. Donors are not beholden nor accountable to citizens, and dictate through their budget allocations what issues will be prioritized. At the same time, citizens in resource-poor settings have little influence in designing large-scale health and development interventions, although their acceptance of these interventions ultimately shapes outcomes. The condom campaign in Mozambique discussed earlier demonstrates donors' lack of accountability: USAID and PSI suffered no consequences from the campaign that failed because of the poor reception from the community.

2.5 Conclusion

As the epigraph in this chapter aptly relayed, AIDS affects populations around the world. While Africa has shouldered most of the burden, there is significant variation in the intensity of the epidemic across the continent, with Southern Africa being the most deeply affected. The African experience with AIDS has been distinct not just in the

---

[30] Shiffman (2009) defines a policy community as a network of individuals and organizations that share a concern for a particular issue (609).

scale of the epidemic, but also in the focus of HIV interventions (e.g., reducing heterosexual transmission) and the late and rationed access to treatment for those sick with AIDS.

The response to AIDS has varied over time and across the continent. Political scientists often focus on government response to AIDS, though as this chapter has shown, governments frequently lagged behind their citizens and local communities (e.g., religious congregations) in responding to AIDS. Many government responses only began in earnest after an influx of funding from the international community.

This chapter also demonstrated the disconnect between interventions as imagined in global capitals and as implemented at the grassroots level. One illustration of this disconnect was the USAID-supported condom social marketing campaign in Mozambique that failed to increase condom use and actually generated a hostile backlash among intended beneficiaries. I have previewed the argument I put forward more concretely in the next chapter, which is that we can attribute this disconnect to a misalignment of priorities in the global supply chain of HIV/AIDS interventions. The model of intervention in Chapter 3 illustrates how governments and their implementation agents can be pulled in different directions by international donors funding responses and the citizens to whom interventions are targeted.

3 | *Principal–Agent Problems and AIDS Interventions in Africa*

But if things go through so many places, justice cannot be done since people want those things as well. From one place to another, many people would want to benefit something. As such, things can't reach far.

Headman Interview #82, Mchinji District, July 11, 2008

Government is soliciting funds from donors for HIV/AIDS cases but in turn the moneys end up being swindled by unscrupulous individuals who have no welfare of people at heart.

Malawian Journals Project, Distonie Daison, April 14, 2005

Imagine two HIV testing counselors, paid the same wage by the Ministry of Health. One works in an area mistrustful of government health initiatives, especially those involving blood tests, and so she puts forth a great deal of effort to mobilize people to get tested; she rides her bike to far-flung villages and holds village meetings promoting HIV testing. Her colleague, however, works in an area where people are more trusting of government health initiatives and where there is already high awareness about and acceptance of HIV testing. This second HIV testing counselor can stay in his office and play games on his mobile phone or read the newspaper while waiting for clients to come by his office to be HIV tested. The end-of-quarter report by the Ministry of Health enumerating the number of people HIV tested could show similar output by these two HIV testing counselors, even though their levels of effort were markedly different. The quantitative nature of reporting gives no indication of the quality of the work nor of accountability to intended beneficiaries (Ebrahim, 2003, 816). Because these HIV testing counselors were paid the same wages, financial incentives cannot explain their different levels of effort. I witnessed many situations like these in Malawi – where people in similar positions differed in how hard they worked for AIDS interventions. The difference I saw in what motivated these agents was their personal experience with AIDS and their consequent preferences that AIDS be prioritized.

The previous chapter substantiated both that AIDS is pandemic in Africa and that there has been an overwhelming response to AIDS by donors, governments, and citizens. Thirty years since its scientific discovery, AIDS continues to take more than a million lives each year and stakeholders have yet to find a "silver bullet" policy solution. Instead, policymakers design and fund interventions that are often disconnected from the contexts in which they are implemented.

In this chapter, I offer a framework for understanding disconnected AIDS interventions. Like other donor-supported health and development initiatives, AIDS interventions in Africa are beset by what social scientists call principal–agent problems. A principal–agent relationship involves two actors: one actor is a principal who delegates a task to another actor, an agent. Principal–agent problems are the challenges that arise when principals delegate tasks to agents. I illustrate in this chapter how delegating implementation of AIDS interventions to local agents challenges intervention success.

A lot of ink has been spilled documenting the failures of foreign aid. As you might expect, the scholars debating why foreign aid has failed have yet to reach a consensus.[1] Although it documents some failed AIDS interventions, this book is not primarily concerned with assessing overall whether aid for AIDS has failed. Instead, my contribution to the literature about "why aid fails" is to develop a better understanding of where and how things can go wrong.

I argue two characteristics doom the global AIDS intervention in Africa. First, nested principal–agent relationships inherent in the multitiered global AIDS intervention produce multiple opportunities for mismanagement. Second, agents actually implementing interventions on the ground act in ways congruent with both their policy preferences and the policy preferences of their fellow citizens, not external donors.

To build to this conclusion, I begin the chapter with an overview of the principal–agent framework and the two primary consequences of the principal–agent problem evident in HIV/AIDS interventions: adverse selection and preference misalignment. Then, I apply the principal–agent framework to the setting of HIV/AIDS interventions

---

[1] The most well-known debate is perhaps that fought between Sachs (2005) and Easterly (2006), but see also Moyo (2009). More connected to the arguments made in this book, however, is the global-to-local study of foreign aid by Gibson et al. (2005).

in Africa, identifying the many actors involved. I devote one section of the chapter to an illustrative example from Kenya of how the global-to-local supply chain of AIDS intervention offers multiple opportunities for corruption. Then, I present and debate the usefulness of some of the solutions scholars have offered for principal–agent problems that arise in health and development interventions. The last section of the chapter draws from the insights of the global hierarchy of AIDS intervention to illuminate a problem not often discussed in the development literature: how agents implementing interventions are cross-pressured by external donors and fellow citizens, whom I call agents' dueling principals.

3.1 Principal–Agent Framework

Moe (1984) defines the principal–agent model as: "an analytic expression of the agency relationship, in which one party, the principal, considers entering into a contractual agreement with another, the agent, in the expectation that the agent will subsequently choose actions that produce outcomes desired by the principal" (756). The principal–agent model formalizes what we call delegation. The principal offers a contract to the agent to produce an output for a wage. The agent chooses to exert effort in order to produce output. Agents want more wages and to exert the least effort possible. Using the language of economists about utility functions, an agent's decision on how much effort to exert is shaped by his goal to maximize his utility from wages and minimize the disutility of his efforts. The principal has different motivations; his utility function aims to minimize wages and maximize output. Ultimately, the agent is accountable to the principal in carrying out the task. Principals can rarely observe agents' efforts, but instead observe agents' output (Miller, 1992, 121).

We can see a conflict of interest when we compare the utility functions of the principal and the agent. The principal wants low wages and the agent wants high wages. Note also that the principal cares not about the agent's effort, but instead derives benefits from the agent's observed output. Certainly, output is some function of the agent's effort, but output is also dependent on conditions of nature.[2]

---

[2] Consider the example of a tenant farmer dependent on rain-fed agriculture: she could exert little effort in tilling the soil for her landlord yet still produce a significant output because of a good rainfall. Miller (1992) offers the example

Principals could elect to produce their desired output themselves, but there are advantages to delegation. Principals can benefit from the skills, knowledge, and abilities of agents. By delegating tasks, principals are then free to devote their effort to other tasks and/or pursue other goals. By delegating a task, however, the principal incurs risk of what is called agency loss. Agency loss is the difference between what a principal wants and what the agent delivers (Müller, Bergman and Strøm, 2003, 23).[3]

Agent Preferences Matter

Much of the scholarship on health and development interventions in Africa has argued that interventions suffer from weakly motivated agents. Work in development economics looks explicitly at incentivizing agents to perform, offering financial reward (punishment) for attendance (absence) (Banerjee, Duflo and Glennerster, 2008; Duflo, Hanna and Ryan, 2012; Cilliers et al., 2014). Institutional design solutions to the principal–agent problem in international aid interventions often overlook agents' preferences and motivations irrespective of wages.[4] Incentivizing agents in the ways proposed by the aforementioned development scholarship relies on the assumption that agents are solely motivated by wages.[5]

Wages are a critical component in shaping agent behavior, but studies of health worker motivation stress the importance of other motivating factors (Franco, Bennett and Kanfer, 2002). Using focus group discussion data from Tanzania, Manongi, Marchant and Bygbjerg (2006) argue financial incentives are insufficient motivation for health workers and convey health workers' prioritization of supportive supervision and performance appraisal. In Benin and Kenya,

---

of a salesperson who devotes great effort to her job only to find a product does not sell because of unforeseen moves by the competition or bad economic conditions (121).

[3] More specifically, agency loss is the difference between the outcome of delegation and what the outcome would have been had the principal done the task armed with unlimited information and resources (Lupia, 2003, 35).

[4] A notable exception is a policy experiment on police performance in India in which the incentive was a transfer to a more desirable post (Banerjee et al., 2014).

[5] Of course, there is some power in this assumption: teachers come to school when offered a financial incentive and students do better on exams when teachers come to school (Muralidharan and Sundararaman, 2011; Duflo, Hanna and Ryan, 2012).

Mathauer and Imhoff (2006) find that nonfinancial incentives and human resource management tools play an important role in increasing motivation of health professionals. And a study in Mali found that increased salary was a distant second to "feeling responsible" as an important motivating factor to health workers (Dieleman et al., 2006).

Agents have personal tastes for some policies and not others. Thus, I expect personal taste for a particular intervention will motivate agent effort. For example, we might expect an agent who is living with HIV to give greater priority to implementing an AIDS intervention, than, for example, implementing an intervention against climate change. Likewise, we should expect an agent more affected by AIDS to give greater priority to AIDS interventions than an agent less affected by AIDS.[6] Relatedly, we could imagine an agent who has never had a personal experience with AIDS or who thinks AIDS is not a priority issue to have little preference in particular for HIV/AIDS interventions.

Principal–Agent Problems: Adverse Selection and Preference Misalignment

Principal–agent problems are the challenges inherent in delegating tasks to agents. The principal–agent problems that can lead to agency loss include moral hazard, adverse selection, and preference misalignment. Moral hazard refers to the problem principals face in being able to keep their agents honest and diligent.[7] Because a principal cannot know for sure to what extent an agent is productive, the principal will rely on proxy measures like quality of reports, timeliness, and diligence; the principal's reliance on proxy measures incentivizes the agent to redirect efforts toward the proxy measures (Moe, 1984, 755). Although I cannot rule out the potential for moral hazard, such problems did not feature prominently in my observations of AIDS interventions in Africa.

---

[6] Chapter 5 offers evidence consistent with this expectation: HIV-positive Malawians gave higher priority to HIV/AIDS interventions than HIV-negative Malawians.

[7] Lupia (2003) offers the classic example of buying life insurance to illustrate moral hazard: "Since the insurer cannot prevent its clients from all risks, it faces a moral hazard problem – its clients may take riskier actions after a policy is issued" (41).

The two features of principal–agent problems prominent in this book are adverse selection and preference misalignment. Adverse selection occurs when a principal may not select the right agent because the principal lacks information about an agent's skills and/or preferences. In AIDS interventions in Africa, principals often choose to delegate to agents precisely because principals lack local knowledge and networks. Thus it is difficult for principals to evaluate and select an agent with the local knowledge and networks necessary to implement a project successfully.

There are adversely selected agents at every level of the hierarchy of intervention. Take for example a woman selected to head Kenya's National AIDS Control Council (NACC), Dr. Margaret Gachara. Gachara lied about her previous salary and qualifications when hired and after an audit brought these facts to light, Gachara was ordered to repay NACC $340,000 (Tanui and Ng'ang'a, 2006). Another illustrative example comes from Gambia, where HIV rates never went higher than 2.1% (UNAIDS, 2016). Many new organizations formed after Gambia received $15 million from the World Bank for HIV/AIDS response in 2001; some saw the funding as a "money-making enterprise" and submitted substandard proposals in hopes of benefiting from the windfall (Cassidy and Leach, 2009a, 19). The overwhelming financial support for AIDS intervention in Africa makes such interventions a potential target for agents interested in personal enrichment. In other words, these well-financed interventions are at risk of recruiting agents who could have an "adverse" impact. Knowledge of AIDS financing is widespread, with citizens remarking "AIDS is money" (Morfit, 2011) and that "there is money in AIDS" (Cassidy and Leach, 2009a).

A second feature of principal–agent problems prominent in AIDS intervention in Africa is preference misalignment. Preference misalignment is the situation in which a principal and agent have different ideal policies and the agent carries out his task in a way that is more congruent with the agent's ideal policy than with the principal's ideal policy. A conversation I had with two bureaucrats working for a development agency illustrates the potential for agency loss from preference misalignment.[8] They were tasked with spending a large sum

---

[8] Meeting with bilateral agency officials in Lilongwe, Malawi, December 17, 2008.

on HIV/AIDS programming[9] but had just learned from the results of my study that their intended beneficiaries prioritized access to clean water over HIV/AIDS programs. The three of us sat in a Lilongwe café trying to brainstorm ways to rework HIV/AIDS program funding to support increased access to clean water. While the officials did not reject their principal's priorities, their ideal policy outcome no longer centered on HIV/AIDS but instead considered the priorities of intended beneficiaries as integral to program effectiveness.

It is possible that an agent and her principal will have conflicting interests, or desire different policies. In situations where an agent and principal have different "ideal" policies, the outcome implemented by an agent will pull away from the principal's ideal policy toward the agent's ideal policy (Romer and Rosenthal, 1978; Lupia, 2003). Especially in a context where a principal lacks information about agent action, the agent does not benefit from implementing interventions in a way that veers from her ideal policy (Lupia, 1992).

Preference misalignment on AIDS interventions in Africa has an important consequence for implementation: when agents have weak preferences for a policy that has been enacted, we should expect little motivation toward achieving output desired by the principal, which can compromise the success of HIV/AIDS interventions. Policy preferences do not have to be opposing for preference misalignment to create agency loss. An example from Morfit (2011) of an NGO working on gender illustrates a very slight deviation from a donor's preference. The NGO director would craft a proposal that incorporated AIDS issues to secure funding, but once that funding was received, it "could be directed to other pursuits" (Morfit, 2011, 70). Misaligned priorities in this case did not necessarily lead to personal enrichment but resulted in AIDS resources being allocated to non-AIDS programming.

Should principals find agents whose priorities align with their own, they may still diverge on preferences for the nature of an intervention. I expect a local agent will prefer that an intervention be designed such that it is congruent with the local context, which may be incongruent with how the principal envisioned the program. For example, a local

[9] Halperin's experience with the development agency USAID paints a similar picture: "USAID missions ... would receive reprimands for not spending their entire annual budgets. And some US government representatives working on AIDS, typically overburdened with bureaucratic responsibilities, often were out of touch with local cultural and other subtleties" (Timberg and Halperin, 2012, 358).

agent working in a socially conservative setting could highly prioritize HIV intervention and prefer HIV prevention campaigns focusing on abstinence rather than condoms. Should this agent's output be measured according to a principal's preference for condom distribution, the agent would be considered unproductive. The agent could even be accused of mismanagement of funds if she reappropriated condom-earmarked resources to provide anti-HIV programming that did not include condoms.

Rather than a simple relationship between a single principal and a single agent, imagine the principal–agent framework as a long chain of relationships. Actors can hold both the role of principal or agent, depending on whether interacting up or down this hierarchical chain. The complicated chain and duality of roles is best described by Moe (1984, 765–6), who wrote:

The whole of politics is therefore structured by a chain of principal–agent relationships, from citizen to politician to bureaucratic superior to bureaucratic subordinate and on down the hierarchy of government to the lowest-level bureaucrats who actually deliver services directly to citizens. Aside from the ultimate principal and the ultimate agent, each actor in the hierarchy occupies a dual role in which he serves both as principal and as agent.

To more directly apply the principal–agent framework I have introduced here to the global intervention against AIDS in Africa, we should make concrete what we mean by principals, agents, effort, and output in this context. Who are the principals, who are the agents, and who along the hierarchical chain holds both roles?

3.2 Principals and Agents of AIDS Interventions

There are so many organizations and agencies involved in the global intervention against AIDS that it can be hard to pin down who the principals and agents are. Figure 3.1 presents a stylized model of the hierarchy of actors involved in the global HIV/AIDS intervention. The left panel uses the Malawian context to offer specific examples of actors and what they are expected to contribute to the global AIDS intervention. The right panel makes explicit the links connecting actors and the long chain through which resources flow from donors to their intended beneficiaries; it also offers a blunt rendering of the decisions actors in the global hierarchy make. I categorize stakeholders according to this hierarchy: international principals, national agents and principals, regional agents and principals, local agents, and ordinary

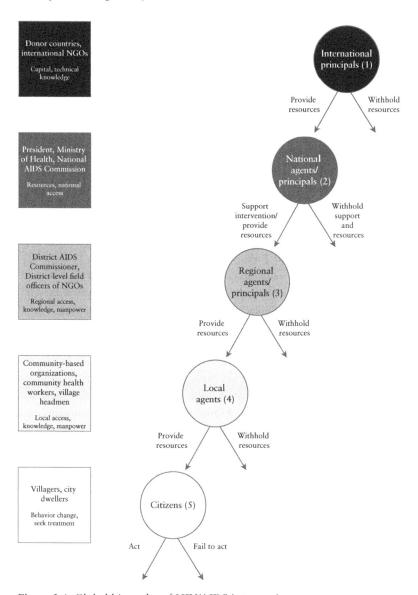

Figure 3.1 Global hierarchy of HIV/AIDS intervention

citizens who also act as local principals. The model could also be represented as a nonhierarchical network of principal–agent relationships,[10]

---

[10] Gibson et al. (2005) offer a related but more complicated "chain of aid delivery" that imagines multiple linked hierarchies, including, for example, a hierarchy of principals and agents in the donor organization and a hierarchy of

however, I adopt a hierarchical representation that is consistent with how resources – especially financial – flow through the global supply chain of AIDS intervention. This hierarchical representation is consistent with the asymmetry of power in global health governance in general and AIDS response specifically (Lieberman, 2009; Patterson, 2018).

International principals (1) are at the top of the global hierarchy, providing resources for HIV/AIDS interventions but lacking capacity to develop and implement programs in each AIDS-stricken country. These international principals include the major donors for HIV/AIDS interventions: bilateral government donors such as the US President's Emergency Plan for AIDS Relief (PEPFAR) and the United Kingdom's Department for International Development (DFID); multilateral donors like The Global Fund and the European Union; and private foundations like the Clinton Foundation and the Bill and Melinda Gates Foundation. External principals also include the international agencies shaping the policies and direction of AIDS response, like the World Health Organization (WHO) and the Joint United Nations Programme on HIV/AIDS (UNAIDS). International principals often contract out their AIDS intervention work to international organizations that can implement interventions, including Population Services International (PSI), World Vision, Marie Stopes, and Save the Children. What this amalgamation of international actors share in common is their involvement in AIDS interventions in Africa and their simultaneous reliance on local agents to implement their interventions. I characterize them as international principals because none of these principals would be capable of implementing without local agents and because they exist external to sites of implementation.

International principals provide resources to and rely on a range of national agents (2) to implement interventions. National agents include a country's National AIDS Commission (NAC) or Ministry of Health and also include national headquarters of some of the aforementioned international principals, e.g., the country office for Save the Children, located in Lilongwe, Malawi's capital city. National agents act as the conduits through which international principals can implement their

principals and agents in the recipient government. While their more comprehensive mapping of the structure illustrates the proliferation of actors involved, my slimmed-down model allows us to focus on the nature of the problem.

HIV/AIDS programming; they are second from the top in the global hierarchy. But national actors – the immediate agents of international principals – are themselves principals; much like international actors, national actors often lack capacity to implement programs, particularly beyond the capital city limits or wherever their headquarters are located. Thus national agents transform into principals themselves, who delegate implementation to regional agents.

Regional agents (3) receive resources and directives to collectively implement national programs in their respective geographic areas. Regional agents include District AIDS Commissioners, District Health Officers, and satellite offices of some of the aforementioned organizations that act as national principals, e.g., the Balaka District office of Save the Children. Regional agents are useful to their national principals because they have specialized knowledge about the area under their jurisdiction, making them capable of implementing interventions. For example, District AIDS Commissioners will know better than the NAC the most at-risk populations in their districts, and are likely to be acquainted with activists or representatives in these populations. So if the NAC initiated, for example, a program to encourage safer sex practices among youth, though the NAC might create standardized campaign materials, these would be used by the District AIDS Commissioners and their offices to generate programming to disseminate information on the campaign to local youth organizations and other institutions where youth congregate (i.e., schools). District-level knowledge can make implementation efficient. But like their national counterparts, regional agents will also act as principals, further delegating responsibility down the chain to local agents for implementation.

Local agents (4) are the penultimate link in the global supply chain of HIV/AIDS interventions. Unlike the national and regional agents above them, they often come into direct contact with intended beneficiaries of AIDS interventions: the people navigating the AIDS epidemic. Local agents of HIV/AIDS interventions in Africa include village headmen, community health workers, clinicians, religious leaders, and community-based organizations. They facilitate or even independently implement interventions on the ground.

The last set of actors in the global hierarchy of AIDS interventions are intended beneficiaries: citizens (5). They decide whether to cooperate with the agents implementing programs and change their behavior to prevent HIV transmission or seek support and treatment if they are sick with AIDS. Citizens are complicated actors: they are not only the intended beneficiaries of the global AIDS intervention but simultaneously the source of an agent's authority. Many agents depend on citizens' everyday cooperation for agents' legitimacy. Citizens expect agents like headmen, religious leaders, and even community health workers to provide for citizens' needs and to represent citizens' interests to outsiders and benefactors. Simultaneous to implementing programs supported by external principals, then, local agents also expend effort in generating outcomes that improve the welfare of their local principals: the citizens over whom they preside (Przeworski, 2003, 56). All the resources and efforts of the global AIDS intervention are expended with the claim of preventing the spread of HIV among these "local principals" and for the subset of them who are already ill, providing life-lengthening treatment. The primary complication, however, is that local principals have their own sets of preferences and priorities and can pressure local agent effort to be devoted to problems other than AIDS.

This global-to-local supply chain of HIV/AIDS intervention illustrates that the nature of the intervention – its multiple nested principal-agent relationships through which resources filter to the grassroots – provides multiple opportunities for leakage and corruption, as the opinions shared by Malawians in this chapter's epigraph suggest. In the next section, I explore at length a corruption case in Kenya to illustrate how people exploited opportunities for leakage at different links in the global supply chain of AIDS intervention.

3.3 How a Hierarchy of Principal–Agent Relationships Goes Wrong: Kenya's KHADREP Corruption Scandal

In 2000, the World Bank contracted with the Government of Kenya to fund an AIDS intervention, the Kenya HIV/AIDS Disaster Response Project (KHADREP). KHADREP's aims were to significantly increase HIV prevention, health care, and AIDS treatment, particularly for vulnerable groups like youth, women of child-bearing age, and high-risk communities. This World Bank commitment of $50 million to the Kenyan NACC was organized along three primary components:

- Component 1, $10.3 million to support government ministries to incorporate HIV/AIDS programming across sectors;

- Component 2, $12.1 million to coordinate programs and project activities by NACC and its decentralized entities; and
- Component 3, $30 million to support implementation of initiatives from civil society, private sector, and research institutions, with a strong priority given to community-driven initiatives (The World Bank, 2007, 3).

KHADREP is – unfortunately – an excellent example of how a hierarchy of principal–agent relationships can go wrong. The Kenyan government and the World Bank commissioned forensic audits of NACC's accounts, involving both the Kenya Anti-Corruption Commission and the Government Efficiency Monitoring Unit. These audits uncovered a wide range of accounting and management irregularities. Auditors found that ministry officials provided price estimates to bidders in exchange for future kickbacks and solicited bribes throughout the implementation process and NACC had internal procurement procedures that fostered collusive practices, biased bid evaluation, and fraud (Department of Institutional Integrity, 2007). The audits and subsequent probes showed that corruption and graft occurred across levels of governance in KHADREP's implementation.[11]

Dr. Margaret Gachara, the director of NACC until her dismissal in 2003, was charged and convicted of taking exaggerated salary and allowances. One report alleged Gachara received a salary seven times higher than she should have. Gachara was ordered to repay NACC $340,000. In August 2004, she was sentenced to 1 year in prison after being convicted of three counts of fraud and misuse of office; however, she was granted a presidential pardon in December 2004 (Tanui and Ng'ang'a, 2006).

Gachara's take from NACC was the largest, but she was not alone: senior managers and permanent secretaries were also accused of embezzlement. NACC's next director, Patrick Orege, was suspended in 2006 amid allegations of graft in disbursement of funding to NGOs.[12] Before Orege's departure, he had to recover $61,039 illegally paid out

---

[11] Caroline Mango, "Unit to Probe Sh19m HIV/Aids Council Scandal," *East African Standard*, July 3, 2002; "NACC: Cotu, MPs Join Fray," *East African Standard*, September 25, 2002; Victor Obure, "Corruption Alleged in Aids Council," *East African Standard*, June 12, 2003; "AIDS Council: Government Asked to Revoke Pay," *East African Standard*, July 31, 2003.

[12] Nixon Ng'ang'a, "Aids Council Boss Interdicted," *East African Standard*, February 28, 2006.

as bonuses to NACC staff.[13] All told, it is unclear how much of the $12.1 million devoted to KHADREP's Component 2 was necessary or effective in carrying out KHADREP's aims of preventing infection and providing care.

Graft and irregular accounting also occurred in the government ministries, particularly in the AIDS Control Units (ACUs) set up in government ministries to incorporate HIV/AIDS programming in each sector (as part of Component 1). Tanui and Ng'ang'a (2006) remarked the money channeled to ACUs was squandered with grants being spent on "needless seminars." The Ministry of Agriculture, for example, spent more than 75% of the $205,000 allocated by NACC from the KHADREP funding on staff accommodation, allowances, and participation fees at HIV awareness-raising events, and almost a third of those expenses are unaccounted for and presumed wasted.[14]

Organizations funded by NACC to implement KHADREP's community initiatives (as part of Component 3) also faced accusations of fraud and corruption. The World Bank audit of KHADREP identified: "(1) payments of bribes by grant recipients to public officials; (2) duplicated, fabricated, or inflated claims by grant recipients; (3) significant grant funds unaccounted for; (4) conflict of interest; and (5) abuse of power by public officials" (Department of Institutional Integrity, 2007, 4). One example of corruption found by the World Bank audit was a grant recipient paying a $430 bribe to a NACC disbursement officer to hasten transfer of NACC funding to the grant recipient's bank account (Department of Institutional Integrity, 2007, 23).

Small-scale regional organizations would submit proposals requesting NACC funding to a Constituency AIDS Control Committee (CACC), a local arm of NACC to which decisions about funding local HIV/AIDS initiatives were decentralized. Over 90% of the $30 million committed via Component 3 to community initiatives was allocated at the CACC level. Interviews conducted as part of the World Bank audit found that Members of Parliament (MPs) had undue influence on their respective local CACCs: grant applicants with personal ties to the MP were awarded grants to the detriment of other, genuinely committed local organizations (Department of Institutional Integrity, 2007, 24).

---

[13] Patrick Mathangani, "NACC Officials Paid Themselves over Sh37million," *East African Standard*, April 28, 2005; Mugo Njeru, "Sh69m for Aids Drive Missing," *Daily Nation*, May 4, 2005.

[14] Nixon Ng'ang'a, "Aids Cash Ended Up in a Bar," *East African Standard*, April 29, 2005.

Local CACC officials also engaged in nepotism: they would compel grant applicants to hire certain people, including him/herself, to write grant proposals for a fee (Department of Institutional Integrity, 2007, 25). One grant recipient reported that instead of paying secondary school fees for orphans, the organization used grant money to pay bribes (Department of Institutional Integrity, 2007, 25). Even before the World Bank audit was conducted, a chairwoman representing community-based organizations in one Kenyan district reported officials in CACCs demanded bribes and kickbacks before approving funding proposals for anti-AIDS programs.[15]

* * *

The KHADREP example highlights the challenge posed by an intervention with multiple nested principal–agent relationships. The World Bank did not have the infrastructure in Kenya to disburse funding for community-level anti-AIDS activities and thus had to rely on NACC. NACC lacked capacity in the various regions of Kenya to review and award grant proposals from community-based organizations to implement AIDS interventions locally and thus had to rely on CACCs. CACCs themselves do not implement interventions, but merely act as "middlemen" in disbursing funding and thus rely on the community-based organizations to implement programming as proposed. Figure 3.2 illustrates the transfer of funds between actors involved in KHADREP and the various opportunities for graft. The evidence of corruption across KHADREP's multiple levels of governance demonstrate how a decentralized AIDS program financed by international principals but implemented by national-level and then subnational agents has multiple opportunities for corruption and inefficiency. While the structure of KHADREP – and AIDS interventions more generally – gives rise to multiple principal–agent problems, scholars have offered potential solutions for overcoming these problems.

3.4 The Problems with Potential Solutions for Principal–Agent Problems

In devising solutions to principal–agent problems, scholars of development focus our attention on agents' behavior and motivation. The most

[15] Joseph Murimi, "Nyeri AIDS Groups Decry Funds Theft," *East African Standard*, July 3, 2003.

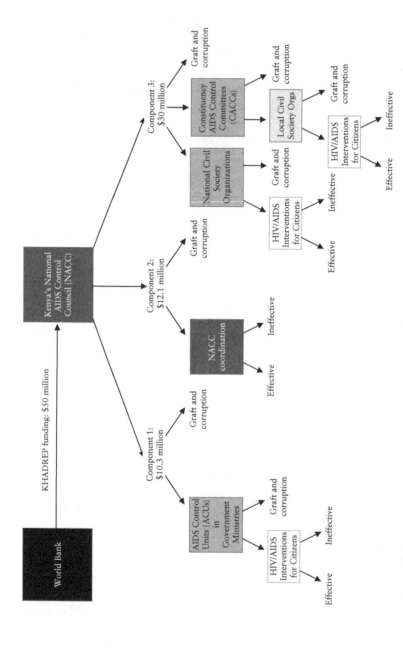

Figure 3.2 Potential for corruption in nested principal–agent relationships, Kenya's HIV/AIDS Disaster Response Project (KHADREP)

commonly studied local agents in developing country contexts – teachers and health service providers – have high absence rates (Chaudhury et al., 2006; Banerjee, Deaton and Duflo, 2004; Banerjee and Duflo, 2006), especially in poor, remote areas (Alcázar et al., 2006). Scholars draw attention to these frontline service providers' lack of motivation: low pay (McCoy et al., 2008), infrequent monitoring by the central bureaucracy (Banerjee, Duflo and Glennerster, 2008; Duflo, Hanna and Ryan, 2012; Cilliers et al., 2014), weak incentives to perform (Björkman and Svensson, 2009; Duflo, Hanna and Ryan, 2012), and generally difficult working conditions (Banerjee and Duflo, 2006; Muula and Maseko, 2006).

Findings from the development economics literature provide institutional design solutions to the principal–agent problem in international aid interventions. These institutional design solutions include the introduction of community-based monitoring (Björkman and Svensson, 2009), the provision of financial incentives to agents (Muralidharan and Sundararaman, 2011), and a combination of monitoring and financial incentives to motivate agents (Duflo, Hanna and Ryan, 2012). Essentially, the idea is that agents just need more incentives from and more monitoring by their principals in order for them to satisfactorily complete their delegated tasks.

Can we attenuate the principal–agent problems intrinsic to the global AIDS intervention in Africa using incentives or monitors? There are no studies to my knowledge that examine the impact of incentives on agents implementing HIV/AIDS interventions.[16] And, as I discussed earlier, scholarship examining health worker motivations found monetary incentives as insufficient motivation. But what about monitoring as a potential solution for principal–agent problems in AIDS interventions?

Monitoring is costly. A dollar spent by a principal on monitoring is one less dollar spent on the actual interventions principals want implemented. Monitoring can also be costly for agents. If in the course of monitoring, a principal finds an agent to be shirking, an agent can suffer a sanction on her wages, reducing them to a fraction of the wages the principal and agent initially agreed upon. And what does the costly

---

[16] There are, however, rigorous studies of the impact of incentives *for ordinary people* navigating the AIDS epidemic that demonstrate incentives can influence positive behavior change that leads to reduced HIV infection (Thornton, 2008; Baird et al., 2012).

action of monitoring buy? To answer that question, first we have to get a sense of what would be monitored.

One challenge to the monitoring solution is that the measures principals ultimately use to monitor agents can be misleading about agent effort. Agents can reach the same level of output with different levels of effort if implementing interventions in places or at times with variable conditions that can shape the intervention's impact.[17] Let's return to the HIV testing counselors example that opened the chapter, where one agent exerted high effort in promoting HIV testing but yielded few people coming for HIV tests because the villages in her area are largely mistrustful of blood testing. Her colleague exerted low effort in a different area not experiencing problems of mistrust among villagers regarding blood testing, and consequently had equal or even higher turnout than his counterpart. If a principal is unaware of the state of nature, his assessment of agent performance would rely only on the output measure, unless the principal chose to expend resources to also monitor effort. But what would measuring agent effort tell us?

Because it is difficult to measure the outcome principals care about (in the case of AIDS interventions, HIV incidence), AIDS interventions are similar to donor-funded projects more generally in that all are often measured by *outputs* rather than *outcomes*. For example, instead of reporting a reduction in HIV incidence (outcome), a project would report on the number of condoms handed out (output). Monitoring outputs instead of outcomes is not just unsatisfying but can also mislead principals as to their programming's impact. In the case of HIV intervention in Africa, we have little evidence of what works in preventing the spread of HIV: there is no vaccine, and thus most prevention interventions are targeted at behavior change, but there is little if any evidence that behavior change interventions have any impact on HIV incidence (Hogan and Salomon, 2005; Independent Evaluation Group, 2009). In reviewing the potential of monitoring as a solution to the principal–agent problem inherent to AIDS interventions in Africa, we have identified at least two information asymmetries[18] that favor agents: knowledge about agent effort and ignorance about interventions' actual impact on the outcomes principals care about.

---

[17] Consider again the example of the peasant farmer under contract with a landlord: she could exert high effort in a dry year and low effort in a wet year, with both years' harvests being equal.

[18] An information asymmetry refers to when in an interaction, one party has more or better information than the other.

Another problem is with the type of monitoring offered as a solution: community-based monitoring. As already alluded to (and as I will show in Chapter 5), the people navigating the AIDS epidemic do not prioritize HIV/AIDS over other health and development interventions. Why should we expect to see these same people for whom AIDS does not register as a priority to come together as communities to monitor whether local agents are following the directives of faraway principals who have interests divergent from their own? If anything, we might expect that if local communities organized to pressure agents on delivering goods and services, then these citizens might instead ask agents to devote efforts to issues of greater importance and higher priorities to citizens.

3.5 Agents Navigate Competing Pressures of Dueling Principals

Practitioners and scholars alike overlook a knotty problem local agents face: competing interests from two principals. Particularly in resource-poor settings, we focus on whether local agents implementing health and development interventions are doing so in line with the interests of the external principals resourcing interventions. But, agents are also beholden to local citizens, principals from whom they derive their legitimacy to act as agents. In contexts where there are multiple, competing principals, policy decision-making shifts to agents who form tradeoffs between these competing pressures (Whitford, 2005, 44).

A basic interpretation of an agent acting in her best interest would predict she allocates time and resources to the effort-minimizing task(s) assigned by the highest-paying principal most closely aligned to her policy preference. Her wages, however, can be modified by sanctions associated with monitoring by her principal. When there are dueling principals, agents thus also consider their principals' varying ability to monitor agents. Relatedly, agents will consider potential for repeated future interactions with each of her dueling principals. A sanction from a principal you only expect to encounter once will be much less costly in the long run than a sanction from a principal you expect to encounter again and again.

Village headmen are great examples of how agents are cross-pressured in the global AIDS hierarchy. Headmen are often sought out by external principals to assist with implementing interventions because – as I show in Chapter 6 – they are informative and influential gatekeepers. Headmen simultaneously act as agents of their villagers, representing their interests to external actors and governing the village according to villagers' interests and needs. Headmen's external and local principals have divergent preferences. International actors greatly prioritize HIV/AIDS interventions, whereas local citizens experiencing the AIDS pandemic firsthand prioritize other health and development concerns (Dionne, 2012; Youde, 2012; Dionne, Gerland and Watkins, 2013; Justesen, 2015).[19] Both principals have power over the headman agent: external principals offer resources, and local principals offer legitimacy and cooperation. How do agents navigate the competing preferences?

For village headmen evaluating tradeoffs between dueling principals in the global AIDS intervention, the context favors local principals. This is largely driven by the differential costs principals face in monitoring agents and the differential potential impact of sanctions. Local principals live in close proximity to agents and thus more frequently observe agent behavior. Local principals also have fewer agents whose behavior they might want to monitor; in the case of a Malawian village, many villagers can monitor the single agent – their village headman. External principals, on the other hand, initiate contracts with multiple agents and typically do not live in close proximity to most of those agents. Because monitoring will be less costly for local principals, agents will expect their activity will more likely be monitored by local principals than external principals.

The differential in potential sanctions for acting inconsistently with a principal's preferences also matters. Returning to the headman example, sanctions from local principals have higher potential costs for headmen agents. Although village headmen are typically unelected, villagers can use mechanisms other than elections to hold headmen accountable. For example, villagers displeased with their headman's actions can complain to an authority over the headman and after adjudicating the dispute, the higher order authority can sanction the headman. Sanctions include removing a headman from power. Although external principals can potentially offer headmen agents significant resources, opportunities with external principals are rare and repeated

---

[19] Chapter 5 provides greater detail on the evidence of high prioritization of AIDS in the international community, weak local prioritization of AIDS from rural Malawians, and mixed demand for increased resource devotion to AIDS services in Africa more broadly.

interactions with the same external principal (e.g., the same district officer of Save the Children) are even more unlikely.

In sum, when an agent is cross-pressured by dueling principals – in the case of Malawi village headmen, external donors and local constituents – we should expect an agent's decision of how to navigate competing priorities to be shaped by the local principal's preferences because the local principal has a monitoring and sanctioning advantage over the external principal.

3.6 Conclusion

This chapter described the global supply chain of AIDS intervention to illustrate how interventions are vulnerable at multiple links in the chain. I highlighted challenges posed by such a complicated hierarchy of stakeholders using insights from what social scientists call the principal–agent problem. Whereas the basic principal–agent model is concerned with one agent and one principal, the reality of the global AIDS intervention is that there are multiple, nested principal–agent relationships spanning different levels of governance. Even if uncommon, it is possible to imagine a scenario where every agent in a global supply chain of intervention acts as their respective principal wishes. Understanding the actions principals and agents take requires understanding the preferences of principals and agents, a task I take on in Chapters 5 and 6. Before diving into the data on policy priorities in Malawi, however, the next chapter provides an overview of the Malawian context and how the data analyzed in the later chapters were collected.

4 | *AIDS in Malawi*

If I say that we don't have people who are suffering from AIDS then I will lie.

Headman Interview #6, Balaka District, August 28, 2008

... as of now I would have been dead but because of these medicines that's why now I am found that I am alive and I am healthy.

PLHIV Interview #8, Mchinji District, July 7, 2007

As a group of men played *bawo*[1] and discussed current events, one shared his ideas about the origins of AIDS and questioned whether condoms are protective against HIV infection. Shortly after, a research assistant wrote down what the man said in a diary,[2] and I quote at length his recording of the man's claims:

The Americans are very clever. You can see that they were seeing the Africans begging [for] their aid time after time. And they [the Americans] realized that this begging was due to overpopulation in the African countries and then the "whites" made a number of meetings in order to find a better solution to avoid the frequent begging from the Africans. And at the end they decided to introduce the disease that is not curable to the Africans so that they should be dying of that disease and that's why they created what is said to be AIDS. And when they saw that the population is not going down, they introduced the condom telling the people that they can avoid getting AIDS if they use the condoms and that is a trick too. The condoms do also give other infections on their own and I have never used the condoms myself and I will never use them in my life.[3]

---

[1] *Bawo*, or *bao*, is a mancala board game of mathematical strategy. It is not uncommon in Malawi to find a group of men in a market or in the village gathered around two men playing.

[2] These observational data come from the Malawian Journals Project, discussed in greater detail near the end of this chapter.

[3] Malawian Journals Project, Diston Geladi, March 20, 2002.

To recap, this Malawian man alleges AIDS was created by Americans as a form of population control in response to African aid requests. He further claims that when the disease failed to control population growth, the "whites" – presumably Americans – introduced condoms because under the guise of protecting Africans from AIDS, condoms would also keep them from reproducing. While only one man's suspicions, the freethinking ideas shared at that *bawo* game offer a glimpse into Malawian perceptions of international interventions against AIDS.

My observations in Malawi have largely shaped my understanding of AIDS in Africa. In this chapter, I describe the Malawian context, including changes in the political and economic setting and the country's experience with AIDS. Then I use two contemporary events – a corruption scandal and contention over an HIV prevention strategy – to illustrate how accountability and alignment challenge AIDS intervention in Africa. I conclude with describing the Malawi data that I analyze in the remainder of the book.

4.1 A Context of Competing Challenges

Malawi is a small, densely populated country of 118,484 square kilometers and 17.2 million people.[4] It is a landlocked country in Southern Africa, bordered by Tanzania to the North, Mozambique to the East and South, and Zambia to the West. Increasingly scarce land in Malawi's population-dense physical environment has become more difficult to farm. Almost 90% of Malawi's population relies on subsistence farming, and nearly all subsistence farming in Malawi relies on rainfed agriculture. Farming has become less productive due to declining soil fertility (Carr, 1997) and more erratic weather patterns in the era of climate change. With limited agricultural opportunities, many Malawians migrate for labor to regional economic hegemon South Africa.

Malawians have significant development needs. They live in one of the poorest nations in the world. Using 2010 data, the World Bank estimated 82% of Malawians live on less than $2 a day (World Bank, 2014). Most (85%) of Malawi's population live in rural areas, where 96% of households rely on firewood for cooking, and only 2% of

[4] This is the mid-2016 population estimate from the Population Reference Bureau (2016).

households have access to piped water (National Statistical Office [Malawi], 2008). One manifestation of this poverty is low educational attainment among Malawians. Although many enter primary school, a large majority (62%) do not finish (Education Policy and Data Center, 2014). Poverty is also borne out physically: Almost half (48%) of Malawian children are stunted, which means they are at least two standard deviations below the international standard of height for age (National Statistical Office [Malawi] and ICF Macro, 2011).

AIDS is the top cause of death in Malawi, but it is only one of a number of significant health threats Malawians face.[5] We can compare the relative threat different diseases pose in Malawi using a measure known as Disability-Adjusted Life Years (DALYs), which are the sum of years of life lost to premature death and years lived with disability (Murray et al., 2013). HIV/AIDS accounted for 20.7% of total DALYs in Malawi in 2013; lower respiratory infections made up 10.7%, diarrheal diseases 9.4%, and malaria and malnutrition each accounted for 3.9% of DALYs in Malawi.[6] In other words, HIV is not the only threat to good health. Malawians simultaneously encounter multiple health threats associated with poverty. The three leading risk factors shaping Malawi's overall disease burden are malnutrition, unsafe sex, and water, sanitation, and handwashing (Institute for Health Metrics and Evaluation, 2016).

AIDS emerged in Malawi during a time of great change. A strong neoliberal shift began in 1981 when Malawi implemented a number of reforms under the auspices of structural adjustment programs (SAPs) supported by the World Bank and the International Monetary Fund. SAPs had serious consequences for Malawians, especially the poor (Chinsinga, 2002, 30–1). After SAPs, Malawians could not depend on publicly provided health services but instead resorted to self-treatment and traditional medicine as the government reduced the share of the budget devoted to health care (Chinsinga, 2002; Lwanda, 2002). These SAP-induced budget reductions precipitated severe scarcities of medicine and medical supplies in government hospitals and health centers (Kalipeni, 2000, 969). A major political shift followed shortly

[5] All comparative health indicators are the most recent figures from the Global Burden of Disease Study (Institute for Health Metrics and Evaluation, 2015, 2016).
[6] The next five leading causes of DALYs in Malawi in 2013 were: tuberculosis, neonatal preterm birth, congenital anomalies, neonatal encephalopathy, and meningitis.

thereafter, from rule by an autocrat to a semi-competitive multiparty system.

4.2 Democratic Shift, Dictatorial Legacy

Malawi is a young state, having only gained its independence from the British in 1964. Hastings Kamuzu Banda of the Malawi Congress Party (MCP) ruled Malawi for 30 years after independence, during which he named himself Life President. Banda was ruthless with any who opposed his absolute rule, and thousands of Malawians were imprisoned, killed, or forced to flee and live in exile during his reign (Posner 1995, 134; see also Mapanje 2011). High-level corruption during Banda's tenure enriched his personal finances as well as those of his close allies. Banda ruled when AIDS was first discovered in Malawi, but it was at that time that he began to lose grip on power. He left office after losing in the first competitive election in 1994, which followed a referendum to reintroduce multiparty competition in 1993. Malawi has since seen multiple alternations in power, but Banda's use of personalist rule[7] is his lasting legacy, even decades after his departure from office and subsequent death.

Ruling immediately after Banda was Bakili Muluzi of the United Democratic Front (UDF) party, who won office in 1994 with 47% of the popular vote. Muluzi won reelection in 1999 with 52% of the vote and attempted but was unsuccessful in amending the constitution so that he could run for a third term.[8] Muluzi's presidency was critical for continuing Banda's legacy of personalist rule into Malawi's new democratic era. As he quietly pursued his third term ambitions, he removed cabinet ministers who harbored presidential ambitions (Englund, 2006, 17).

Muluzi's party was widely criticized for corruption as early as his first term in office (The Economist Intelligence Unit, 1999). Corruption and personalist rule carried into his second term (The Economist

---

[7] Africanist political scientists Robert Jackson and Carl Rosberg (1984) define personal rule as a "political system in which the rivalries and struggles of powerful and wilful men, rather than impersonal institutions, ideologies, public policies, or class interests, are fundamental in shaping political life" (421).

[8] According to Section 83(3) of Malawi's 1994 Constitution, the president is limited to two five-year terms in office. Muluzi and his UDF party overestimated their ability to direct parliament in the quest for removing presidential term limits (Dulani and van Donge, 2005).

Intelligence Unit, 2006), with his administration funneling foreign aid to supporters and for political rather than developmental needs. Political scientist Ryan Briggs (2015) shares the example of an $11.8 million World Bank school project that produced only one-third of its expected outputs. Project evaluation documents pointed to a lack of oversight and overcompensation of contractors. An interview with an official from the Anti-Corruption Bureau (ACB) and leaked testimony from an ACB investigation suggest electoral pressure influenced spending, with school construction funds being used as handouts during campaign rallies (Briggs, 2015). Donors withheld government budget support during Muluzi's second term and called for greater accountability (Resnick, 2013).

Muluzi hand-picked his successor, Bingu wa Mutharika. Mutharika won the 2004 election with 36% of the vote. Once secure in office, Mutharika defected from Muluzi's UDF party in 2005 and created a new political party, the Democratic Progressive Party (DPP). He won reelection in 2009 with the widest margin since the reintroduction of multiparty politics,[9] largely thanks to a fertilizer subsidy program credited with improving food security for Malawi's mostly rural, agrarian population (Smiddy and Young, 2009; Dionne and Horowitz, 2016).

Mutharika took an authoritarian turn during his second term in office, continuing the tradition of personalist rule in Malawi. Like with Muluzi, donors became frustrated with Mutharika's personal enrichment and politicization of aid and removed budget support during his second term (Resnick, 2013). It is perhaps luck that the donor push to increase AIDS treatment in poor African countries like Malawi occurred during Mutharika's first term, when he needed and sought out the support of citizens and donors. Mutharika did not invest significantly in public health provision, and perhaps karmically, he died of a heart attack in the poorly resourced Kamuzu Central Hospital while still in office in 2012 (Dionne and Dulani, 2013).

Mutharika's vice president, Joyce Banda, assumed the presidency upon his death in April 2012. Although she was elected on the DPP ticket with Mutharika in 2009, he had started sidelining her in favor of promoting his brother, Peter Mutharika, as his successor. While still VP, Banda created a new political party, the People's Party. Largely because of a corruption scandal that came to light during her short

---

[9] In 2009, Mutharika won 66% of the popular vote and his main opposition candidate, John Tembo of the MCP, won only 31% of the vote.

tenure, Banda lost the presidency in 2014 to Peter Mutharika of the DPP, who won office with 36% of the vote (Dulani and Dionne, 2014). Banda's short time in office effectively limits any meaningful assessment of her impact, particularly with respect to AIDS, an epidemic that requires not just significant financial and human resources but also long-term planning. Banda had an election to win only two years after taking office, and dedicated much of her time in office to campaigning.

Despite these alternations in executive power, Malawi has yet to register as a "full democracy" as measured by political analysts. A recognized assessor of freedom in the world, Freedom House, has rated Malawi "partly free" since 1999, or the year of the second election following the reintroduction of multiparty competition (Freedom House, 2016). But what does "partly free" actually mean for ordinary citizens?

Political Participation after Malawi's New Dawn

Malawians have the freedom to participate in regular elections, which since multiparty reform in 1993 have been competitive. Malawians thus have a mechanism through which they can effect change in their government – at least once every five years. Voter turnout was high in the 1990s: 67% of registered voters turned out to vote in the 1993 referendum on whether to reintroduce multiparty competition and 81% voted in the first elections in 1994. Turnout increased in 1999, with 94% of registered voters voting, but declined considerably in 2004 to only 59%. Turnout was higher in the last two elections, with 78% voting in 2009 and 71% voting in 2014. These turnout trends track with citizens' satisfaction with democracy; according to Afrobarometer public opinion data, more Malawians report satisfaction with democracy than not, except in 2003 and 2005.

Malawians can also voice their opinions through collective action; freedom of assembly – and thus the right to protest – is also enshrined in the 1994 constitution. A dataset compiling social conflict events – including riots, strikes, and protests – counted 150 such events in Malawi between 1990 and 2015, averaging about six per year (Salehyan et al., 2012). Only a small fraction of Malawians engage in protests; never more than 10% of adult citizens have reported participating in strikes or protests in all six waves of the Malawi

Afrobarometer.[10] Some notable protests specifically voiced citizens' discontent with the rising cost of living and lack of economic opportunities. Unfortunately, such social action has not yielded significant change or response from government. Furthermore, the state's recent use of violent repression of protests discouraged protest participation, particularly among poorer Malawians (Dionne, Robinson and Kadzandira, 2013).

While the 1994 constitution gave Malawian citizens freedoms to express their opinions and priorities, the methods available to engage political leaders are few and far between. Elections only occur every five years and Malawians have grown disenchanted with elections as vehicles for improving their daily lives. Citizens see politicians as faraway elites who only visit their constituencies during campaign season. Although street demonstrations offer another mechanism to voice opinions, the lack of meaningful change following protests and the state repression of protestors diminish the value and impact of demonstrations. More importantly, the poverty faced by the average Malawian brings its own demands of time and effort that displace opportunities to engage in politics.

Other Checks on Executive Power in Malawi

Like in other democratizing countries, it is not just citizens that can check executive power in Malawi. The legislature, courts, and the media have demonstrated independence from Malawi's powerful presidents throughout the AIDS era.

Malawi's 193-seat[11] parliament is its sole legislative body. Its primary responsibility is passing an annual budget. MPs represent geographically defined single-member constituencies and are elected every five years under a first-past-the-post electoral system.[12] Malawi's parliament has become more independent since the one-party regime, when parliament acted as a rubber stamp for Kamuzu Banda. Only for

[10] The highest proportion was reported in the 2008/9 wave of Afrobarometer, when 9.6% of respondents replied affirmatively after being asked if they had attended a demonstration or protest march in the year before the survey interview.

[11] The first parliament after the reintroduction of multiparty politics in 1994 had only 177 seats. The number of parliamentary seats increased to 193 by the second election, in 1999.

[12] There are no electoral quotas or reserved seats for minority groups in Malawi's parliament.

a period of three years since the reintroduction of multiparty democracy, has a majority in parliament come from the same party as the president (2009–12); otherwise, the president has faced either an opposition parliament, often in which his ruling party held a plurality of seats. Both Muluzi and Mutharika faced challenges from parliament, including MPs boycotting parliament and stalling the passage of a budget in response to presidential maneuvers (Dulani and van Donge, 2005).

Significant checks on presidential power by the legislature, however, have been more the exception than the rule. Political scientist Daniel Young (2014) showed that in Malawi's multiparty era, many MPs have switched to the president's political party. Some likely switch to increase their chances of reelection, while others seek benefits usually afforded to only ruling party MPs, such as increased potential in being appointed to cabinet, which would confer tangible benefits like an office, staff, international travel, and a government vehicle (Young, 2014, 107). Diana Cammack, a long-time scholar of Malawian politics, attributes this discretion of the president to appoint cabinet with increasing the president's power and leaving "Malawi's parliament particularly weak" (2012, 383). All told then, Malawi's parliament is not a consistently viable check on presidential power.

The judicial branch of government can also act as a check on the executive. Malawi's courts have demonstrated some independence from the executive, appearing "relatively fearless" in deciding against the government, even when the president is involved in cases (VonDoepp, 2006, 396). Political scientist Peter VonDoepp (2006) attributes the relatively assertive nature of Malawi's judges to institutional protections they have against government backlash; namely, the president cannot act unilaterally to remove judges from the bench. Judicial independence in Malawi may be even stronger at times when the executive's popular support is low (VonDoepp, 2005). Strong presidents with significant popular support may nonetheless seek more control over the judiciary, as President Bingu wa Mutharika did. Mutharika's government used the DPP's legislative majority during his second term to pass a law eliminating the courts' ability to grant injunctions against the government (Dionne and Dulani, 2013, 114). So although the judicial branch has some independence from the presidency, that independence is influenced by the popularity of the president and his party's share of seats in parliament.

Theoretically, the media – or the "fourth estate" – also has the potential to act as a check on government power. Malawi's constitution guarantees freedom of the press and there are a wide range of news sources available to the public. Holding over from the one-party era, however, is the dominance of public media houses in Malawi's media landscape; these continue a long history of pro-government bias (Freedom House, 2015). Furthermore, presidents have found ways to limit the power of the media, whether through passing laws limiting press freedom, harassment or violence targeted at journalists, or co-opting prominent journalists by appointing them to government office. Violence against and harassment of journalists has been common even after the adoption of press freedom with the 1994 constitution (Freedom House, 2015). Journalists reported that harassment often followed publication of stories that offended the government (VonDoepp and Young, 2013, 37).

Essentially, power in Malawi is concentrated in the executive office and presidential politics has never offered much in the way of meaningful change for Malawians at the ballot box (1994 being a major exception). While other branches of government are meant to act as a check on executive power, they have little independence from Malawi's strongly presidential regime. Likewise, Malawi's media has the power to keep the executive in check, but minimal resources combined with harassment and violence against journalists effectively minimizes that power. The only other players with real power in Malawi are the donor community.

4.3 Donor Dependency

Donors wield significant power in Malawi, because it is heavily dependent on foreign aid. In 2009, for example, donor support funded 37% of the government's budget (Ministry of Finance [Malawi], 2011, 19). The level of aid as a share of gross national income has been 24% on average over the last two decades (Resnick, 2013, 110).

The most compelling illustration of the power of donors is how Malawi's government responds to donor threats to remove support. For example, since 2009, when two Malawians – Steven Monjeza and Tiwonge Chimbalanga – were arrested on charges of sodomy, multiple donors threatened to suspend aid to Malawi for violating the human rights of LGBTQ Malawians (Biruk, 2014). After Chimbalanga and Monjeza were convicted and sentenced to 14 years in prison, UN Secretary General Ban-Ki Moon paid a visit to then-president Bingu wa Mutharika. After the visit, Mutharika pardoned Chimbalanga and Monjeza. The Chimbalanga–Monjeza case is just one example in a long history of donors using the threat of aid withdrawal as a tool to change government behavior.

Political scientist Danielle Resnick (2013) characterizes Malawi's relationship with the donor community as cyclical, alternating between close cooperation and mutual distrust. More importantly, Resnick shows how development assistance has bolstered the power of the executive vis-á-vis parliament (2013, 133–4). Perhaps the most significant check on Malawi's executive over the last three decades then has been donors, who have tied conditionalities to their aid and withdrawn support during the tenure of all presidents who have served (Wroe, 2012; Resnick, 2013).

Donor withdrawals, delays, and diversions have serious consequences for Malawians. When donor delays or withdrawals yield shortfalls in funding public services, Malawi's government does not step in. Funding and supplying AIDS treatment programs is, unfortunately, a good example. Malawi's AIDS treatment program has suffered critical drug supply shortages due to delayed release of donor funding and subsequent logistical delays (Ministry of Health HIV Unit [Malawi], 2010, 1,10). A 2009 audit of clinics providing antiretroviral treatment (ARV) found that 15 clinics had no stock of first-line ARV, meaning any patient coming to one of these fifteen clinics for a prescription refill would have left empty-handed (Ministry of Health HIV Unit [Malawi], 2010, 7).

* * *

To summarize the context in which AIDS emerged in Malawi: citizens' day-to-day lives are – on average – materially deficient, and we should expect that to shape their policy priorities. While Malawians enjoy relative freedom today as compared to previous decades of dictatorship, they have little influence over their government. Real power resides in the executive branch of government, and to a lesser extent, with international donors. While donors can act as a check on government power, there are no accountability mechanisms in place that can act as a check on donor power. All told, it should be no surprise that when it comes to responding to AIDS in Malawi, donor priorities take precedence over citizen priorities. Now, we turn to an overview of the AIDS epidemic in Malawi, to give additional necessary context to understanding and evaluating AIDS response.

4.4 HIV/AIDS in Malawi

HIV Prevalence and Transmission

Malawi has a mature epidemic. Retrospective analysis of blood samples collected between 1981 and 1989 from a randomly drawn sample of Malawians in the northern district of Karonga show HIV was circulating in Malawi at least as early as 1982 (Glynn et al., 2001). The first AIDS diagnosis in Malawi was in February 1985 and twelve additional cases were identified later that year (Cheesbrough, 1986). At the same time, HIV prevalence was 2% among women seeking antenatal care at one of the country's largest hospitals, Queen Elizabeth Central Hospital, located in Blantyre, Malawi's commercial capital (Lwanda, 2004). Early data estimating HIV prevalence are likely to significantly undercount HIV-positive Malawians given a short supply of HIV testing kits and delays in testing early in the epidemic (Reeve, 1989, 1568). High rates of HIV among Malawian miners working in South Africa led to the repatriation of all Malawian miners back to Malawi in 1985 and 1986 and of some 13,000 Malawian migrant workers between 1988 and 1992 (Chirwa, 1998). While the repatriation of Malawian migrants was largely a political move by South African politicians responding to domestic pressures (Chirwa, 1998), it had significant consequences for Malawi's emerging AIDS epidemic.

As the village headman simply put it in the quote that began this chapter, there is no denying the toll AIDS has taken. Between 1990 and 2015, an estimated 1.1 million Malawians died of AIDS (Institute for Health Metrics and Evaluation, 2015). One of the most tragic impacts of AIDS has been that borne by those left behind. By 1996, 71% of women and 68% of men reported knowing someone with AIDS or knowing someone who had died of AIDS (National Statistical Office [Malawi] and Macro International Inc., 1997, 73–4).

Malawi is often characterized as the nation with a million orphans, another consequence of AIDS. The National Statistical Office [Malawi] (2008, 15) estimated 12% of the under-18 population have lost at least one biological parent. Services to support orphans and vulnerable children (OVC) is limited: only 6% of OVC households in Malawi received medical support, and only 9% received social/material support (National Statistical Office [Malawi] and United Nations Children's Fund, 2008, 260).

In Malawi, HIV is primarily transmitted through sex. Most people living with HIV (PLHIV) in Malawi contracted HIV in heterosexual relationships, though a significant minority of men became infected through sex with other men. It was only late in Malawi's epidemic that scholars and advocates identified men who have sex with men (MSM) as a major risk group. The first studies of MSM and HIV were not conducted until 2008, more than two decades after Malawi's first AIDS diagnosis (Wirtz et al., 2013).

The overall trend in HIV prevalence is best understood after 1990, when there were sufficient data to measure prevalence nationwide.[13] Since 1990, HIV prevalence increased, peaking at 17.5% of the adult population in 1999 and 2000. HIV prevalence estimates have declined since then,[14] but Malawi has consistently ranked in the top ten countries in the world for adult HIV prevalence (see Figure 4.1). The most recent data estimate Malawi's adult HIV prevalence to be 9.2%, the ninth-highest in the world (UNAIDS 2017). Since the adoption of population-based HIV estimates, then, Malawi has had a generalized epidemic – what epidemiologists define as an epidemic affecting the general population, which occurs when national HIV prevalence passes the threshold of 1%.

HIV prevalence varies across regions and subgroups in Malawi. Prevalence is lowest in the northern region, estimated at 8.2%, and highest in the southern region, estimated at 17.6% (National Statistical Office [Malawi] and ICF Macro, 2011). HIV prevalence is higher in urban areas (17.4%), though the great majority of PLHIV reside in rural Malawi, where prevalence is 9% and where services are the least developed (National AIDS Commission [Malawi], 2014, 6). Wealthier Malawians are more likely to be infected than the poor; among rural

---

[13] HIV prevalence estimates prior to 1990 relied heavily on data from antenatal clinics. After researchers showed how such estimates overestimate prevalence because women seeking antenatal care are not representative of the broader population, HIV prevalence estimates began to also include data from population-based HIV testing.

[14] Some of the decline in HIV prevalence after 2005 can be attributed to adjustments in mathematical models estimating prevalence, rather than changes in the proportion of the population infected (National AIDS Commission [Malawi], 2010).

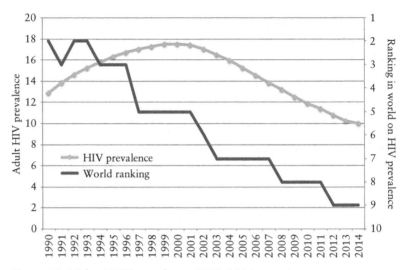

Figure 4.1 Malawi HIV prevalence, 1999–2014

men, Poulin, Dovel and Watkins (2016) found that wealth is significantly and positively associated with HIV infection. HIV prevalence is highest among the Lomwe ethnic group, of which 16.8% tested positive in the 2010 Malawi Demographic and Health Survey, compared to only 7.2% of Chewas and Tumbukas, and 13.1% of Yaos (National Statistical Office [Malawi] and ICF Macro, 2011, 198).

While HIV is a threat to the general population, HIV prevalence is highest among what HIV researchers and practitioners call most-at-risk populations (MARPs). In Malawi, MARPs include female sex workers, who have an HIV prevalence of 71%; police officers, among whom 33% of women and 24% of men are infected; primary school teachers, among whom 22% of women and 24% of men are infected; and female traders on Malawi's borders, who have an HIV prevalence of 23% (National AIDS Commission [Malawi], 2014, 7). Recent research also suggests MSM have increased risk of being infected with HIV in Malawi (Baral et al., 2009). Same sex acts are criminalized and stigmatized in Malawi, making it difficult to precisely estimate HIV prevalence among MSM, but one recent study estimates it is 15% (Wirtz et al., 2013).

Analysts attribute Malawi's high HIV prevalence to a number of factors. A 2010 UNAIDS country profile of Malawi suggests a laundry list of characteristics have fueled the AIDS epidemic there: poverty; low literacy levels; high rates of casual and transactional unprotected sex in the general population, particularly among youth (aged 15–24); low condom use; cultural and religious factors; and stigma and discrimination. While these characteristics are certainly present, their impact on HIV prevalence is less clear. Economist Nicoli Nattrass (2009) argues contextual factors dwarf the impact of economic determinants (e.g., poverty). Her research would suggest Malawi's location in Southern Africa, where HIV prevalence is high, is the primary factor shaping Malawi's high prevalence. Relatedly, historical migration patterns of Malawians to South Africa for labor is also a likely factor driving Malawi's high HIV prevalence. The migrant labor system connecting Malawi and South Africa encouraged high-risk sexual behavior and efficiently transmits HIV over a broad geographic area (Jochelson, Mothibeli and Leger, 1991). Unmentioned in the UNAIDS country profile was Malawi's low circumcision rates, which could also account for Malawi's high HIV prevalence (Poulin and Muula, 2011).

HIV Testing and AIDS Care

HIV testing was limited in Malawi until the 1990s, requiring, for example, transportation of samples to the central hospital laboratory in Blantyre for testing (Reeve, 1989). In 2003, rapid HIV tests that required just a finger prick became available in government hospitals for inpatients. In 2004 and 2005, the Ministry of Health received Global Fund support to scale up HIV testing and counseling to all district hospitals and many rural government-operated hospitals and clinics. Since then, HIV testing services have been offered free of charge. HIV testing coverage expanded considerably in the last decade, with only 17% of women and 30% of men reporting having never been tested for HIV (National Statistical Office [Malawi] and The DHS Program, 2016, 43–4). This is down from 83% of women and men who reported never having been HIV tested in 2004 (National Statistical Office [Malawi] and ORC Macro, 2005, 203).

Access to treatment began in the 2000s and has also expanded considerably over time. In 2002, only three clinics in Malawi offered AIDS patients ARV treatment, but by 2008, that number had increased to 221 (Ministry of Health [Malawi], 2010). By December 2013, there were 689 sites providing ARV services and 472,865 patients alive on ARV, with 102,586 initiated in 2013 alone (National AIDS Commission [Malawi], 2014, 32). As the PLHIV quoted at the start of the chapter shows, the qualitative impact is even more impressive. Unfortunately for a third of those in need of AIDS treatment in Malawi, there is still a shortfall in supply (Government of Malawi, 2015).

The HIV testing and AIDS treatment landscape expanded again in 2016, when the Malawi government adopted the "Test and Treat" initiative. Under this new framework, access to HIV testing would increase and anyone testing positive for HIV would immediately initiate ARV. Increasing the availability of HIV testing expands the population that are aware of their HIV status. Providing ARVs to all people who know themselves to be HIV-positive reduces their viral load, making them less likely to transmit HIV to others. At the population level, the "Test and Treat" strategy is expected to reduce HIV incidence, prevalence, and mortality in countries with severe epidemics (Granich et al., 2009).[15]

The "Test and Treat" initiative has faced serious obstacles. Agents expected to implement the new policy – frontline health workers – were slow to initiate training. At the time "Test and Treat" was introduced, there was lively debate in Malawi about compensation for training, with major donors calling for the elimination of per diems to civil servants to curtail fund mismanagement.[16] Civil servants responded to these efforts by not attending trainings.[17] Meanwhile, PLHIV wanting to initiate treatment and Malawians unaware of their HIV status were left in the lurch.

What Malawians Know and Think about AIDS

Like elsewhere in the world, knowledge about and attitudes toward AIDS in the early period in Malawi drew from fear, denial, and stigma.

---

[15] It is important to note that Powers et al. (2011) concluded from their study conducted in Lilongwe, Malawi's capital, that given the high rate of HIV transmission attributable to early infection (38%), early detection of and prevention of transmission from people with early infection are critical to the potential success of a "Test and Treat" strategy. Unfortunately, the current mode of HIV testing – antibody testing – would result in missed acute infection cases.

[16] Rebecca Chimjeka, "Donors Decry Allowance Culture," *The Nation*, August 13, 2016.

[17] Archibald, Kasakura, "Can of Worms for New HIV Plan," *The Nation*, August 13, 2016.

AIDS interventions were often packaged with family planning interventions (which were unpopular in Malawi), and as the story opening this chapter corroborates, some Malawians claimed AIDS was an "American" family planning plot (Lwanda, 2004, 35).[18] While stigma, denial, and even conspiracy theories about AIDS have been present in Malawi, they do not characterize general understandings of AIDS in the contemporary period.

AIDS is a subject of concern among Malawians, debated in public, even with strangers (Kaler, 2004a; Watkins, 2004). Folklore scholar Anika Wilson (2013) recalls during her first week of fieldwork in northern Malawi how a woman she had just met was sharing with her – and others waiting in a vehicle – how her absent husband was likely having an affair, saying "Marriage is one way to get AIDS" (33). In her study of rural women's strategies to avoid HIV infection, sociologist Enid Schatz (2005) found women will openly discuss with their partners, friends, and relatives the danger of AIDS and how promiscuous sexual behavior increases risk. Analyzing the Malawian Journals Project, sociologists Susan Watkins (2004) and Amy Kaler (2004a) find that during conversations at funerals, drinking sessions, or rides on public transport, Malawians share many ideas about AIDS, its origins, and how it is transmitted – debating how much behavior change can prevent infection.

Malawians' concern about AIDS parallels their relatively high levels of knowledge about HIV transmission and nondiscriminating attitudes toward PLHIV. In a nationally representative survey conducted in 1996, 97% of women and 99% of men reported knowing about AIDS and more than two-thirds of women and just under half of men reported multiple sexual partners as a way to get AIDS (National Statistical Office [Malawi] and Macro International Inc., 1997, 64–9). Malawians' acceptance of PLHIV is high, with 94% of women and 96% of men saying that they would be willing to care for relatives with AIDS at home (National Statistical Office [Malawi] and ORC Macro, 2001, 152–3). While one might attribute high levels of knowledge and accepting attitudes to decades of donor-funded HIV awareness-raising campaigns, these data predate multimillion dollar commitments for

---

[18] Malawians do not have a monopoly on the conspiracy theory of AIDS introduced by white people to kill Africans. See Mshana et al. (2006) for similar findings in rural Tanzania and Cohen (1999) for the same ideas offered by Black Americans.

AIDS response by donors. Malawians' knowledge of HIV and acceptance of PLHIV should not be surprising given how many of them have had personal experiences losing someone to AIDS.

* * *

HIV prevalence is no longer climbing in Malawi, but the HIV/AIDS situation remains serious. Despite significant scale-up of HIV/AIDS services in the last decade, coverage remains limited. Malawians' discussion of HIV and acceptance of PLHIV demonstrate the potential of grassroots response.

4.5 Responses to AIDS in Malawi

There is no silver bullet for AIDS response. There has been a lot of trial and error in crafting responses that identify the infected and prevent further transmission. Malawi's AIDS response has evolved over time. A consistent thread in national-level response is adoption of programs designed by powerful donors keen to support technological advances in treatment and prevention. While the Malawian government and international donors largely shape the nature of national response to AIDS, efforts by citizens and civil society were especially influential early in the epidemic, before AIDS was a priority among government and donors.

Citizen and Civil Society Response

Government response – detailed later – came "well after" ordinary Malawians developed their own strategies for responding to AIDS (Watkins, 2004, 679). In their 20-year study in Zomba district, Peters, Walker and Kambewa (2008) characterized how villagers responded to AIDS as "striving for normality" – not an act of denial, but rather efforts "to *control* the abnormal circumstances of the rising toll of HIV-related illness and death, making huge efforts to channel them into the normal and normative ways of their society" (662, emphasis in the original). Responses by ordinary citizens involved both reducing chances of HIV infection and caring for those sick with and affected by AIDS.

Some strategies to avoid HIV infection include fidelity (or, at least, a modified version), greater attention to partner selection, seeking

HIV tests when suspicious about a partner's behavior, and divorce (Watkins, 2004; Smith and Watkins, 2005; Peters, Walker and Kambewa, 2008; Reniers, 2008). In addition to actions Malawians took to protect themselves, they also made efforts to protect their loved ones. Sociologist Amy Kaler (2004a) writes of maternal uncles – traditionally expected to advise and counsel their sisters' children – advising nephews to change their behavior in order to avoid HIV infection (292).

When many Malawians became ill with AIDS, it was ordinary citizens – not the government or the greater healthcare system – who provided the care they needed. Chimwaza and Watkins (2004) document how relatives – especially women – were the primary source of care for AIDS patients in Malawi. Beyond care of the ill, Mtika (2001) shares the example of caring for the "AIDS-affected": a brother providing financial assistance to his sister, who was caring for 12 grandchildren from her three daughters believed to have died of AIDS. Even after the influx of donor funding and attention to AIDS in Malawi, most of the day-to-day help Malawians facing AIDS receive is from their friends and family (Swidler and Watkins, 2017).

Western medicine did not offer much to Malawians sick with AIDS early in the epidemic, and so PLHIV often sought care from traditional medicine (Lwanda, 2004, 36). For example, one of the first patients diagnosed with AIDS was discharged because his father sought a second opinion from a traditional healer (Cheesbrough, 1986, 6). Traditional healing offered Malawians more financially accessible, feasible approaches (Trinitapoli and Weinreb, 2012, 146).

Mchape, one purported traditional remedy,[19] drew between 300,000 and one million people to a rural village in 1995. It was the invention of Billy Chisupe, a subsistence farmer who claimed that he had dreams where spirits (one recognized as his maternal uncle) instructed him on how to prepare the cure, how it should be distributed (at his home and for free), and that it would both cure and prevent AIDS (Doran, 2007; Mkandawire, Luginaah and Bezner-Kerr, 2011). Doran (2007) offered three reasons why *Mchape* was so popular: people were afraid of AIDS, people believed *Mchape* would cure them, and Chisupe was giving "voice to popular frustration with the conglomeration of Western and government agencies and individuals at the head of the

---

[19] *Mchape* was a liquid made from soaking a special tree bark in water.

national response to AIDS" (400).[20] Seeking Chisupe's remedy meant queuing for many hours with hundreds of other people, and potentially being part of the daily news coverage of Chisupe's village. One thing *Mchape* demonstrates is that even if AIDS was a taboo subject early in the epidemic, hundreds of thousands of Malawians were willing to participate in this public activity in the chance they might be cured.

There were also groups and organizations at the community level responding to AIDS – many without assistance from the government or international donors. For example, sociologists Jenny Trinitapoli and Alexander Weinreb (2012) have documented the important role that local religious congregations have played both in promoting HIV prevention and also in caring for Malawians sick with AIDS. They found that religious congregations – particularly Christian ones – supplemented the care provided by sick Malawians' family members. Schou and Tsoka (2012) report that civil society organizations were also "heavily engaged" in Malawi's HIV/AIDS efforts, while at the same time admitting that evaluating the activity of community-based organizations is challenging because of a lack of reliable information about programming and location.

* * *

These grassroots efforts substantiate that Malawians were willing and able to respond to AIDS, but how well did these efforts inform coordinated response at higher levels of governance? Put another way, how well connected were higher level responses to the efforts already being undertaken by citizens? In the remainder of this section, I describe the response to AIDS by the Malawian government and international donors. Examined together, the differences according to who is responding demonstrates the disconnects in the global-to-local supply chain of AIDS intervention.

Government Response

Malawi government response has not been as robust as local community response, with one scholar calling it "low key" when compared to

---

[20] Hanson (2010) points out, however, that Chisupe's claims that *Mchape* would protect people from AIDS required that those who took it abstain from promiscuous sex afterwards. In other words, even as Chisupe's claim to cure AIDS was false, he offered good HIV prevention advice to all who came to him.

Table 4.1 *A timeline of HIV/AIDS in Malawi*

1985	First AIDS diagnosis in Malawi.
1988	National AIDS Control Programme (NACP) established within the Ministry of Health and Population to coordinate national response to HIV and AIDS epidemic.
1999	President Bakili Muluzi declares HIV/AIDS a national emergency.
2001	NAC established, replacing NACP.
2002	Malawi received final approval from the Global Fund for US$196 million over 5 years to fund treatment, care, and support activities.
2004	ARV treatment became free, but access was limited.
2007/2008	First study conducted explicitly focused on measuring HIV prevalence and risk factors among men who have sex with men (MSM) in Malawi.
2010	Global Fund audit finds financial irregularities and mismanagement by NAC, after which donors either withdraw aid or make significant shifts in channeling financial support.
2014	NACgate scandal revealed in national media, alleging mismanagement of funds with the First Lady and former president both implicated.
2016	Government launches "Test and Treat" strategy to increase number of Malawians who know their HIV status and to increase the proportion of PLHIV on treatment.

governments in other African countries facing severe epidemics (Kaler, 2004*a*, 286). Table 4.1 presents a timeline of Malawi's experience with HIV and AIDS, including important key government actions. Government response to AIDS was initially a lackluster effort, though as politicians began to understand AIDS interventions as a source of foreign exchange, they performed political will (Lwanda, 2002, 2004; Kaler, 2004*a*; Watkins, 2004). Although the first AIDS case was diagnosed in 1985, HIV/AIDS was not declared a national emergency until 1999, when HIV prevalence was at its peak, 17.5%. It was only after the turn of the millennium that the government developed comprehensive policies and programs.

Life President Kamuzu Banda who ruled until 1994 was characterized as having "made only modest efforts to respond to the epidemic"

(Watkins, 2004, 679). The "paralyzing governance" of the Banda era constrained even expatriate practitioners in responding to AIDS as it would involve discussions of sex, which was deemed imprudent for public discussion under Banda's conservative regime (Lwanda, 2002, 152). Likewise, contentious health issues were banned from public debate (Mkandawire, Luginaah and Bezner-Kerr, 2011, 91). Under Banda's repressive rule, tight control over information potentially damaging to Malawi's image could have fostered HIV's spread; Malawian scholar John Lwanda (2002) documents the official suppression of the news about high HIV rates among miners expelled from South Africa in 1985–6, which meant the men were quietly sent home, putting their wives and girlfriends at risk (159).

Banda's successor Bakili Muluzi is remembered as having done more than Banda, but his response was slow and apathetic. Before Muluzi was elected to office in 1994, his party's manifesto set AIDS as a high priority, but with the exception of one high-profile AIDS awareness walk by Muluzi, there were no similar high-profile events until 1997 (Lwanda, 2004, 39). Muluzi's continuity in office was not certain but required substantial voter support, which he bought through a repurposing of foreign aid. The constitutional restrictions limiting office tenure and his narrow win at the polls in 1994 meant Muluzi had a short time horizon, and his health and development policies and spending reflected that. Given AIDS has a long latent phase, Muluzi – like other African leaders – did not invest significantly in responding to AIDS (Dionne, 2011). A government document admits the early response lacked clarity: "Throughout the 80s and 90s, Malawi did not have a clear national HIV and AIDS policy guiding the implementation of HIV and AIDS activities" (Republic of Malawi, 2005).

Assessments of government response to AIDS since the turn of the millennium are mixed. By 2003, Malawi scored better than average on the overall AIDS Program and Effort Index (API) measure discussed in Chapter 2, scoring 77 out of a possible 100, whereas the average overall score in East and Southern Africa was 64 (USAID et al., 2003, 21). Nonetheless, as late as 2008, Malawian analysts characterized politicians' response to AIDS as just "lip service."[21]

HIV/AIDS policies and budget decisions have been the purview of the Office of the President and Cabinet and the NAC. Originally,

---

[21] Kondwani Munthali, "Politicians, Parties Dodging AIDS Fight," *The Nation*, May 25, 2008.

HIV/AIDS policy leadership came through a division in Malawi's Ministry of Health, the National AIDS Control Programme (NACP). NAC replaced NACP in July 2001, after the international community gave Malawi a $35 billion loan to create NAC.[22] Usually with the assistance of external consultants and under the advisement of the Office of the President and Cabinet, NAC creates national AIDS policies and "strategic frameworks" setting goals and priorities for dealing with Malawi's AIDS problem.

HIV policymaking demonstrates disconnect between branches of government and between government and citizens. Take for example the government's position on promoting condom use in its national HIV policy. There was vigorous debate over condoms in Malawi's parliament. Although MPs generally opposed a universal condom policy, government instituted a pro-condom policy in 2003, before the debate on condoms in parliament had even concluded (Mkandawire, Luginaah and Bezner-Kerr, 2011, 96). The government's adoption of a pro-condom policy was also disconnected from citizens' mostly negative attitudes toward condoms. Not only did citizens doubt the technical effectiveness of condoms, as the story that opened this chapter illustrates, people also saw condoms as an unwanted form of population control being instituted by a government they trusted little, whose actions were being supported by donors with potentially malevolent intentions (Kaler, 2004*b*).

NAC created management systems and funding mechanisms purported to mobilize the public and private sectors and civil society. Of course, as the previous section showed, a robust grassroots response to AIDS preceded government response. As Schou (2009) details, NAC established at the regional level umbrella organizations, who were responsible for mobilizing CBOs. NAC also was expected to coordinate the efforts of District AIDS Coordinators, who themselves headed District AIDS Coordinating Committees. Government documents also called for the establishment of Community AIDS Coordinating Committees and Village AIDS Committees. These structures

---

[22] From Garbus (2003, 6): "As of the end of 2000, the government's efforts to grant NACP the autonomy to implement the strategic framework were proceeding slowly. Additionally, NACP remained understaffed, thereby impeding its ability to function. Given the limitations of NACP, the NAC was established in July 2001 to coordinate multisectoral implementation of the strategic framework."

were inorganic and imposed from external actors, which explains why so few communities have them.

Essentially, government response to AIDS has showed little initiative by government and rather a government response to incentives from the donor community. Beyond the examples above, the mimicry of NAC policy documents to policy documents or initiatives supported by international stakeholders like UNAIDS and the WHO show Malawi's government asserts little autonomy in AIDS response.

Donor Response to AIDS in Malawi

Because the resources needed to address the AIDS epidemic place demand on already limited state resources, Malawi depends heavily on international donors to support AIDS interventions: 81% of Malawi's health expenditure and 99% of its HIV expenditure comes from donors (Clinton Health Access Initiative, 2015). According to AidData,[23] donors committed an average of $67 million in annual funding to Malawi for HIV/AIDS programs between 1990 and 2012. The scale of funding for HIV increased dramatically in the late 1990s. The first year for which there is data, 1990, saw only $671,929 in aid commitments, but by the end of the decade, the annual aid commitment for AIDS in Malawi was at more than $22 million (Peratsakis et al., 2012). Foreign aid for AIDS in Malawi was so remarkable that it shifted Malawi's development sector to favor AIDS programming above all else (Morfit, 2011).

In addition to the greatly increased volume of aid for AIDS, there was a proliferation of international agencies and organizations in Malawi's AIDS industry. In addition to major players like the Global Fund and US agencies, other multilateral and bilateral donors engaged in AIDS interventions in Malawi include Médecins sans Frontières, the United Kingdom's Department for International Development, Population Services International, Save the Children, World Vision, Catholic Relief Services, the Clinton–Hunter Initiative, and the European Union. There were also many smaller outfits engaged in anti-AIDS efforts that brought "altruists from afar," whether representatives from mid-sized

---

[23] AidData is a publicly supported initiative to collect and report data on foreign aid around the world. AidData also has a special foreign aid database for Malawi between 1994 and 2014 that captures roughly 80% of all aid projects supported by foreign donors (Peratsakis et al., 2012).

international NGOs or small Christian missionary groups from North America (Swidler and Watkins, 2017).

Depending on donors for AIDS response has proved unsustainable in Malawi. A 2010 audit by the Global Fund identified mismanagement of funds, after which the Global Fund suspended its current grant to Malawi, demanded a refund from the Malawian government, and rejected new proposals for HIV/AIDS funding from Malawi (Anderson and Patterson, 2017). It was at this same time that multiple bilateral donors withheld or redirected aid to Malawi (Wroe, 2012; Resnick, 2013; Anderson and Patterson, 2017). These shifts and withdrawals led to a funding crisis in Malawi's health sector (Anderson and Patterson, 2017), as the drug stockouts described earlier in the chapter demonstrate. A subsequent scandal at NAC also highlights donor power through aid withdrawal, while also illustrating the potential of civil society, the media, and parliament in holding NAC accountable.

Donors are central in two important aspects of AIDS response: accountability and alignment. In the remainder of this section, I present these two concepts through two examples: a corruption scandal that interrupted Malawi's AIDS response and donor promotion of male circumcision as HIV prevention.

Response to Response: Accountability and the 2014 NACgate Scandal

Reports began emerging in late 2014 of a corruption scandal at NAC; media dubbed the scandal "NACgate."[24] Implicated in the scandal were two organizations loosely connected to sitting president Peter Mutharika: Beautify Malawi (BEAM) Trust, which is headed by First Lady Gertrude Mutharika; and Mulhako wa Alhomwe, a cultural group that represents the interests of the Lomwe ethnic group, which was initiated during Mutharika's brother's first term in office and to which both Presidents Mutharika ascribed. In an initial investigative report, *The Nation* found the two groups were awarded $30,000

[24] NACgate followed a widely publicized corruption scandal known in Malawi as "Cashgate." In 2013, local investigative reporters broke the Cashgate scandal, in which officials siphoned tens of millions of dollars in government funds through fraudulent payments and loopholes via Malawi's Integrated Financial Management Information System payment platform.

from NAC to fund activities having nothing to do with AIDS.[25] Later reports exposed how the previous administration – of President Joyce Banda – was also tied to improper benefits from NAC, including vehicles borrowed from NAC during the 2014 election campaign period and increased funding to Banda's private foundation, the Joyce Banda Foundation International.[26] No one has refuted the claim that resources were misused as resources given to NAC were meant to fund its mission of leading national response to HIV and AIDS in Malawi, and none of the activities supported by these grants had to do with AIDS response.

Both parliament and civil society responded promptly to reports of NAC's mismanagement of funds meant for AIDS response. In parliament, an opposition MP and the chairperson of the Budget and Finance Committee, Rhino Chiphiko, asked the Minister of Finance, Goodall Gondwe, to comment on how the government was dealing with ineligible expenditures made using Global Fund money.[27] Civil society organizations and Malawian NGOs working on health and HIV/AIDS issues threatened that they would demonstrate in the streets if BEAM Trust and Mulhako wa Alhomwe did not pay back the funds from NAC.[28]

Following NACgate's revelation, and upon closer investigation of NAC finances, the Global Fund demanded a refund of $3.3 million from Malawi's government, saying it had abused funds.[29] The Global Fund also redirected all of its HIV/AIDS funding away from NAC, channeling their funding instead through Malawi's Ministry of Health and two international NGOs, Action Aid and World Vision.[30] This maneuver allows the Global Fund to support anti-AIDS efforts while bypassing government structures alleged to have misappropriated funds. The Global Fund takes the risk that the Ministry of Health

[25] Rebecca Chimjeka, "Beam Trust, Mulhako Bombard NAC with Funding Requests," *The Nation*, November 22, 2014.

[26] Rebecca Chimjeka, "NACgate: Audit Exposes Abuse at NAC, Funding to JBF," *The Nation*, February 14, 2015.

[27] Rebecca Chimjeka, "Explain Refunds to Global Fund–Chiphiko," *The Nation*, February 20, 2015.

[28] Rebecca Chimjeka, "Global Fund Pens NAC over BEAM Funding," *The Nation*, December 13, 2014.

[29] Lucky Mkandawire, "Malawi Paying Global Fund Refund," *The Nation*, May 20, 2015.

[30] Mabvuto Banda, "Global Fund Redirects $574 Million from Malawi AIDS Council," *Reuters*, March 25, 2015; Rebecca Chimjeka, "Global Fund Dumps NAC," *The Nation*, February 21, 2015.

or Action Aid or World Vision could also mishandle funds, as did their predecessor, NAC.

These actions by the media, civil society, parliament, and the international donor community suggest a context of accountability in Malawi's AIDS response, indicating that domestic watchdogs can be vigilant in monitoring anti-AIDS spending, even if anti-AIDS funds are externally provided. Likewise, donors electing to fund programming they support through alternative channels demonstrate a willingness to sanction government. Despite these pressures, however, government has not responded to the NACgate scandal in a meaningful way. No arrests have yet been made nor have there been reports of misappropriated funds being returned. The lack of action against high-level officials or organizations tied to the current and former presidents is consistent with Malawi's earlier experiences with corruption scandals.

Misalignment and Male Circumcision as HIV Prevention

I used a tool dubbed the "PEPFAR dashboard" to create Figure 4.2, which offers a glimpse of just a few links in the global supply chain of AIDS intervention in Malawi. On the left are US government agencies from whose budgets funding flows. Immediately to their right are the organizations who have won contracts to implement programs. These organizations include universities based in the United States, such as the University of Washington, and "local" NGOs, like Partners in Hope, which is a faith-based charity hospital in the capital city Lilongwe that was started by an American doctor. To the right of these organizations are the initiatives or programs for which the organizations have been funded to implement. The far right column includes PEPFAR's 15 different "budget codes," identifying the programming areas under which each of these grants fall. The budget code accounting for the greatest proportion of PEPFAR funding in Malawi is HTXS, which includes all funding spent on adult treatment.

We can follow one programmatic example through the diagram: "Support to MDF," a program funded by PEPFAR through the US Department of Defense (DOD) and contracted to be implemented by JHPIEGO, a nonprofit organization affiliated with Johns Hopkins University and by Project Concern International (PCI), an international NGO with an office in Malawi. The program's goal was to reduce HIV infection among soldiers in the Malawi Defence Force (MDF). PCI's task is to "create demand" for voluntary medical male circumcision

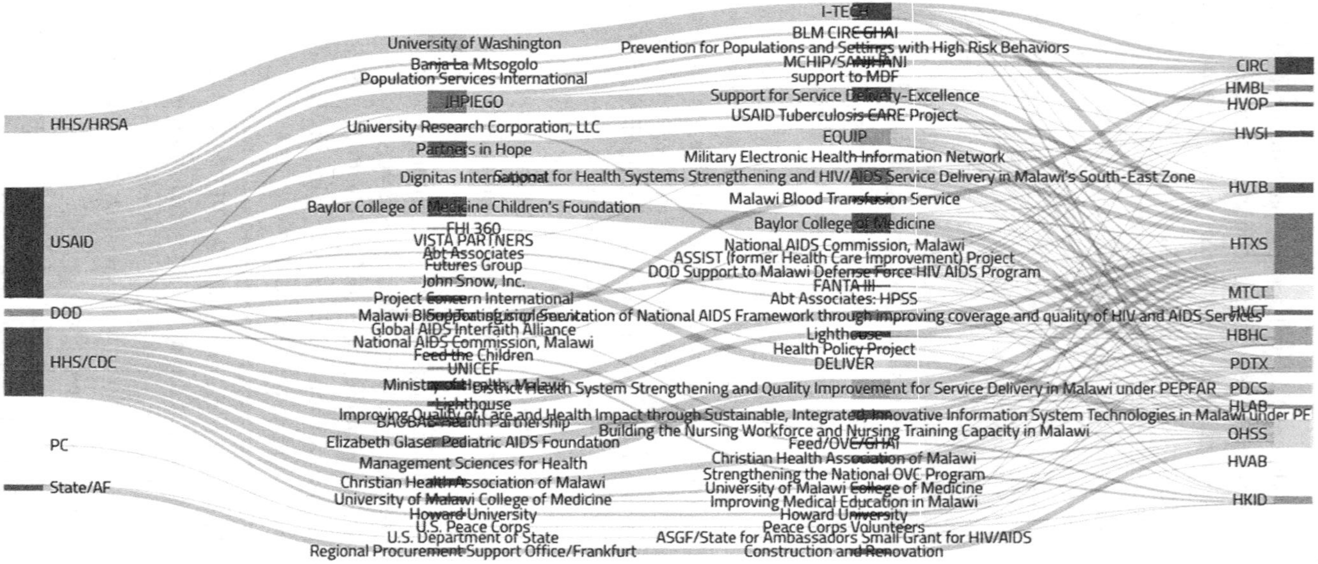

Figure 4.2 PEPFAR funding flow in Malawi, 2014

Source: U.S. President's Emergency Plan for AIDS Relief (2015)

(VMMC) and JHPIEGO's task is to provide VMMC to 5,000 MDF soldiers. That activity is ultimately categorized under the "CIRC" budget code, which accounts for all funding spent on VMMC programs. The planned funding in 2013 and 2014 for the "support to MDF" initiative was $750,000 ($300,000 in 2013 and $450,000 in 2014) (U.S. President's Emergency Plan for AIDS Relief, 2015).

PEPFAR support of VMMC programs in Malawi is part of a push in the international community to promote VMMC as essential in HIV prevention. This push followed the results of three randomized controlled trials that demonstrated the protective properties of VMMC against HIV in Africa (Auvert et al., 2005; Bailey et al., 2007; Gray et al., 2007). UNAIDS issued a policy statement in March 2007 recommending VMMC. The March 2007 endorsement urged countries with high HIV prevalence and low levels of male circumcision (MC) to increase access to MC as part of a comprehensive package of HIV prevention services. By May 2007 – only two months after the endorsement – there had been "a considerable evolution of thinking about MC," noticed during a meeting of the Eastern and Southern Africa Consultation on Safe Male Circumcision and HIV Prevention held in Harare, Zimbabwe (World Health Organization, 2007). Participants at the Harare meeting[31] strongly endorsed MC as an HIV prevention strategy. As the PEPFAR example above illustrates, international donors also began committing significant funds to support providing VMMC in high-prevalence countries.

Using the key concepts in Chapter 3 to relate the PEPFAR example to the book's broader argument, PEPFAR and the Department of Defense are the *international principals*. Their goal is to reduce HIV infection by increasing male circumcision among Malawians – particularly those in the military. PCI and JHPIEGO are the *agents* tasked with implementing the intervention and must partner with the Malawi Defense Force (a *local agent*) in doing so. The success of "Support to MDF" relies on PCI to effectively mobilize Malawian soldiers to want VMMC, which – as I will show below – is no small task. The program also relies on JHPIEGO to adequately carry out 5,000 circumcisions (the target goal), requiring equipment, facilities, and trained medical professionals. Ultimately, however, the decision to "receive"

---

[31] The 65 participants in the Harare meeting represented ministries of health, faith-based organizations, nongovernmental organizations, UN agencies, and development partners (World Health Organization, 2007, 7).

the intervention remains with the Malawian soldiers offered VMMC (*citizens*). But the "Support to MDF" program is a powerful illustration of misalignment between *international principals* who design and fund interventions and ordinary *citizens*, whose decisions on whether to accept internationally supported intervention ultimately decide the fate of the intervention.

On average, Malawians have negative opinions about male circumcision and they openly question whether it is actually protective against HIV. As the Malawi media reported on results from the three African VMMC trials,[32] I asked colleagues their assessments of MC as protective against HIV.[33] None of my Malawian friends or colleagues thought the procedure would work in Malawi, even those from an ethnic group that regularly practices MC. Their rejection of MC as protective against HIV drew from their understanding of regional differences in HIV rates: HIV prevalence is highest in Malawi's southern region, which is also where the population who practices male circumcision – the Yao – live in greatest numbers. The logic was that if MC was protective against HIV, then the southern region that has so many Yaos who circumcise should not have such high HIV rates. I would point to a working paper (later published as Poulin and Muula (2011)), which used data from Malawi's Southern Region to show that women with circumcised spouses have a lower probability of HIV infection compared to those with uncircumcised spouses. Even with these data, I could not convince my Malawian friends and colleagues that MC was partially protective against HIV.

These conversations with Malawians who questioned whether male circumcision was protective against HIV inspired research with sociologist and demographer Michelle Poulin, where we examine survey data from Malawi on opinions about male circumcision (Dionne and Poulin, 2013). We find few Malawians think circumcision is protective against HIV; only 14% of survey respondents reported that male circumcision decreases the chances of HIV infection. When asked their opinion about a hypothetical situation in which a friend decided to get circumcised, a majority (57%) offered negative responses like "He would risk getting a disease" or "He would be foolish" (Dionne and

[32] Gospel Mwalwanda, "About Male Circumcision," *The Nation*, November 5, 2007.
[33] These conversations were not unlike those Malawians were having among themselves starting in 2005 after newspaper and radio coverage of the South African VMMC study began (Dionne and Poulin, 2013, 610).

Poulin, 2013, 611–12). Most interestingly, we found attitudes toward circumcision varied by ethnicity and region and argued acceptance of circumcision as a tool for HIV prevention could be low in societies divided by ethnoregional identities that also shape the practice of circumcision. We expected VMMC to face low demand in Malawi because of these attitudes.

The push to scale up VMMC in Malawi has not been very effective. Of the 14 countries identified as priority countries for VMMC scale-up, Malawi performed the worst in achieving progress toward the goal of 80% male circumcision coverage, having managed to perform less than 2% of the circumcisions needed to reach its goal (World Health Organization Regional Office for Africa, 2013, 12–13). While a WHO report lists a number of obstacles to VMMC scale-up in Malawi, that list does not include the attitudes of Malawian men who are the targeted beneficiaries of VMMC interventions. Instead, the report pointed to Malawi's lack of a VMMC champion at the national and local levels (World Health Organization Regional Office for Africa, 2013, 5). Parkhurst, Chilongozi and Hutchinson (2015, 18–19) document resistance to VMMC by local officials, who perceived the initiative as one being "forced" upon Malawi by donors. The promotion of VMMC in Malawi is, unfortunately, an example of how well-funded anti-AIDS interventions that use technological advances are handicapped by important disconnects between the donors that support them and the population these interventions are meant to serve.

Misaligned preferences for male circumcision is just one example of disconnect in the global-to-local supply chain of AIDS responses in Malawi. In the remainder of this book, I examine misalignment on AIDS more generally in Malawi, particularly the misalignment of priorities between benefactors and beneficiaries. Measuring priorities for AIDS interventions requires original data collection, the description of which I turn to next.

4.6 Malawi Data Used in This Book

Data Collection

Between 2006 and 2010, I conducted research in rural Malawi to learn more about local demand for and provision of HIV/AIDS programs. Between June and August 2006, I was a graduate student research assistant on an NIH-funded panel study on HIV and I worked primarily in Mchinji and Balaka districts in Malawi's central and southern regions, respectively. The research project was the Malawi Longitudinal Study of Families and Health (MLSFH), a demographic survey conducted in rural areas of Mchinji, Balaka, and Rumphi districts (Kohler et al., 2015). In this book, I primarily analyze the 2008 wave of the MLSFH. The survey for the 2008 wave was 27 pages long and took on average two hours to complete. The questionnaire was written in English and translated to Chichewa, Chitumbuka, and Chiyao, the languages in which the interviews were conducted by experienced Malawian enumerators. Typically, a month after the survey, respondents were revisited by the research team, this time by Malawians specially trained and certified to administer rapid HIV tests. A brief questionnaire accompanied the HIV test, and the overall visit took less than an hour to complete on average. All interviews were conducted face-to-face using pen and paper, in a private location in or near the respondent's home.

My responsibilities in 2006 were to assist with coding qualitative data and quality checks of survey data. The MLSFH qualitative study I was charged with was the Malawian Journals Project, from which this chapter's opening story draws. The aim of the Malawian Journals Project is to capture Malawians' knowledge, attitudes, and opinions about AIDS as they naturally emerged in everyday conversations. These were recorded by advanced Malawian research assistants in exercise books and later typed as transcripts. There are more than 2,000 journals that span from 1999 to 2015.[34] In addition to my responsibilities to the MLSFH project in 2006, I took field notes and conducted informal interviews to get a sense of the availability of HIV/AIDS services in rural areas and the funding of AIDS community-based organizations in Balaka District.

In 2007, I partnered with two other students affiliated with the MLSFH to conduct semistructured interviews of HIV-tested villagers and their near neighbors in Mchinji district. Our research assistants conducted open-ended interviews in June and July 2007 alongside a study on HIV testing and treatment surveillance led by the University of Pennsylvania in conjunction with the Mchinji District Office of the Ministry of Health. Our study interviewed 30 respondents sampled

---

[34] See Watkins and Swidler (2009) for more detail on the journals and the "hearsay ethnography" method they use.

from clinic registers of people who were recently HIV tested. We also interviewed 19 of their "near neighbors," a quasi-randomly selected sample of people who lived in the same village and were of a similar age and gender, but their inclusion in our study did not rely on their having sought out HIV/AIDS services (Angotti, Dionne and Gaydosh, 2011). This pilot project studied experiences with HIV/AIDS services and explored how AIDS patients, Malawians who knew themselves to be HIV-negative, and other villagers prioritized different potential policy interventions. Participants' opinions and ideas on village priorities informed my later research strategies, including my design of a survey question aimed at measuring villagers' policy priorities.

From June 2008 to January 2009, I participated again in MLSFH data collection, this time introducing new questions on the survey to measure rural Malawians' policy priorities. Another original contribution I made to the study was interviewing village headmen in MLSFH villages. The headmen survey was conducted between June and August 2008. The 15-page survey was written in English and translated into Chichewa, Chitumbuka, and Chiyao. Skilled enumerators were native or fluent speakers of the languages in which interviews were conducted. We successfully interviewed a representative from each village in the MLSFH sample; these were primarily with headmen, or if he was absent, with an assistant headmen or with a headman's designated councilor. All interviews were conducted face-to-face using pen and paper and in a private location in or near the participant's home. The survey took 90 minutes to complete on average. We asked background information about the headmen, their villages, and the duties assigned to them by the government and higher-level traditional authorities. We also asked headmen's opinions about politics and development. In 2010, I joined the MLSFH team again for an additional wave of survey data collection.

When participating in survey data collection, I also collected qualitative data as needed to verify and understand the survey data. These included 85 in-depth interviews with key informants on HIV/AIDS interventions at the national, district, and local levels. Some of these interviews were with a purposefully selected subset of MLSFH headmen that followed their survey interviews. Follow-up interviews with headmen gave me a broader understanding of their role in implementing HIV/AIDS interventions. I personally conducted – in English – interviews with district- and national-level officials, and research assistants interviewed local officials, including headmen, in Chichewa. We all followed a question guideline, but allowed interviews to flow like a conversation. On average, interviews were an hour long and typed transcripts of these conversations were 15 single-spaced pages. I further supplemented these interviews with focus groups of villagers in villages where headmen actively promoted HIV testing campaigns, and with archival data of government documents on HIV/AIDS and health interventions and newspaper articles on the HIV/AIDS situation and response in Malawi.

My analyses also draw on field notes taken by me, three Malawian research assistants, and one village headman. My field notes were captured in brief in a notebook during a day's fieldwork, and then typed up in more detail upon reflection each evening. The time period covered by my field notes spanned June 2008 to January 2009. Research assistants would describe their interactions with headmen and their observations of headmen in the village. Their journals had on average five entries per week and spanned July 2008 to June 2009. The village headman kept a journal that chronicled different meetings he had with villagers as well as outsiders. He wrote in Chichewa and his journals were translated into English by a local research assistant. His journal usually had daily entries and spanned September 2008 to January 2009.

But who am I to collect these data? I am a mixed-race Korean American woman who visited Malawi in my late 20s and early 30s, first on my own, and then accompanied by my husband and young daughter. During my first visit to Malawi in 2006, men with access to important people or important data were very friendly and open to my requests. During my extended stay in 2008 with my family, these helpful gestures by professionals in urban areas were replaced by longer, more in-depth conversations with village headmen, who now thought of me as having reached adulthood because I had a child. I presented myself to the people I interviewed as a graduate student researcher. It is possible some of them thought I was also attached to some international NGO in the AIDS industrial complex, not least because I often asked their opinions about the work such organizations were doing.

It was rare that Malawians I met through my interviews would offer negative opinions about the United States, US-supported health and development interventions, or foreign aid more broadly. It was less rare among close Malawian friends I had made or in conversations I had and overheard with Malawians during minibus rides or while shopping in markets or queuing at banks. If ever Malawians challenged the hegemonic foreign aid industry in Malawi, it was often subtle and spoken as if a question, lilted at the end of the sentence. When Malawians who weren't my close friends learned my research was about AIDS, they often performed for me all of the behavior change campaign language or other buzzword phrases on how to avoid infection and why the epidemic was so bad in Malawi. Their performances showed more than their HIV knowledge; they also demonstrated what Malawians thought an American woman studying the AIDS epidemic wanted to hear: AIDS was a terrible threat in Malawi and more needs to be done in response to this threat.

Among close friends or during longer conversations or interviews, Malawians would perform less and talk more openly with me about what other issues mattered to them. In these longer relationships and conversations, Malawians would reveal their curiosity about my identity – my not seeming entirely "white" and my peculiar, Asian-sounding given names. I often shared more about my background; being raised by an immigrant mother and qualifying for public assistance made me seem to my Malawian friends as less "white" and less American. Perhaps their perceptions of my social distance to a typical *azungu*[35] gave more space for them to share less sanguine views about American (and other Western) intervention in their country.

I hired and trained a small team of research assistants to conduct in-depth interviews for two reasons. First, I am not fluent in any of Malawi's local languages. Research assistants thus conducted all interviews with respondents preferring to speak in a local language. I relied on this same team to translate these interviews into English. Second, I learned during my time in Tanzania in 2004 and my first trip to Malawi in 2006 that my presence elicited social desirability bias[36] toward prioritizing AIDS. Rather than conducting interviews with villagers and headmen on my own, I worked with the MLSFH survey to learn about

---

[35] *Azungu* is the plural and honorific form of *mzungu*, which translates from Chichewa to English as European or white person and derives from a literal meaning of "wonder maker" (Paas, 2005, 317). It has equivalents in other Bantu languages; for example, as *Mzungu* in Kiswahili.

[36] Social desirability bias refers to research participants offering responses during interviews they perceive to be "correct" or socially acceptable to avoid embarrassment or to project a favorable image (Maccoby and Maccoby, 1954; Fisher, 1993).

Malawian policy priorities as captured in interviews conducted by experienced Malawian enumerators fluent in local languages and less likely to elicit the social desirability bias I had experienced.

Study Sites

The research sites selected for the study are rural because like in many other African countries, Malawi's population is predominantly rural. When MLSFH began in 1998, one district from each of Malawi's three administrative regions was selected into the study: Rumphi in the north, Mchinji in the center, and Balaka in the south. In each district, villages were drawn using a cluster sampling strategy.[37] Though the original sampling strategy in 1998 was not designed to be representative of the rural population in Malawi, the sample's characteristics are very similar to those of the rural population interviewed by the Malawi Demographic and Health Surveys (DHS) that covered nationally representative samples.

Figure 4.3 is a map indicating the three research sites; each region of Malawi is represented in the study as are the four largest ethnolinguistic groups and two major world religions. Rumphi in the north is dominated by the Tumbuka, who largely practice Christianity. Mchinji in the center is mostly Chewa (though with a sizable Ngoni population) and Christian. Balaka in the south is majority Yao who practice Islam, and also includes a nonnegligible Lomwe population who are predominantly Christian.

In 2007, the urban sentinel surveillance site in Rumphi had an HIV prevalence of 11.0%, the rural site had a prevalence of 6.7%; Balaka's urban site had a prevalence of 17.4% and a rural prevalence of 15.5%; Mchinji's urban site had a prevalence of 8.8%, whereas the rural site had a prevalence of 6.3% (Republic of Malawi and National AIDS Commission [Malawi], 2008).

HIV/AIDS services had expanded in Malawi prior to the start of my research, but access was still quite limited for respondents in our research sites.[38] For example, in 2007 we interviewed a widow whose

---

[37] Watkins et al. (2003, 6–8) and Kohler et al. (2015) provide more details on sampling, including the sampling of individuals in the main MLSFH survey and how it approximates Malawi's rural population.

[38] Our study sites were not special in this regard. Access to HIV/AIDS services during my study period was limited for most rural Malawians, who faced prohibitive costs of transport to service locations (Zachariah et al., 2006).

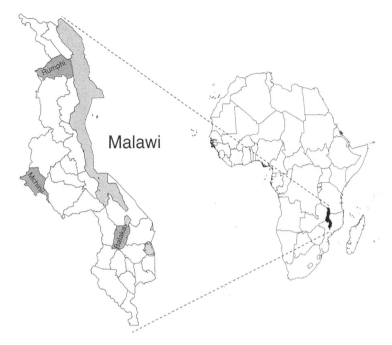

Figure 4.3 Map of Malawi Research Sites

husband had died of AIDS in 2001. Though she was HIV-positive and very sick (the interview transcript is peppered with interruptions and "coughing" typed in brackets), she was not yet sick enough to be eligible for ARV, which was available at the district clinic where she was HIV tested.[39] It is important to recognize that low prioritization of HIV/AIDS programs to be described and analyzed at length in Chapter 5 is not a result of saturated service coverage following the scale-up of services. In other words, Malawians aren't ranking AIDS a low priority because they now have incredible access to AIDS services.

Participant observation by a local research assistant working at the major AIDS clinic in Mchinji district describes services as difficult to access during the period when much of the data analyzed in this book was collected. As of 2008, Mchinji district had eight sites providing free HIV testing and two government-supported clinics treating AIDS patients. On average, it would take a villager in the Mchinji study area

---

[39] PLHIV Interview #7, Mchinji District, July 3, 2007.

a half day to learn her HIV status: about one hour to travel to the nearest testing site,[40] an hour waiting to be seen by the clinician, 30 minutes to be counseled and tested, then 30 minutes to await the results, be post-test counseled, and finally another hour to travel home. Accessing treatment from a village in the Mchinji study area would take considerably longer, as the nearest AIDS treatment clinic is a further distance and the wait to see a clinician is longer, as is the time spent in the clinic being examined and treated. An AIDS clinic visit would take an average of two hours spent in transit, two hours spent waiting to be seen, and one hour spent being examined and dispensed treatment, essentially consuming a full day for a villager from the Mchinji study area.

These time estimates assume that villagers can pay for transport and that when villagers seek testing or treatment, the clinics are staffed and stocked. Traveling from these villages to testing sites or clinics normally requires two forms of transport (bike taxi and minibus) because of the lack of paved roads and infrequent motor traffic. Additionally, during the study period, AIDS treatment clinics in rural Malawi were officially only open three days per week and HIV testing sites had limited business hours.

4.7 Study Sample Characteristics

MLSFH Villager Study

Table 4.2 provides summary statistics of the MLSFH sample during the 2008 wave. The 2008 wave included 3,384 women and 2,631 men, of which 4,183 (70%) were successfully visited by the research team. There are more women in the sample than men, owing to the original sampling frame's focus on ever-married women. Just more than half of the villagers interviewed in 2008 were "middle-aged," or between 25 and 49 years old. Most had attended some school, but few completed secondary school. While respondents from Malawi's biggest ethnolinguistic groups were all interviewed, the Yao, Chewa, and Tumbuka have substantially more representation in our dataset. There are more Christians than Muslims in our study sample, with Catholic and

---

[40] Fleming and Yeatman (2008) found that persons seeking HIV testing in Mchinji would travel on average 8.6 kilometers from their home to an HIV testing clinic. My estimate that it would take an hour to travel to the nearest testing site relies on the person seeking testing to walk at a fast pace and to attend the nearest testing facility, which Fleming and Yeatman (2008) suggest is the modal choice.

Table 4.2 *Summary statistics of MLSFH study sample*

Demographics

Female	58.1%
Age group: 15 to 24	18.3%
Age group: 25 to 49	52.3%
Age group: 50+	29.4%
Education: No school	25.1%
Education: Primary level	62.1%
Education: Secondary level	12.5%
Education: Higher education	0.3%
Ethnicity: Yao	26.2%
Ethnicity: Chewa	31.1%
Ethnicity: Tumbuka	29.3%
Ethnicity: Ngoni	5.4%
Ethnicity: Lomwe	4.4%
Ethnicity: Other	3.6%
Religion: Muslim	25.3%
Religion: CCAP	18.1%
Religion: Catholic	17.2%
Religion: Indigenous Christian	14.0%
Religion: Church of Christ	10.4%
Religion: Pentecostal	3.5%

Shocks and safety nets

Experienced agricultural loss in last 5 years	73.9%
Received food aid in last 3 years	31.2%
Received agricultural subsidy in last 3 years	87.7%

HIV-affected variables

Ever tested HIV-positive	4.6%
Recent household death likely AIDS	2.0%
Knew someone who died of AIDS	94.2%
Knew someone who is HIV-positive	72.7%
HIV-positive family member in MLSFH	3.13%

Source: MLSFH 2008; $N = 4,052$.

Protestant (CCAP) denominations accounting for more than a third of our respondents.

My study's focus on policy priorities requires a basic understanding of the lived conditions of respondents as well as their recent experiences with shocks and safety nets. Agricultural production is central to the lives of MLSFH study participants as nearly all are farmers. Many (73.9%) experienced a severe shock to their agricultural production in the five years preceding the survey, including poor crop yields, crop loss to disease or pests, or loss of livestock to theft or disease. While some (31.2%) MLSFH study participants reported receiving food aid in the previous three years, many more (87.7%) had received a government subsidy to support purchase of agricultural inputs.[41]

Experience with HIV and AIDS in our sample tracks with other data collected in rural Malawi. Few in the MLSFH sample had ever tested HIV-positive (4.6%), but nearly all (94.2%) knew someone who died of AIDS. While the proportion of our respondents who tested HIV-positive is only slightly more than half the HIV prevalence of Malawi's rural population as measured by the DHS (8.9%), subgroup patterns of HIV infection in our sample are consistent with the DHS sample. Specifically, the proportion of HIV-positive respondents is highest in our southern research site. Likewise, the major ethnic group with the highest proportion of respondents who tested positive in our sample was the Lomwe, as in the DHS (National Statistical Office [Malawi] and ICF Macro, 2011, 198).

MLSFH Headmen Study

Table 4.3 provides summary statistics for the MLSFH Headmen Study. We successfully interviewed a representative from each village in the MLSFH sample; 82% of interviews were with headmen, 15% were with assistant headmen, and the remaining interviews were with headmen's councilors. In interviews with assistant headmen or headmen's councilors, respondents were instructed to answer as if the village head (i.e., responding with the length of the village headman's tenure in office, not the assistant village headman's tenure).

Headmen ranged in age from 23 to 94; the average age was 58. Experience of headmen also ranged: some were installed the same year of

[41] More precisely, these respondents had received an Agricultural Input Subsidy Programme (AISP) coupon for fertilizer and seed. See Dionne and Horowitz (2016) for more on MLSFH study participants receiving AISP coupons.

Table 4.3 *Summary statistics of villages and their headmen*

Characteristics of village headmen	Mean	Std. Dev.
Male	0.91	0.29
Age	57.54	16.30
Years in office	12.81	11.78
Education level	1.37	1.03
Elected to office	0.13	0.34
Village characteristics	**Mean**	**Std. Dev.**
Number of adults	222.04	313.64
Health Surveillance Assistant resident in village	0.28	0.45
Has traditional healer	0.37	0.48
Has Village AIDS Committee	0.28	0.45
Has Village Development Committee	0.75	0.44
Simpson's diversity index (ethnic diversity)	0.21	0.20
Village AIDS experience	**Mean**	**Std. Dev.**
Number tested HIV-positive in MLSFH	1.51	2.28
Number of funerals headman attended in last month	4.75	4.28

Notes: $N = 122$. Source: MLSFH and MLSFH Headman Study, 2008. Education level is an ordinal variable where 0 signifies no formal schooling, 1 signifies attending primary school, 2 signifies attending and completing primary school, 3 signifies attending secondary school, and 4 signifies attending and completing secondary school. Elected to office is a self-reported binary measure on whether the headman was elected to office (1 = elected). Presence of a Health Surveillance Assistant, traditional healer, Village AIDS Committee, and Village Development Committee are binary variables (1 = present). The Simpson's diversity index for each village is bounded by 0 and 1, with 0 indicating an ethnically homogenous village and values approaching 1 indicating high ethnic diversity. Number tested HIV-positive in MLSFH is the count of villagers in a village that had ever tested HIV-positive during MLSFH data collection. Number of funerals headman attended in last month is a count reported by the headman.

the survey, and one headman had been in office 64 years; the average headman had 13 years experience. Respondents were predominantly male; only 10% were women.[42] Headmen's ethnic identity typically

[42] Peters (1997) found even in the predominantly matrilineal societies of the Shire highlands in Malawi – where women are the "owners" and "builders" of the village – most headmen are men. Eggen (2011) cites Malawi's 2008 Welfare

mirrored that of his villagers: most in Mchinji were Chewa, in Rumphi Tumbuka, and in Balaka Yao. A handful of interviews were conducted with Ngoni, Senga, and Lomwe headmen. Most headmen were Christian, though headmen interviewed in Balaka were predominantly Muslim.

4.8 Conclusion

The arrival of AIDS is only one of a number of significant changes Malawians have faced in the last 30 years. As Malawians grappled with the new health threat, they also struggled to adjust to austerity measures imposed under a new neoliberal order and began to experience new freedoms associated with the end of dictatorship. At the same time, this mostly agrarian country wrestled with new challenges to agricultural production largely brought on by the more erratic weather patterns associated with climate change.

While responses to AIDS in other parts of the world meant shunning and stigmatizing the sick, in Malawi families took care of the ill and endeavored to keep their children HIV-negative. These families were supported in their efforts by their local communities and religious congregations, before the Malawian government or international donors took meaningful steps toward AIDS response.

Because political power continues to be vested in Malawi's executive branch and because donors wield considerable influence in this aid-dependent country, much of the national-level response to AIDS in Malawi is driven by donor interests and priorities. Often overlooked in AIDS interventions are the opinions of ordinary citizens who are navigating the epidemic and an understanding of the broader context of competing challenges Malawians face. The failure of donor-supported campaigns to promote male circumcision as HIV prevention that I described in this chapter is one example of the disconnect in global AIDS interventions: though Malawians have generally negative views of male circumcision, donors see it as similar to a vaccine in its potential to reduce HIV infections. In the next chapter, I draw on the data I have described in this chapter to examine more systematically one particular disconnect in the global response to AIDS: the misalignment of priorities between the international community and the people navigating the AIDS epidemic.

Monitoring Survey as calculating 12% of households are in villages with female chiefs.

5 | *Policy Priorities in the Time of AIDS*

Some problems can be forgotten if the assistance goes only to one side. We have other problems like boreholes. Hence this [AIDS] money could also go to other areas ... People suffering from other diseases too should be helped.
Headman Interview #48, Mchinji District, July 10, 2008

The success of international health and development interventions depends on how they are received by local populations. Judging from the scale of resources, international actors highly prioritize AIDS intervention. Little is known, however, about the policy priorities of the people in whose name powerful donors send assistance. This chapter examines empirically what is often overlooked: Africans' attitudes about development and health interventions for which they are the intended beneficiaries. While it is true that Africa has suffered the most from AIDS, we cannot presume that HIV is the most important problem facing Africans.

Earlier chapters substantiated that AIDS is pandemic in Africa and presented an argument that the global AIDS intervention is plagued by principal–agent problems inherent in the multitiered intervention against AIDS in Africa. That argument relies on the assertion that policy preferences for AIDS intervention are misaligned. In this chapter, I empirically substantiate the misalignment of AIDS prioritization between two important constituencies: the international donors who largely decide global priorities and the people who are their intended beneficiaries.

The chapter is structured as follows: the first section details the prioritization of AIDS in the international community, primarily among powerful donors, using data on official development assistance (ODA). I then draw from existing scholarship to examine what shapes citizens' policy preferences, and focus on two expectations: that people living with HIV (PLHIV) stand to benefit most from AIDS interventions and will thus give higher priority to AIDS; and that HIV-affected people – people related to and potentially caring for PLHIV – will also give

AIDS higher priority. The next two sections analyze public opinion data, which substantiate ordinary Africans give relatively low priority to AIDS interventions and provide evidence that experience with HIV/AIDS makes people more likely to prioritize AIDS (even if only weakly). Then I explore alternative measures of AIDS prioritization and alternative explanations for low prioritization of AIDS by ordinary Africans. The chapter concludes with a discussion of some implications of the misalignment of priorities.

5.1 Prioritization of AIDS in Corridors of Power

AIDS is a priority for major bilateral and multilateral donors. Of the $51.5 billion committed as ODA to sub-Saharan African countries in 2013, $4.7 billion (or 9.1%) was earmarked for HIV/AIDS programs and services (Organisation for Economic Co-operation and Development, 2015). AIDS as an issue has been increasingly important to donors over time; political scientist Jeremy Shiffman (2006*b*) points out there was a 28-fold increase in annual funding to address HIV/AIDS in low- and middle-income countries between 1996 and 2006. Figure 5.1 shows the trend for HIV donor funding – as well as overall health ODA commitments – from 1995 to 2013.[1]

Judging from data on donor spending, AIDS is exceptional, especially if you compare it to other health issues. Figure 5.2 has a series of bar charts with mortality estimates in sub-Saharan Africa for both HIV and malaria. Layered over these bar charts are line graphs of the ODA committed for HIV/AIDS and malaria. Though malaria is just as deadly as AIDS (and in some years, more deadly), AIDS funding far outpaces malaria funding. The lack of close correspondence between disease burden and donor funding is not specific to these two initiatives, but is consistent with analysis by Shiffman (2006*a*) covering 20 high-burden communicable diseases and related funding from 42 major donors between 1996 and 2003.

AIDS does not just eclipse other diseases in its funding levels; funding for AIDS has also overshadowed support for health generally. For

---

[1] More specifically, HIV donor funding corresponds to the sector OECD titled "STD Control Including HIV/AIDS" and overall health ODA is a sum of OECD's two categories "Health, Total" and "Population Policies/Programmes & Reproductive Health, Total," the latter measure including as one of its components "STD Control Including HIV/AIDS" (Organisation for Economic Co-operation and Development, 2015).

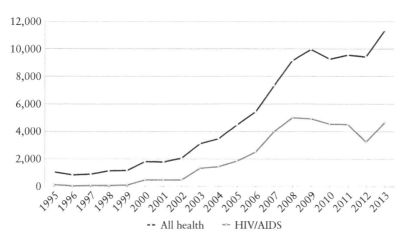

Figure 5.1 Official development assistance for health and HIV in sub-Saharan Africa, in millions (USD)
Source: Organisation for Economic Co-operation and Development (2015)

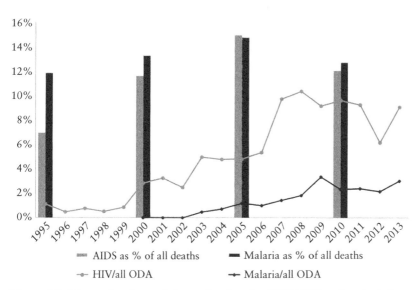

Figure 5.2 Disease burden and donor funding for HIV/AIDS and malaria in sub-Saharan Africa
Sources: Organisation for Economic Co-operation and Development (2015) and Institute for Health Metrics and Evaluation (2015). Note: OECD has no data on malaria funding prior to 2000.

example, in 2003, Rwanda received $187 million earmarked for AIDS programs from three major international donors – PEPFAR, Global Fund, and World Bank – which was more than five times the government's annual budget ($37 million) for health (Shiffman, 2006b).[2] Because donor funding for AIDS is subsumed under health funding, it is technically impossible for AIDS funding to be larger than health funding. However, comparing donor funding for AIDS against donor funding for all other health initiatives, AIDS funding was greater than health funding in 2007 and 2008 and was nearly equal in 2009 and 2010.[3]

Donor funding for AIDS has also outpaced donor funding for other development interventions. From 2003 to 2011, donor funding for AIDS was greater than that for agriculture and for water supply and sanitation initiatives. From 2007 to 2011, donor funding for AIDS even outpaced donor funding for education.[4]

These snapshots of donor funding provide some evidence of how the international community prioritizes AIDS compared to other health and development initiatives. At the turn of the century, AIDS became as important as other issues to the international community and by 2005 began to overtake other issues, at least as measured by donor funding commitments. While other diseases are equally deadly (e.g., malaria), AIDS has been exceptional in garnering donor attention and support. As the remainder of the chapter shows, however, this AIDS exceptionalism is characteristic of donors, not citizens navigating the AIDS epidemic.

5.2 What Influences Whether Citizens Prioritize AIDS?

Because AIDS is fatal, and because AIDS is epidemic in Africa, people often assume African citizens would prioritize efforts against HIV and AIDS, failing to appreciate that the majority of Africans are

[2] I should note that Rwanda has very low HIV prevalence when compared to other sub-Saharan countries. In 2003, when these funds were disbursed, Rwanda had an HIV prevalence of 4.3%; 17 other African countries had higher HIV prevalence estimates (UNAIDS, 2016).

[3] According to OECD data, in 2007, donor funding for AIDS was $4 billion and for all health (less AIDS) was $3.35 billion. In 2008, donor funding for AIDS was $5 billion and for all health was $4.2 billion.

[4] To calculate comparisons in OECD data, I used the sectors "STD Control Including HIV/AIDS," "Agriculture, Forestry, Fishing, Total," "Water Supply & Sanitation, Total," and "Education, Total."

HIV-negative and that other problems may take precedence for both HIV-positive and HIV-negative citizens alike. African public opinion data established that though concern about HIV has risen over time, AIDS has yet to register very high on the "people's agenda" (Afrobarometer, 2004; Whiteside et al., 2004; de Waal, 2006), and some scholars question the prioritization of HIV/AIDS intervention (Shiffman, 2008; Independent Evaluation Group, 2009; Dionne, Gerland and Watkins, 2013), particularly when spending on HIV/AIDS has been at a cost to general health systems improvement (England, 2007; Garrett, 2007; Grépin, 2012) or displaces funding for equally deadly diseases like malaria (Lordan, Tang and Carmignani, 2011). Like activists and policymakers, some scholars assert the provision of HIV/AIDS services is a public good (Ainsworth and Teokul, 2000; Walton et al., 2004; Kim and Farmer, 2006; Patterson, 2006; Lieberman, 2007, 2009), the provision of which would improve outcomes indiscriminately in a population. However, HIV/AIDS services cannot be characterized as public goods because their use is neither nonrival nor nonexcludable.[5]

Treatment and care for those sick with AIDS inherently benefits HIV-positive individuals. For example, the lion's share of funding for HIV/AIDS services focuses on AIDS treatment, which has limited availability and is beneficial only to the small minority in the population who is sick with AIDS. Accordingly, I do not assume African citizens perceive HIV/AIDS services as public goods. Rather, I expect policy priorities to be driven by citizens' perceptions that such services are limited and exclusive to the population that is HIV-positive. In other words, if we presume citizens to be self-interested, we should expect only those affected by HIV to prioritize AIDS interventions.

There is a long literature on how self-interest shapes policy opinions. Sears, Hensler and Speer (1979) define a "self-interested attitude" as "one which is directed toward maximizing gains or minimizing losses to the individual's private well-being." Early studies of public opinion on issues in American politics questioned the relevance of self-interest in shaping policy opinions (Berelson, Lazarsfeld and McPhee, 1954; Campbell et al., 1960) and later analysis shows that self-interest has

---

[5] To be clear, a good or service is a public good if one's use of the good does not compete with another's use of the same good, and use of the good cannot be restricted to a certain population. A common example of a public good is clean air.

not been of major importance in explaining the American public's political preferences (Sears and Funk, 1990). For example, individuals rarely form preferences for economic policy on the basis of economic self-interests (Mansfield and Mutz, 2009, 433). Even scholars skeptical of the role of self-interest concede, however, that there are exceptions. Sears and Funk (1990, 159–61) highlight cases in which self-interest affects policy preferences: in situations with clear, substantial costs and benefits; in cases with both severe and ambiguous threats; and during the course of events politicizing self-interest. I find it difficult to characterize AIDS prioritization in Africa as meeting the latter criterion, but argue the former two criteria are applicable: AIDS is a severe and ambiguous threat and increasing the availability of AIDS treatment would provide a clear, substantial benefit to anyone sick with AIDS.

The self-interest public opinion scholarship leads us to predict AIDS prioritization will vary across populations differentially impacted by HIV and AIDS. If we consider HIV/AIDS services as excludable goods available to self-interested individuals, we should expect that people who stand to benefit will demand the good, and those who expect no benefit will prefer resources be devoted to a different policy issue. The group that stands to benefit most from increased availability of HIV/AIDS services are HIV-positive people. Analyzing individual-level data, we should see HIV-positive individuals giving higher priority to HIV/AIDS services than HIV-negative individuals. At the national level, we should expect countries with higher HIV prevalence to have a higher aggregate demand for HIV/AIDS services. But HIV-positive people are not the only people *affected* by AIDS, and thus not the only group likely to prioritize AIDS interventions.

Because attitudes are made, maintained, or modified through interpersonal processes (Erickson, 1988, 99), we should also consider how connections to HIV-positive people may affect individuals' policy priorities. Imagine an HIV-negative villager who gives high priority to HIV/AIDS interventions compared to other health and development interventions. What benefit would HIV/AIDS services bring to someone who knows she's not infected? It may be that she is the primary caretaker of someone sick with AIDS and her close connection to someone who would benefit from AIDS treatment influences her prioritization of AIDS. I expect relatives of HIV-positive respondents would give higher priority to HIV/AIDS services because relatives are the primary source of care for the sick, especially women (Chimwaza and

Watkins, 2004). Spouses in particular will not just carry the burden of caring for a sick spouse, but could also prioritize AIDS because they might need AIDS services in the future.

I operationalize "affected by AIDS" two ways: (1) whether a person knows or suspects someone close to them to be sick with or have died of AIDS and (2) whether a person is a spouse, parent, or child of someone with HIV. At the individual level, we should see these AIDS-affected respondents to give higher priority to AIDS. Whereas our first expectation proposes studying how HIV status impacts AIDS prioritization, this second expectation gets at whether those indirectly affected would also prioritize AIDS.

5.3 Prioritization of AIDS in Africa

Demand across Africa for Devoting Resources to AIDS

I use data from Afrobarometer, a cross-national public opinion survey, to study how citizens across Africa prioritize AIDS. A question on the 2005 survey asked respondents to choose which of the following two statements they agreed with:

Statement A: The government should devote many more resources to combating AIDS, even if this means that less money is spent on things like education.

Statement B: There are many other problems facing this country beside AIDS; even if people are dying in large numbers, the government needs to keep its focus on solving other problems.

Fewer than half of the 24,000 Afrobarometer respondents agreed with Statement A, that more resources should be devoted to AIDS. Excepting South Africa and Lesotho, African countries with the highest HIV prevalence rates (e.g., Botswana, Zimbabwe, Namibia, and Zambia) demanded resources be devoted to problems other than AIDS. Figure 5.3 plots the proportion of Afrobarometer respondents supporting more resources be devoted to AIDS in each country against national HIV prevalence. There is no significant relationship between national HIV prevalence and demand that resources be devoted to AIDS. Data aggregated to the national level, then, fails to confirm the expectation that higher HIV prevalence rates should predict prioritization of resources for AIDS response.

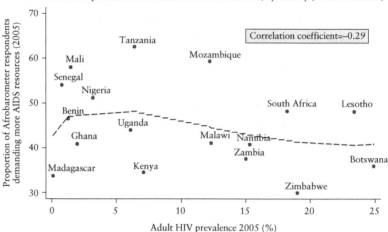

Figure 5.3 HIV prevalence and demand for AIDS resources
Sources: Afrobarometer Round 3 Data and UNAIDS (2008)

Afrobarometer data also allow us to examine whether AIDS-affected individuals give higher priority to AIDS. Figure 5.4 separates responses about AIDS resources by whether the respondent knew someone who died of AIDS. Those who reported not knowing someone who died of AIDS were split on whether to devote more or fewer resources for AIDS. However, those who seemed to be more impacted by the disease – people who knew someone close to them who died of AIDS – were less likely to demand additional resources be devoted to combat AIDS, and were more likely to demand resources be devoted to other problems. The difference is statistically significant, even though the substantive difference is relatively small. This same result holds in each of the countries surveyed by Afrobarometer.[6]

Overall, the 2005 Afrobarometer data show that citizens were mixed on whether to demand more government resources be devoted to AIDS. Afrobarometer data also showed that experience with AIDS is not associated with wanting more resources devoted to AIDS.

---

[6] In some cases, country-level analysis shows a breakdown similar to the aggregated data for respondents who report not having someone close to them to have died of AIDS; in others the disparities are even wider; in Tanzania, for example, respondents not knowing someone close to them to have died of AIDS were even more likely to prefer resources devoted to AIDS (70% preferred resources devoted to AIDS, 30% to other problems).

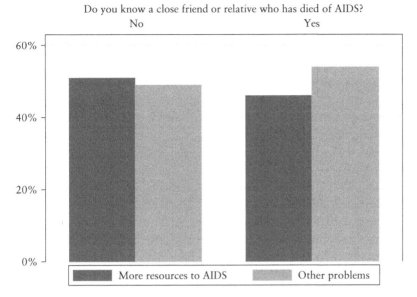

Figure 5.4 Should government devote more resources to AIDS?
Source: Afrobarometer Round 3 Data. N = 22,614. Differences between groups of respondents are statistically significant.

A Broader Question, a Broader View

Another Afrobarometer survey question is less direct in probing how ordinary citizens prioritize HIV/AIDS. In multiple waves, Afrobarometer asked an open-ended question that reads, "In your opinion, what are the most important problems facing this country that government should address?" Responses were captured verbatim and then later coded into roughly 30 categories, one of which was specifically HIV/AIDS. Less than 3% of respondents in the first wave (1999–2001) of Afrobarometer mentioned AIDS as an important problem that government should address. The proportion was higher in Botswana (20%), Namibia (11%), and South Africa (8%), where HIV prevalence was higher. No respondents mentioned AIDS in Ghana, Mali, Nigeria, or Zambia in the first wave. By the second wave (2002–3), a greater proportion (10%) of respondents mentioned AIDS as one of the top three problems.[7] There were no countries in Round 2

---

[7] There are two challenges with comparing data across waves. First, the countries included in Afrobarometer grew over time, and thus complicates comparison across waves of opinions of all Afrobarometer respondents. Second, the

in which respondents did not mention AIDS, though it was noticeably unimportant in Mali (only 6 of 1,283 respondents mentioned it). Botswana again topped the list, with 29% of respondents mentioning AIDS as an important problem government should address. Scholarship analyzing data from these early waves was the first indication that AIDS failed to register high on the public agenda, even in high-prevalence countries (Afrobarometer, 2004; Whiteside et al., 2004; de Waal, 2006).

Later waves of Afrobarometer similarly show low salience of AIDS among African citizens (Dionne, 2012; Justesen, 2015). By the third round in 2005, the proportion of respondents mentioning AIDS as an important problem went down to 7%. Botswana continues to top the list, with 27% of respondents naming AIDS as a top problem; South Africa was second (24%), with Namibia close behind it (23%). AIDS continues to decline in importance in later Afrobarometer waves, with only 4.2% of respondents in Round 4 (2008–9) and only 3.1% of respondents in Round 5 (2011–13) mentioning AIDS as one of the most important problems government should address.

In sum, Afrobarometer data on responses to the open-ended question asking what are the most important problems government should address corroborate earlier analysis on the weak prioritization of HIV. In the full Afrobarometer sample, AIDS is not often mentioned as one of the most important problems.

5.4 Prioritization of AIDS in Malawi

As part of the MLSFH, a longitudinal study on the consequences of HIV/AIDS in Malawi, we surveyed 4,183 villagers to learn their policy priorities and to examine more specifically whether AIDS-affected Malawians were more likely to prioritize AIDS.[8] Four measures in our study capture the AIDS-affected population: HIV status of respondents; HIV status of spouses, parents, or adult children using linked data; reported household member deaths attributable to AIDS; and suspected HIV infection or AIDS deaths of people known to the respondent.

---

  question changed slightly after Round 1 in that all respondents were given the option to name three (rather than only two) important problems in response to the question.
[8] Of the five waves of the MLSFH, my analysis focuses on the fourth wave, conducted in 2008. See Chapter 4 for more detail on the MLSFH data.

In 2008, 4.3% of MLSFH research participants tested positive for HIV, but this is likely an underestimate of HIV prevalence in our sample. Of 211 respondents who refused to be HIV-tested in 2008, 17 (8%) tested positive for HIV in a previous MLSFH round.[9] I use 2004 and 2006 test results to impute HIV status of anyone who refused testing in 2008, resulting in a sample in which 4.6% of respondents are HIV-positive. In the analysis then, HIV status is a binary measure equal to 1 if the respondent ever tested positive in MLSFH biomarker collection, 0 otherwise.

In most cases, married respondents are linked in the MLSFH data; in fewer cases, respondents are also linked to parents or adult children.[10] Because of marital and intergenerational links in the data, we can use HIV test data to identify all those who are linked by familial connection in the dataset to someone who has tested HIV-positive. Respondents with spouses, parents, or children whoever tested HIV-positive in MLSFH biomarker collection make up 3.1% of our sample.[11]

Moving beyond sero-status of respondents and their linked family members, we asked respondents whether they knew someone who died of AIDS or is sick with AIDS as another measure of being affected by AIDS. Of the 784 respondents who reported a household death in the last two years, 85 (10.8%) of the deaths were reported to be likely or very likely attributable to AIDS, but overall, the population reporting a recent household death attributable to AIDS was only 2% of our sample. In our sample, 3,781 respondents (94.2%) report having known someone to have died of AIDS. Nearly three-quarters of respondents (2,936 or 72.5%) report knowing someone who is HIV-positive. HIV prevalence is lower than the national average in our study population and household AIDS deaths are reported to affect only a small group. However, considering the number of respondents who report

---

[9] It is probable that additional respondents refusing to be tested in 2008 also know themselves to be HIV-positive, but were made aware of their status not by our study; among individuals who know their status, HIV-positive individuals are four times as likely to refuse HIV testing than HIV-negative individuals (Reniers and Eaton, 2009).

[10] In 2008, the MLSFH introduced parents of respondents into the sample. Not all parents were interviewed: dead parents and parents residing outside the village of their adult child respondent are excluded.

[11] This is an underestimate of respondents with an HIV-positive nuclear family member: it is likely that additional respondents also have HIV-positive parents and/or children but these relatives were simply not included in the MLSFH sample.

knowing someone to be sick with HIV or having died from AIDS, the AIDS-affected population in rural Malawi is as significant as one could expect in the country whose HIV prevalence ranks ninth highest in the world.

To measure how Malawians prioritize AIDS interventions, we asked our study participants to rank in order of importance five public policy priorities: clean water, health services, agricultural development, education, and HIV/AIDS programs.[12] A score of 1 was assigned to the most important policy, 2 to the second most important policy, and so on until a score of 5 was assigned to the least important policy. Figure 5.5 presents the responses graphically. Most notably, nearly half of the respondents ranked HIV/AIDS services as the least important public policy intervention among the five options. The priority ranking of HIV/AIDS programs has a mean of 3.8.

To study the relative influence of different factors on how citizens prioritized AIDS, I use an ordered logit regression where the outcome (dependent variable) is the priority ranking of HIV/AIDS programs and the independent variables are the AIDS-affected measures. The model controls for the respondent's level of education, gender, age, wealth, and region. Table 5.1 displays the results. HIV status operates in the anticipated direction and is statistically significant, confirming the expectation that respondents whoever tested HIV-positive are more likely to prioritize HIV/AIDS services. Attribution of a recent household death to AIDS, knowing someone who is HIV-positive, or having an HIV-positive familial link in the MLSFH dataset do not predict higher prioritization of HIV/AIDS programs, failing to confirm the expectation that AIDS-affected people give higher priority to AIDS. However, if a respondent reports knowing someone who died of AIDS, the respondent is more likely to prioritize HIV/AIDS programs.

Figure 5.6 presents the findings graphically; holding other variables at their means, I use the regression results from Table 5.1 to generate predicted probabilities of the HIV/AIDS priority rankings across two populations: respondents who had ever tested HIV-positive compared to those who had not. Respondents that ever tested HIV-positive have a lower predicted probability of ranking HIV/AIDS programs as the least important public policy and higher predicted probabilities of

---

[12] This list of policy options was informed by a pilot study conducted in Mchinji, Malawi, in 2007, described in greater detail in Chapter 4.

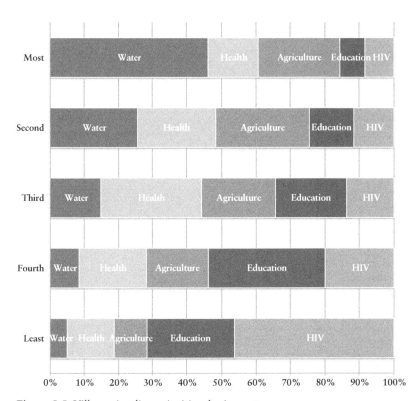

Figure 5.5 Villagers' policy priorities, by importance
Source: MLSFH 2008

ranking HIV/AIDS programs most important (as well as second most important, third most important, and fourth most important).

In sum, the analysis of villagers' policy preferences confirms our first expectation that PLHIV give higher priority to AIDS but has mixed results for our second expectation that AIDS-affected people (friends, family connected to someone who is HIV-positive) would give higher priority to AIDS. There are two primary takeaways: First, proximate experience with AIDS – either being HIV-positive or knowing someone who died of AIDS – makes one more likely to prioritize AIDS programs and while this finding is statistically significant, substantively, the effect is not large. Second, and perhaps more importantly, AIDS is a very low priority among rural Malawians when compared to other pressing issues they face, and this is true even for HIV-positive Malawians.

Table 5.1 *Ordered logit regression of villager prioritization of HIV/AIDS*

Ever tested HIV-positive	0.277*
	(0.142)
Recent household death likely AIDS	−0.355
	(0.209)
Knew someone who died of AIDS	0.311*
	(0.134)
Knew someone who is HIV-positive	−0.120
	(0.072)
HIV-positive family member in MLSFH	−0.075
	(0.171)
Female	−0.091
	(0.062)
Age group	−0.306***
	(0.046)
Education	0.000
	(0.056)
Subjective wealth	−0.019
	(0.037)
Region	−0.138***
	(0.038)
Observations	3,989

Notes: Statistical significance levels: $*p < 0.05$; $**p < 0.01$; $***p < 0.001$. Standard errors are shown in parentheses below coefficients. Model uses an ordinal logit regression where the outcome variable of interest is prioritization of HIV/AIDS programs, rescaled for easier interpretation from 1 to 5, where 5 indicates HIV/AIDS is the most important priority and 1 indicates HIV/AIDS is the least important priority. Source: MLSFH 2008.

5.5 Alternative Measures of Prioritizing AIDS

The primary descriptive result I present here – that HIV is a relatively low priority among ordinary Africans – runs counter to the narrative offered by the Pew Global Attitudes Project (Pew GAP), a series of cross-national public opinion surveys that measure – among other things – people's policy priorities. Pew GAP published a report in 2014 titled, "Public Health a Major Priority in African Nations: Improving Hospitals, Dealing with HIV/AIDS Are Top Issues." Based on survey data collected in 2013 in Ghana, Kenya, Nigeria, Senegal, South

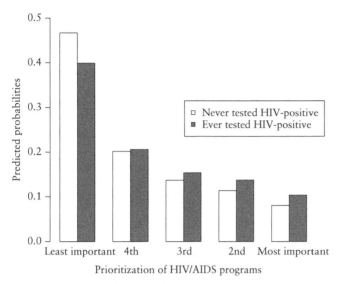

Figure 5.6 Predicted probabilities of villagers' prioritization of HIV/AIDS programs

Africa, and Uganda, Pew GAP reports, "76% [of respondents] believe preventing and treating HIV/AIDS should be one of the government's most important priorities" (Pew Research Center, 2014, 2). The proportion of respondents saying "preventing and treating HIV/AIDS" should be "one of the most important priorities" for government to improve public health and health care were similarly high in African countries surveyed by Pew GAP in 2007 (Kaiser Family Foundation and Pew Global Attitudes Project, 2007).

How does Pew GAP come to a different conclusion about African opinions on prioritizing health? The answer lies in how Pew GAP asked its survey questions. A major difference between my data and Pew GAP data is question wording. The questions asked by Pew GAP limited the scope of prioritization to public health and health care and omitted other development issues. In other words, citizens prioritized AIDS when it was compared only to other health-related issues. The narrative of the Pew GAP report focuses on absolute prioritization, rather than relative prioritization. We should expect many people living in high-prevalence contexts will agree that HIV is a serious problem, but it is more realistic to consider policy responses in a context of resource constraints.

In an attempt at measuring relative prioritization, Pew GAP asked a follow-up question after asking about seven potential public health policy improvements (of which preventing and treating HIV/AIDS was one) probing respondents to report which of the seven "should be the most important priority for the government." There are no remarkable patterns in the responses to this question, but it was only in South Africa that the plurality (35%) of respondents named HIV/AIDS as the most important priority, edging out the unread but voluntarily offered option "All equally important," which was reported by 32% of South Africans in the survey. Again, this relative prioritization is only pitting HIV/AIDS against other health issues.

Pew GAP asked another prioritization question in the 2002 and 2007 waves offering a list of problems and asking respondents to evaluate each problem as very big, moderately big, small, or not a problem at all. On Pew GAP's list of problems was crime, group conflict, corrupt political leaders, poor quality of drinking water, terrorism, poor quality schools, immigration, outmigration for labor, illegal drugs, pollution, and the spread of HIV/AIDS and other infectious diseases. In 2002, 87% of respondents in African countries said the spread of HIV and other infectious diseases was a very big problem. For comparison, 82% of African respondents reported crime was a very big problem. Fewer African respondents (77%) thought the spread of HIV and other infectious diseases was a very big problem in 2007, but it garnered more responses than crime (67%) or corrupt politicians (65%). The wording of this question is also problematic, however, because like the previous question, it only measures absolute instead of relative priority. Furthermore, the question lumps HIV/AIDS together with other infectious diseases, including deadly and widespread diseases like malaria and diarrheal disease.

There are three important limitations of the Pew GAP data. First, the Pew GAP does not collect data on HIV status or on respondents' experience with HIV/AIDS, and so we cannot use it to study whether and how these and other important factors drive citizens' prioritization of HIV in their countries. Second, there are too few African countries included in the Pew GAP – especially when compared to Afrobarometer – and this not only limits the scope to which we could generalize any findings but also precludes us from spatially joining the Pew GAP data to other datasets that capture AIDS affectedness, which would permit us to study factors influencing citizens' priorities. Third, the wording of the questions used by Pew GAP gives us little leverage in understanding relative priorities in populations where many problems can impact everyday lives. Though the 2014 Pew GAP report was technically correct in framing survey responses from Africans as evidence that public health (and AIDS specifically) is a priority, many issues asked about in surveys in the same way could generate similar responses. What is really a priority if everything is a priority? The lack of nuance in studying Africans' policy priorities could generate a misconception among key actors in the policy community that intended beneficiaries would be supportive (even demanding) of more resources being devoted to AIDS. My analysis of Afrobarometer data and data from Malawi would suggest this would be a miscalculation of priority alignment on AIDS.

5.6 Alternative Explanations for Low Prioritization of AIDS

I have focused on the power of personal experience in shaping citizens' prioritization of AIDS. But what are the rival explanations for why most rural Malawians fail to prioritize HIV/AIDS despite high HIV prevalence in the country? In this section, I consider three alternative arguments for why AIDS ranks so low on Africans' priority list: poverty, stigma, and lack of awareness.

Poverty and AIDS Salience

A related but distinct argument for why AIDS salience is low in Africa is high poverty. Like in my study, political scientist Mogens Justesen (2015) analyzes multiple waves of Afrobarometer data and shows citizens do not attach great importance to AIDS. He argues AIDS as an issue is crowded out by other day-to-day concerns impoverished Africans face. Justesen (2015) draws from the logic that the long latent period between infection and death is the reason people do not worry about AIDS (Dionne, 2011): AIDS is a long-term problem and impoverished Africans are "compelled to worry about pressing material concerns" in the short term (Justesen, 2015, 92). Justesen (2015) relents that personal experience likely also shapes AIDS salience, but emphasizes his distinct argument that low AIDS salience is due to widespread poverty on the continent.

One testable implication of Justesen's argument is that AIDS salience will be lowest among the poor – and, indeed, this is what Justesen finds in his analysis. However, because of data limitations, Justesen's analysis suffers from what scientists call confounding or omitted variable bias. For poverty to affect AIDS salience separately from experience with AIDS, poverty would have to be unrelated to experience with AIDS. Data increasingly show, however, that in many African contexts, wealth (the inverse of poverty) increases a person's risk of becoming HIV infected (Poulin, Dovel and Watkins, 2016). It is possible, then, that the poor in Africa rationally rank AIDS as a less important issue not necessarily because they are too concerned about other pressing material concerns but because given their poverty, they find it unlikely they will engage in behavior or be connected to sexual networks that will increase their exposure to HIV. As I mentioned earlier, one major drawback of nearly all public opinion surveys conducted in Africa to study opinion on AIDS is the dearth of concrete measures of being AIDS-affected. The MLSFH is truly exceptional in that it captures both opinions on AIDS priorities and HIV status.

Stigma Makes AIDS Too Taboo for Survey Responses

Could low prioritization of HIV/AIDS as measured in face-to-face interviews actually be due to stigma or denial? This argument would suggest our Malawian research participants might have reported low prioritization of HIV/AIDS programming because the disease is so stigmatized that it would be socially desirable to answer that HIV/AIDS is less deserving of attention.

Herek (1999) defines AIDS-related stigma as "prejudice, discounting, discrediting, and discrimination directed at people perceived to have AIDS or HIV, and the individuals, groups, and communities with which they are associated" (1107). Stigma toward PLHIV in Africa is generally presumed given the AIDS-related stigma in the early years following its discovery in the United States.[13] And, there are multiple accounts of PLHIV in Africa experiencing stigma.[14] However, it is

---

[13] In addition to the review by Herek (1999), see Shilts (1987) and Cohen (1999). On group stigma, see Farmer (1992), who details the significant discrimination against Haitians in the United States, labeled as a major at-risk population early in the epidemic.

[14] Suzanne Daley, "AIDS Is Everywhere, but Africa Looks Away," *New York Times*, December 4, 1998. See also Kaleeba (2004).

unclear if these accounts are representative of general attitudes toward PLHIV, especially in the current period.

AIDS is not so stigmatized in Malawi that people feel uncomfortable talking about it. HIV and AIDS are part of the daily media in Malawi, from saucy, fictional radio dramas, to reports of ARV drug shortages in newspapers. Messages about preventing HIV infection or caring for those sick with AIDS are often featured in church sermons (Trinitapoli and Weinreb, 2012), and rural Malawians talk about AIDS in open spaces and with strangers (Kaler, 2004*a*; Watkins, 2004). Additionally, data presented here show that individuals are willing to share with strangers – in this case, interviewers – that someone close to them has died of AIDS. In our open-ended interviews in 2007, respondents frequently reported their HIV status without prompting. Of the MLSFH respondents reporting in 2008 to having ever been tested for HIV, 90% shared their results with their partner and 54% shared results with friends, relatives, and others. Malawi is not exceptional; in the contemporary period most Africans hold opinions that are accepting of – not discriminating toward – PLHIV. Below I analyze existing data on discriminatory attitudes toward PLHIV to show that AIDS-related stigma is not a big problem in Africa.

In 2007, the Pew GAP asked about perceptions of HIV stigma. Across the African sample, 38% of respondents said PLHIV face a lot of prejudice and discrimination, 30% said some, 18% said only a little, and 12% said none. There is some variation by country, however. More Nigerian respondents (68%) said PLHIV face a lot of prejudice and discrimination than in Uganda, where only 19% of respondents answered PLHIV face a lot of prejudice and discrimination[15]; the modal response in Uganda was "only a little." Senegal had the highest proportion (34%) of respondents say PLHIV face no prejudice and discrimination. These exceptions notwithstanding, the figures suggest that in Africa in 2007, PLHIV faced significant stigma.

If HIV stigma were so strong, why did so many Pew GAP respondents report a willingness to be tested for HIV? In Pew GAP's overall African sample in 2007, 60% were willing to be tested, 19% had

---

[15] For the sake of comparison, the question was also asked by Pew GAP of a nationally representative sample in the United States, and 40% of respondents said there is a lot of prejudice and discrimination against people with AIDS in their country, which is slightly higher than the average across the African sample and more than twice as high as in Uganda (Kaiser Family Foundation and Pew Global Attitudes Project, 2007, 31).

already been tested, and 18% said they were unwilling to be HIV-tested.[16] Unwillingness to be tested was somewhat higher in Ghana (30%) and Senegal (29%) and lower in Tanzania and Uganda (both 10%). HIV prevalence was much lower in Senegal and Ghana at the time of the survey, estimated at 0.8% and 1.9%, respectively, compared to 6.5% in Uganda and 6.6% in Tanzania (UNAIDS, 2016). In sum, stigma toward PLHIV was not so strong as to stop people from sharing their willingness to be HIV-tested with the stranger sent to interview them by Pew GAP.

The World Values Survey (WVS) also measures AIDS stigma, through asking respondents to name what groups of people they would or would not want as neighbors. Looking only at the 12,097 respondents in the seven African countries covered by the WVS in 2006 and 2007, 26% of respondents mentioned people who have AIDS,[17] but there is variation across countries. In South Africa, less than 8% of respondents mentioned people who have AIDS when asked who they wouldn't want to have as neighbors; in Ghana, it was 47%. HIV prevalence estimates at the time of the survey were 1.9% in Ghana and 18.2% in South Africa. The large difference suggests that discriminating against PLHIV would severely limit one's social circle in high-prevalence countries. In South Africa, where there is sufficient WVS data to examine trends over time, we see stigma declined: 38% of respondents said they would not want people who have AIDS as neighbors in 1996, 25% in 2001, and less than 8% in 2006.

Afrobarometer asked a similar question in 2014 and 2015 in 33 African countries. In 26 of the 33 countries surveyed, a majority of citizens reported they would like or would not mind having PLHIV as their neighbors (Dulani, Sambo and Dionne, 2016). The countries with higher intolerance of PLHIV have low HIV prevalence. In Southern Africa where prevalence is high, "intolerance for [PLHIV] might be tantamount to rejecting one's close family members and friends" (Dulani, Sambo and Dionne, 2016, 11).

The best available data on HIV stigma, however, are collected by the DHS, a USAID-funded initiative to collect nationally representative data on health and population trends in developing countries. Though

---

[16] Unfortunately, this question about willingness to be HIV-tested was asked only in African countries and so no US comparison could be made.

[17] As a comparison, in the US survey in 2006, 16% of respondents mentioned people who have AIDS.

Pew GAP and WVS are perhaps more widely known data sources among the general public in the West, the DHS has better coverage of African countries, more frequent data collection, and most importantly for the measurement of HIV stigma, better survey questions regarding social acceptance of PLHIV.

Since 2000, the DHS has asked questions to measure AIDS stigma and discrimination: willingness to care for a relative sick with AIDS; willingness to purchase fresh vegetables from an HIV-positive shop-keeper; and acceptability of an HIV-positive teacher to continue teaching.[18] These questions were asked across 79 surveys in 36 different African countries.[19] Averaging across the 79 surveys conducted since 2000, 83% of men and 78% of women reported they were willing to take care of a family member sick with AIDS. In the 29 surveys conducted since 2010, 87% of men and 81% of women reported they were willing to take care of a family member sick with AIDS. Smaller but still majority proportions of DHS respondents reported willingness to purchase fresh vegetables from an HIV-positive vendor and agreed that an HIV-positive teacher should be allowed to continue teaching. In 69 surveys conducted since 2000, 57% of men and 50% of women reported willingness to buy vegetables from an HIV-positive vendor; in the 29 surveys conducted since 2010, the proportions were higher: 62% of men and 56% of women.

AIDS stigma and discrimination are real. But in a context where AIDS is a generalized epidemic and more people are learning their HIV status, discriminating against or stigmatizing someone with AIDS is difficult to do without affecting one's family and friends. It is perhaps for these reasons that available data show discriminatory attitudes against PLHIV are on the decline. Additionally, even if in early surveys respondents perceived AIDS stigma to be high, those same respondents professed to be willing to get HIV-tested, demonstrating that whatever stigma may have been present, it was insufficient in deterring people

---

[18] An additional question asked about willingness to disclose a relative's HIV-positive status. I do not include this question in my analysis because it conflates measuring stigma and measuring respect for confidentiality. For a nuanced discussion of contentious expectations of disclosure, see Benton (2015).

[19] The AIDS stigma and discrimination questions were asked multiple times in some countries and only once in others. For example, though only asked once in Gabon (in 2012), the questions were asked in five surveys in Tanzania (2003, 2004, 2007, 2010, and 2011).

from acting against AIDS, at least at the personal level. In sum, available data measuring AIDS stigma suggest it is not so prevalent that we should be concerned it significantly impacts how citizens report prioritizing AIDS against other policy issues.

Lack of Awareness about AIDS in Africa

Could respondents' low ranking of HIV/AIDS programs merely be an indication that respondents are unenlightened and not aware that AIDS is fatal or of their risk in contracting HIV? The short answer is no. The 2004 Malawi DHS reported 82% of women and 92% of men knew that a healthy looking person can have the AIDS virus; similarly, 76% of women and 85% of men know that HIV cannot be transmitted by supernatural means (National Statistical Office [Malawi] and ORC Macro, 2005). For the sake of comparison to a context perhaps more familiar to readers, the 2004 Malawi DHS reported 82% of women and 90% of men know HIV infection is not transmitted by food, whereas 51% of Americans surveyed by the Kaiser Family Foundation in 2009 stated they would be uncomfortable having their food prepared by an HIV-positive person (National Statistical Office [Malawi] and ORC Macro, 2005; Kaiser Family Foundation, 2009).

Malawians' life experiences make it almost impossible for them to be unaware of the dangers of AIDS. On average, Malawians in our study attended four funerals a month. Their social autopsies of the dead suggest they knew very well the danger of AIDS and how HIV is transmitted (Watkins, 2004). Rather than underestimating their risk of HIV infection, most Malawians overestimate the chance they will become HIV-positive in their lifetime (Anglewicz and Kohler, 2009).

Malawians are not exceptional among Africans in their knowledge of HIV. Again, averaging across the 79 surveys DHS conducted since 2000, 97% of men and 95% of women reported having heard of AIDS. On average, most people knew that a healthy-looking person can have HIV (79% of men, 71% of women), that AIDS cannot be transmitted by either mosquito bites (59% of men, 56% of women) or supernatural means (75% of men, 68% of women), and that one cannot become infected by sharing food with someone who has AIDS (74% of men, 69% of women). Like in measuring discriminating attitudes, HIV knowledge has changed over time, with populations becoming increasingly more knowledgeable in the last five years. For example, in Nigeria in 2003, only 37% of women knew AIDS could not be transmitted by mosquitoes; by 2013, 67% of women knew.

5.7 Conclusion

This chapter uses survey data to show people in Malawi and other African countries with high HIV prevalence do not give high priority to AIDS. These findings are consistent with analysis of qualitative data gathered through participant observation in rural Malawi conducted around the same time (Verheijen, 2013). The data were collected during the same period when policymakers, activists, and scholars in the international community advocated for and began implementing a massive scale-up of HIV/AIDS services. The village headman quoted at the start of this chapter warned that "some problems can be forgotten," and spoke of the need for boreholes and health services for people suffering from diseases other than AIDS. In the rush to stem the tide of the AIDS pandemic, international actors failed to consider the priorities of Africans. The data demonstrate a misalignment of priorities in the global AIDS intervention.

While leading scholars have characterized HIV/AIDS services as public goods, HIV/AIDS services are more accurately characterized as excludable goods because certain populations stand to benefit more from them, namely those who have been personally affected by HIV. Though the findings in this chapter suggest a higher prioritization of HIV/AIDS services among those affected by HIV, AIDS prioritization remains relatively low.

This chapter's findings ought to change how people in the West think about AIDS as it is experienced by rural Africans. If a villager is HIV-positive, she may want ARV therapy to prolong and improve the quality of her life; however, because of a compromised immune system, she is especially vulnerable to other diseases prevalent in Africa. She may prioritize general health services and generally improved public health via water and sanitation projects because diseases other than HIV and opportunistic infections are a major threat to her quality and length of life. One PLHIV we interviewed admitted that while she personally would benefit from a clinic specifically providing AIDS services, she preferred resources be devoted to a general services clinic, saying ". . . because anyone who is HIV-positive or negative they both get sick with malaria so we need a hospital which can help anyone in the village."[20]

When asked what the government could do for people to be healthy, another PLHIV said the biggest problem needing to be addressed was water.[21] While she reported feeling healthy at the time of the interview, she also shared that she had not yet been able to gain access to ARVs, that her recently separated husband and co-wife were frequently sick, and that her second youngest child had also frequently been ill. Her prioritizing water above having a well-stocked and staffed clinic nearby or expanding access to highly rationed ARVs demonstrates the importance of including intended beneficiaries in decision-making about interventions to improve their condition. One way to learn citizens' policy priorities is to ask them.

This chapter documents the divide in preferences across actors in the global-to-local supply chain of interventions to improve the human condition. Ferguson (1990) and Li (2007) found that local attitudes and preferences are often underappreciated or ignored when implementing interventions designed and/or supported from the outside, and my study suggests more of the same is happening. The context of my study – fighting AIDS in Africa – is somewhat unique in that it may pose a challenge for citizens to engage their governments and relevant international agencies to reconsider their priorities because AIDS is exceptional (Whiteside, 2009; Dionne, Gerland and Watkins, 2013; Benton, 2015). In the 2001 Declaration of Commitment on HIV/AIDS, 189 nations agreed that AIDS was an international development issue of the highest priority (UNAIDS, 2007). Former United Nations Secretary General Kofi Annan called AIDS "an unprecedented threat to human development" (UNAIDS, 2004, 7). AIDS exceptionalism presents a particularly salient obstacle for African citizens who prioritize other policies.

One question this chapter raises is whether we will see diversion of resources earmarked for HIV/AIDS at the grassroots level because villagers fail to prioritize the same issues as international and national actors. The disconnect can create opportunities for corruption. A study of HIV/AIDS community-based organizations (CBOs) in Malawi highlighted how local communities had little influence on CBO's decisions or day-to-day work (Schou, 2009). In one of the districts of Schou's

---

[20] PLHIV Interview #4, Mchinji District, June 29, 2007.
[21] PLHIV Interview #24NN, Mchinji District, July 18, 2007.

study, four of the 25 CBOs funded by the National AIDS Commission to provide HIV/AIDS programming in the community were financially mismanaged, and one of those organizations was suspected to be fake (2009, 163). When citizens do not prioritize the issue for which funding is meant to address, how can we expect citizens to monitor the agents spending those funds and keep agents accountable? The next chapter focuses on local agents who citizens often hold accountable – village headmen – and documents their role in the global AIDS intervention.

6 | Seeing Like a Village: Headmen as Agents of the Global AIDS Intervention

Officials from our district hospital came to the villages to talk with the people without involving chiefs but that was not fruitful at all. People trust chiefs a lot.

> Headman Interview #157, Mchinji District, July 20, 2009

A chief is just like a doctor. He can keep secrets and I see no reason why he should not know the [HIV] test results of his people. It is important because the villagers turn to the chief for all their problems ... The village headman will always be there for his people.

> Headman Interview #159, Balaka District, August 26, 2009

While the previous chapter documented the perspectives and priorities of international donors and ordinary citizens, this chapter shifts perspective to detail what a headman[1] sees as he faces the AIDS epidemic in his village. This chapter's primary goal is to describe local agents, their priorities, and the context constraining their decision-making. Local agents implementing HIV/AIDS interventions in Malawi and elsewhere in Africa include community health workers, local religious leaders and congregations, and community-based organizations, but these have already been well-studied in the scholarship on AIDS.[2]

---

[1] A note on terminology: The range of terms defining the form of village leadership relevant to this study include headman, chief, traditional authority, and traditional leader. The first three terms connote specific positions in Malawi's chieftaincy hierarchy. As such, I avoid using these terms interchangeably and use each of these three terms as needed to distinguish between levels of hierarchy. I recognize "chief" or "traditional authority" may be more appropriate in other African settings and thus retain the terms used by scholars who study other settings when citing their work. I use the term "chieftaincy" to refer to the broader institution, encompassing all levels in the hierarchy. For a deeper discussion on the variety of names given to village leaders (and their superiors) in Africa, see Ray (2003) and West and Kloeck-Jenson (1999).

[2] On community health workers, see Mwai et al. (2013), Maes and Kalofonos (2013), Schneider, Hlophe and van Rensburg (2008), and Hermann et al.

I highlight less well-studied agents – Malawian headmen – because as elsewhere in Africa, most of Malawi's population (80%) live in rural areas, where chieftaincy remains important in provision of goods and services. In Malawi, no local development happens without the assent and participation of village headmen, and this chapter thus contributes to our understanding of their role in health and development interventions as well as the constraints they face. The quotes from village headmen in this chapter's epigraph also suggest headmen are trusted, effective helpers of their villagers, at least as reported by headmen.

A secondary goal of this chapter is to build on existing literature about chieftaincy and representation in Africa. To this end, I first substantiate the alignment of priorities between village headmen and their local principals – the villagers among whom they live. Then I also explore what shapes headmen's priorities. Contributing to the ongoing debate on chieftaincy in Africa, this chapter is the first empirical analysis to my knowledge that examines the fit between policy priorities of villagers and those of their headmen.

Village headmen provide a unique local perspective. Public opinion data has been useful in capturing local demand for and satisfaction with health policies and interventions in Africa (Afrobarometer, 2004; Bratton, 2009, 2012; Deaton, Fortson and Tortora, 2010; Bratton, 2012; Dionne, 2012; Youde, 2012; Dionne, Gerland and Watkins, 2013), but limits our understanding of policy priorities to an aggregation of individuals' preferences. In querying village headmen, we ask not what they want for themselves but what they want for their villages. Their answers tell us what goods and services are of greatest priority at the lowest level of a "public."

In his book *Seeing Like a State*, James Scott (1998) argues the view from which the state operates constrains its ability to improve the human condition; he juxtaposes a stylized bureaucratic state against an inaccessible local context, or at least, local contexts too diverse to aggregate into an intelligible administrative order. I adapt Scott's perspective to a lower level of governance. Although village administration varies across localities, I argue village leaders – like Scott's state bureaucrats – have shared constraints shaping their efforts to

(2009). On local religious leaders, see Trinitapoli and Weinreb (2012) and on religious congregations, see Klaits (2010). On community-based organizations, see Kalibala and Kaleeba (1989), Kalibala, Rubaramira and Kaleeba (1997), Schou (2009), and Schou and Tsoka (2012).

improve the human condition. I re-situate Scott's argument to the village level and suggest that we can better understand the challenges facing HIV/AIDS interventions if we take the perspective of a village headman and "see like a village."

The chapter begins with a review of the literature on chieftaincy in Africa and then draws on published scholarship and my field research to describe chieftaincy in Malawi. I then analyze qualitative data to detail some of the responsibilities headmen have taken on or adapted in the age of AIDS, including: resolving marital disputes brought on by the specter of AIDS, promoting HIV testing, and identifying AIDS orphans as beneficiaries of programs initiated by external donors. Most importantly, we learn from the qualitative data that when pressed to favor either external or local principals, headmen side with local principals – their villagers. The following section matches headmen surveys to surveys of their villagers[3] to examine local alignment of policy priorities and explore what influences headmen's priorities, specifically their prioritization of AIDS. The end of the chapter considers alternative settings and alternative agents of AIDS interventions and makes a case for why headmen might be the most effective agents through whom external principals can enact interventions to improve the human condition.

6.1 Chieftaincy in Africa

Scholars have long studied chieftaincy in Africa, documenting roles, responsibilities, and influence. Early scholarship is mostly descriptive, characterizing selection processes and chiefly duties (Gluckman, Mitchell and Barnes, 1949; Fallers, 1955; Buxton, 1963; Comaroff, 1978). Contemporary studies of chiefs' influence primarily focus on land tenure (Ntsebeza, 2006), however, the control many chiefs exercise over land has contributed to their broader political influence (Ribot, 1999; Herbst, 2000, chapter 6). There has been a resurgence of chieftaincy in the multiparty era (Englebert, 2002; Kyed and Buur, 2007), and with that a resurgence in the study of chieftaincy (see especially Baldwin, 2015). Many rural Africans rely on headmen and chiefs to help navigate the changing political landscape (Williams, 2010). Rather than being viewed as competing with democratic party politics,

---

[3] The data used in this chapter was collected as part of the MLSFH, described in greater detail in Chapter 4.

headmen and chiefs have been sought after as supporters of politicians and political parties (West and Kloeck-Jenson, 1999; Posner, 2005; Baldwin, 2013; Koter, 2013).

Much of the scholarship on chieftaincy in Africa is critical, with negative appraisals of chiefs' effectiveness (Bloom et al., 2005), neutrality (Muriaas, 2009), or representativeness (Chiweza, 2007*a*). The most widely cited work on chieftaincy depicts chiefs as "decentralized despots," and argues chieftaincy is a colonial artifact (Mamdani, 1996). Beall (2005) characterizes the "decentralized despot" view as seeing chieftaincy as "integral to sub-Saharan Africa's problems, operating as a brake on democratisation." The rules of chieftaincy run counter to democratic ideals: chiefs are often appointed, not elected; appointment is hereditary and for life; and the system is hierarchical and patriarchal, marginalizing women (Beall, Mkhize and Vawda, 2005).

There is evidence to support the chiefs-as-despots narrative. Ntsebeza (2008) finds contemporary traditional authorities in South Africa similar to the much-hated Tribal Authorities of the Apartheid era in being unelected, unrepresentative, and unaccountable. Sierra Leone provides some evidence of the negative impact chieftaincy can have. Fanthorpe (2005) found corrupt rule by chiefs contributed to rural youths' grievances, with some crediting their having joined rebel movements to exact revenge on chiefdoms. Comparing Sierra Leonean chieftaincies that have more ruling families to those with fewer shows those with fewer ruling families – and thus more power vested in the chief – had worse development outcomes; chiefs with fewer checks on their power presided over areas with lower literacy rates and educational attainment (Acemoglu, Reed and Robinson, 2014).

The negative appraisals of chieftaincy stand in contrast with the continued salience of chiefs and headmen (West and Kloeck-Jenson, 1999; Baldwin, 2013), whose influence is "widely accepted as a given" (Logan, 2009).[4] Political scientist Carolyn Logan (2009, 112) explores data across eight countries to show that in all but one (Namibia), ordinary Africans consistently rate traditional leaders as more trustworthy than elected officials. In later work exploring popular support for traditional authorities in 19 African countries, Logan (2013) found that while citizens find flaws in traditional leaders, they also believe

---

[4] Of course, there are exceptions. In the 19 African countries studied by Logan (2013), traditional authorities' influence is small in Tanzania and Madagascar.

traditional authorities have an essential role in local governance, particularly in resolving local disputes.[5] Their popularity was remarkably high, with 58% of respondents saying traditional leaders' influence should increase, compared to only 8% saying traditional leaders' influence should decrease (Logan, 2013).

Headmen as Knowledgeable, Influential Gatekeepers

The predominantly negative assessment of chieftaincy in the scholarly literature notwithstanding, governments and organizations rely on chiefs and headmen in rural Africa because they are gatekeepers to rural populations, have influence over villagers, and have specialized information.[6] Headmen wield significant power through their ability to grant or deny external actors access to villagers. Makuwira (2004) reports NGOs could not implement rural education initiatives in Malawi without first seeking traditional authorities' consent. Relatedly, chiefs can act as efficient facilitators by gathering villagers in meetings to distribute information or resources on behalf of external actors. For example, rarely in implementing an HIV information and awareness campaign would an organization have the resources to go door-to-door; it would instead invite villagers to a meeting held in the village center.

Headmen are also influential. Politicians look to headmen and chiefs when seeking the votes of their villagers (Baldwin, 2013). Chiefs can act as electoral intermediaries influencing the voting preferences of their dependents (Koter, 2013). Headmen influence health-related behaviors as well: two of three primary suggestions from research in Togo on how to increase child vaccination rates involved the village chief using his influence to increase social pressure and support behavior change of mothers (Eng, Glik and Parker, 1990).

Finally, a headman will typically know more about his village than any other local agent. Natural resource management projects in Senegal relied on village headmen's knowledge of villagers' preferences to act as representatives of rural populations (Ribot, 1999). In Zambia, politicians look to chiefs for information on development projects

---

[5] However, in Benin, Madagascar, South Africa, and Tanzania, the role of traditional leaders in resolving local disputes is marginal (Logan, 2013, 360).

[6] Government or NGOs working with village headmen is not confined to Africa. For example, Jacobs and Price (2006) discuss village chiefs' involvement in the Cambodian government's poverty alleviation program.

because they know "what the problems are" (Baldwin, 2013). In Malawi and other predominantly rural countries, district-level bureaucrats and district-based NGOs are too overwhelmed to know very much at the village level, whereas a headman is typically resident in the village and will know his community's needs and capacity to address those needs.

Constraints on Village Headmen

Headmen are cross-pressured by two constituencies: external actors like NGO or donor agency representatives who offer headmen resources to implement interventions, and local villagers whom the headmen are expected to represent. In the language of Chapter 3, the NGO or donor agency representative is an *external principal* who provides resources to the headman, who in turn acts as an *agent* implementing the intervention on behalf of the external principal. Similarly, the villagers are the *local principals* who delegate to their *agent* – the headman – the responsibility of governing in the village's interest. As the previous chapter showed, these principals have opposing preferences; while the global community (external principals) has prioritized AIDS response over other health concerns in Africa, African citizens (local principals) give relatively low priority to HIV/AIDS programs. Village headmen are agents for both local and external principals and operate like middle men between these *dueling principals*. A particularly stark example of dueling principals comes from the sunset of Apartheid in South Africa, where chiefs were "fiscally and institutionally dependent on the Apartheid government, but socially and politically dependent on angry and rebellious communities" (De Kadt and Larreguy, forthcoming, 7).

Scholars and development practitioners often focus on external principals, who provide resources to headmen in a context of resource scarcity. External principals can monitor village headmen's actions and sanction those straying from an agreement about how resources would be used to implement an intervention. We expect headmen won't jeopardize their access to resources from external principals. Perhaps more important but less well studied are the constraints local principals impose on headmen.

Some have raised concern that chieftaincy limits citizens' ability to keep headmen accountable (Chiweza, 2007a), but I contend headmen are constrained by their local principals, the villagers to whom interventions are targeted. A Yao proverb, *Chitela changakula ngali nyambi* (in English: A tree does not grow without branches), signifies how headmen depend on villagers for status. To be influential, headmen need villagers to cooperate. To imagine this in the context of this study, an external principal would have no need for a headman who could not mobilize villagers to attend a village meeting.

Headmen must appease villagers – especially influential ones – to retain their power. An historical example is of the administrative staff of Ugandan colonial chiefs, who acted as a check on the chief's power; if the chief failed to govern within customary limits, the staff might support a rival prince and drive the chief from his position (Fallers, 1955, 297). West and Kloeck-Jenson (1999, 475) report on a contemporary example from Mozambique: "should an angered population protest that an *autoridade gentilica* ['traditional authority'] did not truly represent his people ... he might be dismissed from office by an administrator who no longer found him useful." Williams (2010) writes of the fall of a chief in South Africa as frustration over lack of development and ineffective local government reached its breaking point. Quinlan and Wallis (2003) argue that in Lesotho there is a continuous struggle between the rural populace and chiefs as villagers reassess what chiefs do and act to keep the chieftainship relevant to its needs (152). These examples from multiple countries suggest that in Southern Africa at least, there is space to hold chiefs accountable.

During my fieldwork, a few villages experienced challenges to village leadership related to headmen's accountability to villagers. One headman said his drive to work hard for his villagers was motivated by his predecessor's poor performance and subsequent ousting.[7] Sociologist Ann Swidler (2013) recounts the village-led departure of one Malawian village headman:

A village headman who was driven out of his village in a particularly humiliating way – the women of the village surrounded his hut jeering and hurling insults – was described by an informant as someone who if the roads needed repairing would say he saw no need, but if there were a training in the nearby district capital for which he would receive a per diem, "he would be there at nine sharp." As dissatisfaction with the chief's leadership grew, he retaliated by expanding the village graveyard so that it encroached on a dissident family's land. This unjust use of his powers precipitated his being deposed and driven from the village (333).

[7] Headman Interview #61, Mchinji District, June 23, 2008.

Removal from office is only one potential threat to headmen and to the institution of chieftaincy more broadly. Chieftaincy must compete with other recognized institutions for power and legitimacy. For example, headmen's traditional courts compete with the formal judicial system. In Rumphi, the northern district in our study, multiple headmen remarked that there was an increase in divorces and that many of these were being sought in the formal court system, rather than arbitrated by village headmen. The paramount chief in the area attributed these diversions from traditional courts to an increasing presence and salience of human rights organizations promoting gender equality.[8] Mediating disputes is one of the few responsibilities widely understood to be in the purview of headmen. Should women feel the village proceedings discriminate against them, they can vote with their feet by seeking redress in the formal courts. These observations by traditional leaders in Rumphi District – though focused on belittling gender rights campaigns – are an indicator of how headmen do not wield unchecked power, even against traditionally marginalized populations. Because chiefs' power draws considerably from their role in adjudicating local disputes (Swidler, 2013), the loss of cases to an alternative legal venue is a serious threat to their authority. The forum-shopping for divorce proceedings show that villagers could opt to seek redress from another recognized institution should headmen be discriminatory in their arbitration, which further exemplifies the pressure citizens can put on their village headmen.

6.2 Chieftaincy in Malawi

The state has incorporated headmen in governing rural areas in Malawi since the colonial era. The colonial British regime found it difficult to collect taxes and govern the local population without local leaders (Baker, 1975), and thus fashioned a form of "indirect rule" through the *Native Authorities Ordinance of 1912*, which codified chiefs' roles in tax collection and over a traditional court system (Chiweza, 2007*a*). Chiefs gained considerable power with the introduction of the *1933 Native Authority Ordinance*, which allowed them to issue minor legislation for peace and order. Perhaps more importantly, the new ordinance allowed chiefs to establish treasuries that they could

---

[8] Interview with Paramount Chief Chikulamayembe, Rumphi District, October 21, 2008.

use to fund public development initiatives in their localities (Chiweza, 2007*b*, 145).

Following Malawi's independence in 1964, President Hastings Banda asserted that democracy in Malawi would be "based on the old African institutions" (Short, 1974, 260), and retained the institution of chieftaincy. In practice, however, ruling party operatives usurped chiefs' power by interfering in traditional courts (National Democratic Institute for International Affairs, 1995). Nonetheless, chiefs and headmen remained influential in rural areas. During the multiparty transition in the early 1990s, focus groups identified chiefs and headmen as the most important leaders in the day-to-day lives of Malawians (National Democratic Institute for International Affairs, 1995).

In contemporary rural Malawi, the highest authority in a village is a headman.[9] Village headship is formally hereditary across regions and ethnic groups (Chiweza, 2007*a*, 55). Succession procedures vary, usually depending on group traditions of patriliny or matriliny. For example, among the Ngoni, headmen are succeeded by their eldest sons by their chief wives (Gluckman, Mitchell and Barnes, 1949, 100). The Yao, a matrilineal group, transfer chieftaincy to the first-born son of a man's eldest sister (Mitchell, 1949). Succession procedures do not always adhere to these guidelines, rather the successor's personal qualities are also taken into account (Mitchell, 1949, 141).

Figure 6.1 presents one version of the chieftaincy hierarchy in Malawi.[10] Paramount chiefs are at the apex and typically preside over an entire cultural group, e.g., Paramount Chief Chikulamayembe presides over the Tumbuka of northern Malawi. Ruling just below paramount chiefs are senior chiefs. All persons in the chieftaincy hierarchy are associated with a geographically defined community at the lowest level: a village. In other words, a village headman presides over his village, a group village headman (GVH) presides over his village

---

[9] See Cammack, Kanyangolo and O'Neill (2009) on "town chiefs" in urban Malawi.

[10] The chieftaincy hierarchy is obviously not static over time and space. For example, in Rumphi District during the time of my study, there were additional positions between the Group Village Headman and the Traditional Authority, such as the Principal Senior Group Village Headman. Likewise, some of the villages I studied in Balaka District fell under a sub-TA – someone whose rank was also between GVH and TA. Figure 6.1 is a simplified model of the average village in which I collected data in 2008 and 2009.

Figure 6.1 Malawi's chieftaincy hierarchy

and other villages under his group, a traditional authority (TA) presides over his village, the other villages under his group village, and the group villages and villages under his traditional authority and so on. The responsibilities of TAs and higher-level chiefs are often so onerous that they delegate day-to-day duties of presiding over their home villages to assistant headmen and/or trusted councilors. Although any authority from village headman to paramount chief would be called *amfumu*, the Chichewa honorific form of "chief," this study focuses on the lower rungs of chieftaincy in Malawi: village headmen and GVH.

The *Chiefs Act of 1967* empowers the president to appoint chiefs according to customary law; the president can also remove chiefs. The appointment power of lower-level traditional authorities – TAs, GVH, and village headmen – is delegated to the chief or subchief (Patel et al., 2007), though my interviews suggested appointments were usually made the level above an office (i.e., the TA appoints the GVH, the GVH appoints the village headman). These appointments are normally made in consultation with the "subjects" of traditional authorities, particularly those in the former headman's family. The nature of headman selection involves a number of steps and varies considerably. In my study, 13% of headmen surveyed reported being elected to their post. Most reported inheriting the post (43%), and a large group reported being appointed by elders (38%). Open-ended interviews with headmen reporting to have been elected demonstrate that election participation is typically limited to elders in the village.

Villagers unhappy with their headmen can complain to the GVH or TA. Headmen can be reprimanded by those higher up the chain.[11] Villagers can also complain to district officials, who are responsible for distributing headmen's honoraria. Interviews with headmen demonstrate a healthy concern with keeping villagers happy for fear of action against them. Oustings of headmen like the one in Mchinji District discussed in the previous section seem infrequent. Because the sanction is large, I suspect few headmen risk behaving in ways that could lead to dethronement.

Malawi's constitution and formal legal framework partially recognize the power of traditional leaders. While the functions and position of chiefs are not specifically defined in the constitution, a number of sections recognize the existence of headmen and suggest roles headmen can play, such as in the provision for traditional courts being presided over by chiefs (Chirwa, Patel and Kanyongolo, 2013, 27). The *Local Government Act of 1998* was introduced to support decentralization and create a framework for democratic local government institutions, but contrary to its guidelines, traditional leaders maintain influence over local governance such that "in many places, the chief's word is final" (Chiweza, 2007b, 159). While headmen are remunerated with an official honoraria from the government, the amount has typically been small and thus insufficient to rely on for a living.

The most important power Malawi headmen hold is authority over land. Headmen mediate land disputes and, where available, allocate parcels of land. Headmen also handle dispute resolution more generally at the community level, including divorce proceedings, witchcraft accusations, and property inheritance.[12] Headmen are essentially in charge of all local matters, including presiding over funerals and

---

[11] One headman had spoken ill of his TA and was "dethroned" by the TA. Following an investigation by the paramount chief, the headman was reinstated and the TA admonished publicly by the paramount chief. The transcript of his interview – which followed his reinstatement – showed some reluctance to express unsympathetic views about the TA. Headman Interview #102, Rumphi District, October 17, 2008.

[12] Though headmen settle disputes in their communities, their power to do so is not enshrined in law and they are not recognized as part of the formal judicial structure, so in principle, they can only mediate between parties (Gloppen and Kanyongolo, 2007, 117).

cultural or religious ceremonies as well as collecting funds for communal purposes (Eggen, 2011, 320). In addition, a number of duties were delegated to headmen with the implementation of Malawi's Decentralization Policy.[13]

Because many Malawian villages have few government-supported services or infrastructure, the headman is critical in organizing and mobilizing people and resources to meet village needs (Swidler, 2013). In my research, I encountered no local development project that occurred without the assent and participation of the village headman. My interviews were consistent with earlier focus group data that found headmen "placed great importance on their role as initiators and supervisors of community development activities" (National Democratic Institute for International Affairs, 1995, 5).

Village headmen are trusted information sources in rural Malawi (Sturges and Chimseu, 1996) and typically the conduits through which government and NGOs engage rural communities. The headman alone acts as the gatekeeper between the government and the village (Eggen, 2011). For example, as part of the agricultural input subsidy program in 2006, which provided coupons for subsidized fertilizer, government relied on headmen to provide names of eligible villagers and headmen assisted with distribution. Even scholars note the importance of seeking traditional authorities' advice and permission before conducting research (e.g., Posner, 2004, 532). District officials I interviewed reported relying on headmen to identify community needs and capacity.

Afrobarometer surveys collected in Malawi substantiate the continuing influence of traditional authorities. When asked in 1999 if they have a chief, 93% of Malawian respondents said yes; 87% of the no responses were from urban Malawians. A number of questions across rounds help us to understand citizens' expectations of traditional authorities. For example, when asked in 2003 who resolves conflicts, a plurality (36%) of Malawians' first responses pointed to traditional chiefs/elders/mediators. A majority (57%) of Malawians in 2012 named traditional authorities as the person they would go to first for assistance if a victim of a crime. Malawians view chiefs as primarily responsible for solving local disputes and allocating land. These chiefly responsibilities likely draw – at least in part – from the high

---

[13] For example, as of 2008, all headmen are required to keep records of all births and deaths in their village using a government-provided register.

opinions many Malawians have of their village headmen. In 2008, traditional leaders were perceived to often (34%) or always (32%) listen to their constituents. A majority (71%) of respondents in 2008 thought the influence of traditional leaders should increase, compared to 21% who believe their influence should stay the same and 6% who believe traditional leaders' influence should decrease.

6.3 How Village Headmen Act against AIDS

Village headmen have a mixed reputation in Malawi's HIV/AIDS response. News stories portray village headmen as obstacles in the fight against AIDS,[14] who are ignorant about the disease[15] and act as guardians of cultural practices that facilitate HIV's spread.[16] My research goes beyond the headlines to study how Malawian headmen have actually responded to AIDS. In this section I detail three ways many headmen responded to AIDS: resolving marital disputes related to HIV testing or suspicion of extramarital affairs, promoting HIV testing to their villagers, and identifying AIDS orphans as beneficiaries of programs by external actors.

Resolving Marital Disputes in the Age of AIDS

Headmen regularly encounter AIDS-related problems in the course of their day-to-day responsibilities. The most common way headmen face AIDS is in resolving disputes. As noted earlier, respondents in Malawi's Afrobarometer survey viewed chiefs over any other actor or institution as primarily responsible for solving local disputes. Many of the local disputes headmen arbitrate are marital disputes.

While resolving marital disputes is not a new responsibility for village headmen, the arrival of AIDS has changed – even complicated – this responsibility. A headman's journal showed he often arbitrates marital disputes. One marital dispute he encountered related

---

[14] Phaless Chisenga, "Karonga Chief Condemns Condoms," *The Nation*, May 26, 2005.
[15] Peter Makossah, "No AIDS in Malawi – Village Headman," *The Nation*, February 28, 2003.
[16] Patrick Zgambo, "Bending a Few Customs to Stop Aids," *The Nation*, November 12, 2001; Edwin Nyirongo, "Ngoni Chiefs Agree to Review Practices," *The Nation*, July 12, 2005; Lucas Bottoman, "Chewa Chief to Assess Dangerous Traditions," *The Nation*, September 28, 2005.

specifically to HIV and the headmen found the case to be sufficiently important to refer it higher up the chieftaincy hierarchy:

There was a case involving marriage … a man came to complain that his wife wants to kill him … he said that he married his wife long time ago, and the wife is involved in small-scale business. She went to the hospital and was found to be HIV-positive. Because of this, [the husband] suggested using condoms. The woman refused … When the woman was asked to respond, she said that the husband was saying the truth … I as village head, after noticing that it involves a disease having no cure, I referred the case to the Group Village Headman.[17]

Another headman narrated a similar marital dispute:

Last year, 2008, a certain man in my village left his wife and two children to look for employment in Blantyre … after 10 months the man came home for the first time since he left. But … the wife … refused to have sex with him. She demanded that he should first go for HIV test because he had been away too long. The woman had gone for the test earlier on and was found to be HIV-negative. The husband complained to me about what was happening. I advised the gentleman to go for the test. He was found to be HIV-positive and they were both counseled at the testing center.[18]

One headman reported he initiated action against a man who was "taking advantage of his wife" by seeing other women. Rather than letting a problem he saw fester to the point where it could end in divorce – which the headman remarked was slowing his village's development potential – the headman opened a case in his court against the husband "for being cruel."[19] He warned the husband that his actions could lead him to "catch AIDS" and that "this is not acceptable by the government" or by the headman. This example shows headmen don't necessarily wait for disputes to arise but as residents in the village they oversee, they can spot issues on the horizon and deal with them before it's too late.

Promoting HIV Testing

One important area in which headmen have been influential is in encouraging HIV testing, especially among men. The introduction of

[17] Headman Journal, Balaka District, November 22, 2008.
[18] Headman Interview #160, Balaka District, August 26, 2009.
[19] Headman Interview #6, Balaka District, August 28, 2008.

routine HIV testing among women attending antenatal clinics in 2003 increased the number of women tested for HIV in Malawi, but there has been a gender disparity in rates of HIV testing. While 73% of Malawian women reported having ever been tested for HIV, only 52% of men reported the same (National Statistical Office [Malawi] and ICF Macro, 2011, 209–10). To increase men's HIV testing rates, women are encouraged to bring their partners to the antenatal clinic to also be tested for HIV, and this is one form of "couples testing."

Couples testing is a protocol that offers HIV tests and counseling to couples rather than individuals. With individual HIV testing, an individual assumes the burden of disclosing HIV status to her partner, but in couples testing, mutual disclosure is immediate (World Health Organization, 2012). Couples currently constitute the largest risk group in Africa for HIV transmission; most heterosexual HIV transmission takes place within marriage or cohabitation (Dunkle et al., 2008). Scholars studying HIV concordance and discordance in couples argue that couples should know their joint HIV status and have access to information enabling them to reduce risk of infection both in marriage and outside marriage (Painter, 2001; Malamba et al., 2005; Dunkle et al., 2008).

Even before couples testing was widely adopted in the international community as an HIV intervention strategy, village headmen were already promoting HIV testing among couples, typically associated with their role in resolving marital disputes. One headman recounted a number of married couples he counseled about HIV testing. In three marital disputes he arbitrated regarding HIV testing, the wives already knew their HIV status and were asking their husbands to be tested; his arbitration led to two of the husbands to get HIV tests.[20]

Headmen also promote HIV testing at the behest of outside actors. In at least one of my study villages, district health officials and the local community health worker asked the headman to call a meeting to encourage couples testing. At the same time, the headman was arbitrating a divorce case that followed a husband's refusal to be tested after his wife tested positive for HIV.[21] The headman reported only providing introductory and closing remarks at the meeting he called, leaving

---

[20] Headman Interview #152, Balaka District, August 27, 2009.
[21] Thirty-five-year-old woman, focus group in village #8, Balaka District, 1 pm, September 4, 2008.

health workers to encourage HIV testing. It was stressed at the meeting that spouses refusing testing should be reported to the chief because "he has the powers to force this person to go to [the] hospital [and be tested]."[22] The same headman stated that health workers subsequently reported an increase in men coming for HIV testing. The headman said he continues to encourage HIV testing at village meetings.

To confirm that the headman was not overstating his HIV prevention efforts, we conducted eight focus groups with 46 villagers following the headman's interview. Participants were asked to recall meetings called by the headman and what impact the villagers thought the meetings had. In none of the focus groups was discussion of HIV or AIDS prompted by the focus group facilitator. All but one focus group reported a recent meeting with health officials promoting couples testing and subsequent encouragement from the headman to test for HIV.[23] One participant remarked, "Our village headman does keep on encouraging us that we should be going and have those HIV tests and he does sometimes even say about this even when that meeting has got nothing to do with AIDS issues."[24]

The headman used his influence to call a meeting to address a problem associated with HIV testing scale-up: the low uptake of testing by partners of women seeking antenatal care. His summoning the village was in response to health officials' request, but also stemmed from his experience adjudicating a divorce case; furthermore, the headman continued to promote HIV testing at meetings when health officials were absent. Supportive messages about HIV testing by village headmen were not exceptional in the area where MLSFH had been conducting surveys since 1998. It was possible, however, that the decade-long presence of an international research team studying sexual behavior and health may have inadvertently shaped village openness to such discussion.

To be sure village headmen's promotion of HIV testing was not limited to villages studied for over a decade by HIV researchers, a research assistant conducted in-depth interviews with 10 village headmen and

[22] Headman Interview #8, Balaka District, August 27, 2008.
[23] The meeting about HIV testing was most frequently recalled by focus group participants. Other recent meetings called by the headman reported by participants included political campaigns, organizational meetings about agricultural subsidy distribution, and discussing a mosque building project.
[24] Forty-year-old male grocer, focus group in village #8, Balaka District, 3:45 pm, September 4, 2008.

group village headmen outside the MLSFH study area in July and August 2009. The purpose of these interviews was to see if other headmen were similarly encouraging their villagers to test for HIV. Of the 10 headmen interviewed, 9 reported having meetings specifically to encourage HIV testing; these meetings were usually led by government health personnel. All 10 reported having encouraged testing beyond formal village meetings: some reported to have encouraged villagers who have often been sick, some encouraged younger villagers preparing to marry, and some reported using well-attended fertilizer subsidy meetings and funerals to encourage HIV testing.

One Group Village Headman we interviewed in this follow-on study was engaged in the issue of couples HIV testing. He encouraged villagers to get tested at multiple village meetings – including ones whose topics were unrelated, e.g., regarding fertilizer subsidy coupon distribution. He also privately counseled men whose wives were pregnant, telling them they had to accompany their wives to the antenatal clinic and be HIV-tested, which is a routine part of antenatal care in Malawi (Angotti, Dionne and Gaydosh, 2011). The GVH would then follow up afterward with the husband to see if he had followed the GVH's orders. He suspected one villager misrepresented accompanying his wife with actually being HIV tested, and so the GVH asked the wife if her husband was also tested. He remarked, "Husbands lie, so you have to call wives as well to ascertain the truth." When the GVH learned the husband had not been tested, he ordered him to go to the district hospital to be tested and to return to the village with evidence of his test.[25]

Identifying AIDS Orphans

External actors often rely on headmen to decide who among their villagers will benefit from development interventions targeting the poorest of the poor. Headmen reported they were frequently asked to enumerate the needy in their village.[26] In the time of AIDS, many of these external requests for enumerating the needy involved identifying AIDS orphans. When asked how an NGO recently targeted food

[25] Headman Interview #158, Mchinji District, July 20, 2009.
[26] This is consistent with another scholar's observations in Malawi; he concluded, "Only the chief can provide the local information necessary for identifying and mapping beneficiaries ..." (Eggen, 2011, 323).

donations for AIDS orphans, a headman said, "They first come to the village headman and say they are here to assist orphans. So they ask for the total number of orphans in the village and have their names written."[27] The headman gave names to the NGO and the NGO returned later with assistance for the orphans.

How do headmen know how many AIDS orphans are there in their village? In addition to living among villagers and thus being familiar with those in the community, villagers will often seek headmen's help when fostering orphans makes it difficult for them to make ends meet. One headman reported starting a club for these foster parents where the headman and the group members each make a small financial contribution, from which group members can withdraw when they require assistance.[28] The headman also referred foster guardians to a local organization in the district capital that provided food and clothes for AIDS orphans.

Headmen enumerating the needy for external actors is a regular responsibility: "They ask us to tell them the number of orphans and aged [elderly]. So we give them the numbers. So they register them and call them to the usual place where they meet."[29] Village headmen also identify beneficiaries when they gather with other headmen to discuss and plan area development projects. In recounting his preparation for a recent area development committee meeting, a headman said, "So the first thing that the chief should know [is] the number of orphans living in his area."[30]

Headmen say the assistance offered typically falls short. For example, the headman who reported an NGO targeting food donations to orphans in his village had this to say about the assistance they brought: "Of course, there are still some who were left out … five were not helped."[31] Another headman reported that there are a number of orphans in his village, "such that people do come to record names but in the end there is no assistance."[32] An entry in the Balaka headman's journal relates a meeting he attended with the other village headmen in his group village during which they learned a goat-raising project for orphans never materialized; the GVH said during the meeting,

[27] Headman Interview #69, Mchinji District, July 11, 2008.
[28] Headman Interview #154, Balaka District, August 26, 2009.
[29] Headman Interview #68, Mchinji District, July 11, 2008.
[30] Headman Interview #107, Rumphi District, October 13, 2008.
[31] Headman Interview #69, Mchinji District, July 11, 2008.
[32] Headman Interview #153, Balaka District, August 24, 2009.

"I am not happy at all because a lot of people and organizations promise a lot of things to [orphans] but not all fulfill it."[33] One headman also remarked on the type of assistance orphans received. A local NGO provided blankets and *likuni phala* – a local porridge – to some of the orphans in the village. The headman asked why they could not provide more useful assistance, like clothes or *nsima*, a staple in Malawians' diet.[34]

Headmen face other obstacles when engaging with external actors regarding orphan beneficiaries, namely in defining who is an orphan. In 2006, an NGO gave some headmen in Balaka District a week to identify up to 100 orphans, each of whom the NGO would provide a blanket, a kilogram of maize flour, and five bars of soap.[35] The headmen drew up a list and the NGO came with a pickup truck to distribute the goods. Upon arrival, however, agents of the NGO learned that some of the orphans still had a living parent. Essentially, the NGO anticipated their 100 orphan beneficiaries would be "double orphans," or children who have lost both parents. The NGO told the headmen it would not distribute to any orphans listed who had only lost one parent. The headmen of the area refused, saying all 100 children would receive benefits or none would. After some time, one headman calmed down the anxious crowd and it was announced that all listed orphans would receive the donated goods.

* * *

Headmen are expected to advise villagers, mediate disputes between them, and represent their needs to external actors. HIV's arrival has added a new dimension to those responsibilities. Headmen's actions against AIDS are often adaptations or extensions of what headmen already consider to be their responsibility. The examples I have shared in this section of headmen mediating marital disputes, promoting HIV testing, and assisting NGO initiatives for orphans demonstrate both their engagement in AIDS programming and their potential as advocates for their AIDS-affected villagers. In none of our interviews did headmen report ever being consulted about how to assist AIDS orphans. Rather, headmen were merely expected to "write the names"

---

[33] Headman Journal, Balaka District, January 19, 2009.
[34] Headman Interview #57, Mchinji District, July 4, 2008.
[35] Malawian Journals Project, Chikondi Balalika, November 11, 2006.

of the needy. They did as asked, and when they had the power to challenge the narrowing of assistance by external actors, they fought on behalf of their villagers. I expect, however, that headmen would be even more effective agents of AIDS interventions if external principals had a better understanding of how headmen see and prioritize the epidemic.

If a headman's goal is to "care for his village" – as many headmen we interviewed claimed – then all other things equal, we should expect to find that villages particularly affected by a problem will have headmen who prioritize that problem. In the next section, I analyze survey data to study what shapes headmen's policy priorities.

6.4 Village Headmen and Their Priorities

We asked headmen to name the three most important issues facing their village. Responses were open-ended and coded into 20 possible categories. Access to clean water was the most common response. Other issues consistently reported as important were relevant to food security and agricultural development, diseases besides AIDS, and poverty. Of the 124 headmen we interviewed, only 10 mentioned HIV or AIDS as one of the most important issues facing their village.[36] The open-ended nature of the "most important issue" question is sufficiently vague that it may have been a poor measure of AIDS priority. Thus, we posed to them the same policy priority question we asked the villagers under their care. We asked headmen to rank in order of importance five public policy priorities: clean water, health services, agricultural development, education, and HIV/AIDS programs.

Figure 6.2 presents headmen's policy priorities graphically. Like the villagers under their care, headmen gave highest priority to access to clean water, and ranked HIV/AIDS last among the five possible policy priorities. On average, headmen ranked health services fourth most important (though a plurality of headmen ranked it third most important).

In follow-up interviews we asked headmen to explain these priority rankings. Headmen said that if there were clean water, they would

---

[36] Seven of these villages had MLSFH respondents who had tested HIV-positive. One of the three headmen whose village did not have any MLSFH respondents test HIV-positive declared himself to be HIV-positive during the interview (unprompted). Headman Interview #85, Mchinji District, July 8, 2008.

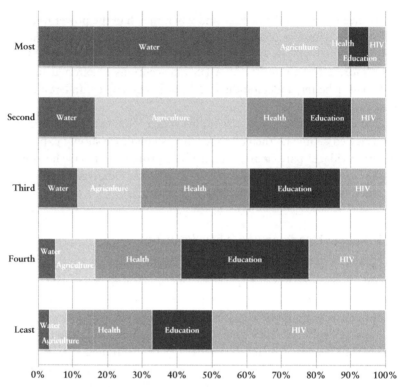

Figure 6.2 Headmen's policy rankings, by importance
Source: MLSFH Headman Study, 2008

not need health services. We asked, "but what about the people in your village sick with AIDS?" Responses ranged. Some headmen conceded that those people needed services but reminded us that even their HIV-positive villagers need clean water and regular access to food to stay healthy. For example, one village headman who spoke at length about the people in his village who were HIV-positive and receiving ARVs pointed out the importance of nutrition when taking treatment. In his words, "These ARVs demands one to eat."[37] Similarly, headmen prioritized agricultural development programs because they reasoned that those who are HIV-affected need nourishment and thus need more inputs for their farm so that they can harvest more without having to

---

[37] Headman Interview #161, Salima District, September 23, 2008.

work as hard.[38] Even headmen who gave high priority to HIV focused their conversations on the agricultural-economic impact of AIDS. For example, one said:

> I want my people to be healthy. Imagine our chickens are gone because of deaths. Even much of our wealth is gone because of funerals. Even herds of cattle are gone too.[39]

Locally Aligned Priorities

A running concern about chieftaincy in Malawi and elsewhere in Africa is that an appointed, unelected leader is unlikely to represent the interests of villagers (Chiweza, 2007a; Ntsebeza, 2008). This concern calls attention to the need to examine village headmen as representatives of their villagers. One way to do this is to ask: How aligned are village headmen's priorities with those of their villagers?

In the previous chapter, I showed that the most important policy concern among villagers was access to clean water. Second most important was agricultural development. Health services was third most important, and education was fourth. Most notably, villagers ranked HIV/AIDS programs last among the five options.

Figure 6.2 showed that at the aggregate level, headmen and villagers mostly agree: clean water is the most important, agricultural development is the second most important, and HIV/AIDS is the least important public policy problem. The prioritization of education and health services is reversed between villagers and headmen (either third or fourth most important). A potential problem of comparing distributions of villagers' and headmen's policy priorities is that aggregate alignment could occur without reflecting headmen's responsiveness to their own villagers. For example, villagers in village A might prioritize water but not HIV/AIDS, the opposite of villagers in village B. However, if village A's headman ranked policies in line with village B's villagers and village B's headman gave preferences in line with village A's villagers, we could not identify local misalignment by comparing aggregate trends.

Disaggregating data by village, I compared headmen's policy priorities against their own villagers' policy priorities. For each village and

---

[38] Traditional Authority Interview #3, Mchinji District, November 8, 2008.
[39] Headman Interview #102, Rumphi District, October 17, 2008.

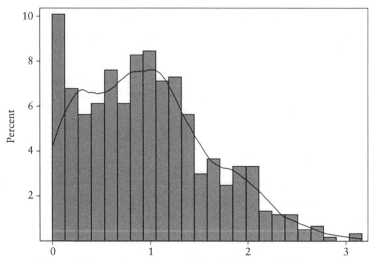

Distance between policy preference rankings of headmen and their average villager

Figure 6.3 Comparing headmen and their villagers

each of five policies, I took the difference between the headman's policy ranking and the average of a village's policy ranking. Figure 6.3 is a histogram illustrating the close match between headmen's and villagers' priorities. Most headmen had policy rankings within one unit of his average villager's ranking of a policy (59%); nearly all observations are within two units (94%).[40]

The matched villager and headmen's datasets support the idea that headmen are representative; at the least, headmen's policy rankings are close to the rankings of their villagers. The data cannot distinguish whether headmen's preferences were formed based on assessment of villagers' preferences or if headmen simply share villagers' lived experience. It is also possible headmen shared their policy preferences with villagers, leading villagers on how to rank their preferences. While I cannot rule out the latter, headmen surveys were collected only after all villager surveys were completed, usually weeks later. Headmen were also not made aware by the research team of the content of villager surveys during data collection.

---

[40] As a comparison, I generated random scores for each village's average policy rankings. In the random assignment, 35% of headmen's responses are within 1 unit and 64% of headmen's responses are within 2 units.

In Malawi, headmen live in close proximity to the intended beneficiaries of rural health and development interventions, and thus have a close-up view of what is most important or desired by their communities. My analysis here suggests that if a headman was sought out to advise on his village's needs, his responses would likely align with villagers' priorities. While this local alignment of priorities comports with normative goals of representation at the grassroots, external principals of health and development projects employing headmen as agents of intervention should be cautioned that their agents – village headmen – may not share principals' priorities, as the next section demonstrates.

Headmen's Priorities Shaped by Village AIDS Experience

Having established that, on average, headmen's priorities are aligned with and thus representative of their respective villagers' priorities, in this section I examine potential influences on headmen's priorities. Building on the findings from Chapter 5 on villagers' priorities, I expect headmen in villages more heavily affected by AIDS will give greater priority to AIDS. More specifically, I expect a headman's prioritization of AIDS will be a function of HIV prevalence and recent AIDS deaths in his village.

There is no village-level data on HIV prevalence or AIDS mortality, so I use two proxy measures. To approximate village HIV prevalence, I use the number of villagers whoever tested HIV-positive in MLSFH data collection.[41] As a proxy measure for AIDS death, I use the headmen's reports of funerals in the last month.[42]

I also examine the explanatory power of a rival argument about AIDS response as being shaped by ethnic boundaries (Lieberman, 2009). One implication of that argument would be that headmen of

---

[41] There are likely more villagers in a given headman's village who are HIV-positive than were captured in MLSFH data because the survey only interviewed and HIV-tested a sample of villagers in each village. Additionally, as detailed in Chapter 4, the MLSFH is a cluster sample. This means that no village's respondents will be a representative sample of the village. While this is a "noisy" measure, it approximates the contrasting contexts between villages with many HIV-positive villagers from those with few.

[42] Of course, AIDS is not the only cause of death in our study villages. However, given the high percentage of deaths attributed to AIDS just prior to this study – estimated at nearly 75% by Doctor and Weinreb (2003) – it seems a reasonable proxy.

Table **6.1** *Headmen prioritization of HIV/AIDS programs*

	(1)	(2)	(3)
# HIV-positives in village	0.217***		0.226***
	(0.080)		(0.085)
# of funerals headman attended	0.082*		0.084*
	(0.061)		(0.047)
Village ethnic diversity		1.110	−0.045
		(0.855)	(0.950)
Headman education level	−0.247	−0.279	−0.235
	(0.184)	(0.196)	(0.179)
Male headman	−1.017*	−0.760	−1.072*
	(0.496)	(0.509)	(0.569)
Observations	120	119	119
Pseudo R^2	0.067	0.025	0.071

Notes: Statistical significance levels: $*p < 0.10$; $**p < 0.05$; $***p < 0.01$. Robust standard errors are shown in parentheses below coefficients. Models 1–3 are ordinal logit regressions where the outcome variable of interest is prioritization of HIV/AIDS programs, rescaled for easier interpretation from 1 to 5, where 5 indicates HIV/AIDS is the most important priority and 1 indicates HIV/AIDS is the least important priority. Source: MLSFH and MLSFH Headman Study, 2008.

ethnically diverse villages should give lower priority to HIV/AIDS than headmen of ethnically homogenous villages. Though earlier research might suggest ethnic homogeneity in Malawi's villages (Posner, 2004), Malawian villages are often comprised of people from multiple ethnic groups. Only 21% of MLSFH study villages had surveys with respondents from only one ethnic group. It is possible that some of those villages are also more ethnically diverse than survey data would suggest as sampling was drawn by village cluster, not by village. The only available data to measure ethnic diversity in MLSFH study villages is aggregating by village reported ethnicity of the survey sample. I construct a Simpson's diversity index for each village where 0 indicates a village where all MLSFH respondents reported having the same ethnic identity and values approaching 1 indicating high ethnic diversity among MLSFH respondents in the village.

Table 6.1 displays the output of an ordered logit regression where the outcome of interest is a headman's prioritization of HIV/AIDS programs, controlling for headmen's gender and education. Headmen who had many more HIV-positive villagers gave higher priority to HIV/AIDS programs. The number of funerals a headman reported attending in the previous month has a positive effect on increasing headmen's prioritization of HIV/AIDS, though the effect is only weakly significant. Headman gender also had an effect, with women more likely to prioritize HIV/AIDS than men. This finding fits with the Malawian context: women have higher HIV prevalence than men, women are more likely to know their HIV status, and women are more likely to act as caretakers when someone falls ill with AIDS (Chimwaza and Watkins, 2004). Village ethnic diversity, however, does not seem to have a significant effect on how headmen prioritize HIV/AIDS.

Using output from Model 1 in Table 6.1, I hold all other variables at their means and vary the number of HIV-positive villagers from 0 (the 10th percentile value in our population) to 3 (the 90th percentile value in our population) to generate predicted probabilities of village headmen prioritizing HIV/AIDS. Figure 6.4 displays graphically the distribution of predicted probabilities. The main takeaway from the graph is that most headmen give low priority to HIV/AIDS programs. A secondary takeaway is that as the number of HIV-positive villagers increases, headmen have a higher predicted probability of giving greater priority to HIV/AIDS.

6.5 Chiefs Acting against AIDS beyond Malawi

How well do my findings on headmen's response to AIDS travel beyond Malawi? Because the influence of headmen and chiefs and the contours of the AIDS pandemic vary across Africa, we should expect the response to AIDS by chiefs and headmen to also vary across space. Given my findings that village headmen are more likely to prioritize AIDS when faced with a more serious epidemic, we should not expect to find many headmen active against AIDS in places with low HIV prevalence.

Focusing on the Southern African nations hardest hit by AIDS, we can use reported trust in traditional leaders as an indicator of potential for headmen to act as effective agents of AIDS interventions. Afrobarometer survey data collected in 2008 show a majority of respondents in Botswana (54%), Lesotho (54%), Malawi (55%), and Zambia (53%) put a lot of trust in their traditional leaders. A plurality of respondents in Mozambique (47%), Namibia (40%),

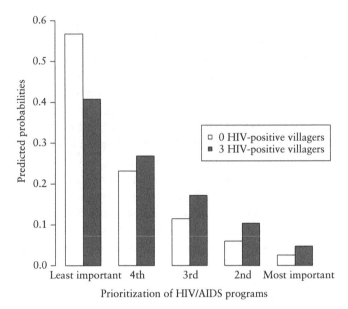

Figure 6.4 Predicted probabilities of headmen's prioritization of HIV/AIDS programs

and Zimbabwe (35%) put a lot of trust in their traditional leaders. In South Africa, however, reported trust in traditional leaders is mixed, with the largest proportion (22%) of respondents saying they do not trust traditional leaders at all. Afrobarometer survey data are suggestive of the potential role traditional authorities could play in the fight against AIDS, though at the same time caution us about how that potential varies across countries. Below I draw from published literature on the other countries where a majority of citizens trust traditional leaders – Botswana, Lesotho, and Zambia – to take stock of chiefs and headmen responding to AIDS there.

Botswana

Botswana offers an interesting example of traditional authorities acting against AIDS. As part of the initiative to increase uptake of male circumcision to protect against HIV, chiefs are combining traditional rites with modern clinical procedures. Shortly after his installation, the chief of the Bakgatla revived the tradition of *bogwera*, a coming-of-age initiation ceremony for boys in which male circumcision is a central part. Addressing villagers, the chief explained *bogwera* would be assisted by doctors and scientists and was part of Botswana's fight against HIV's spread (Dow and Essex, 2010, 116–22; Timberg and Halperin, 2012, 361).

Chiefs were not always champions of AIDS response in Botswana. Owing at least in part to the disempowerment of chiefs in the modern era, Botswana's chiefs were sidelined in favor of elected village-level committees for health and AIDS who report to governmental bureaucratic structures (Allen and Heald, 2004; Heald, 2006). Like the Malawian village headmen in my study, chiefs in Botswana did not independently advance AIDS as a major problem in their villages (Heald, 2006, 37). Even under these constraints and while chiefs did not prioritize AIDS as a problem, Heald (2006) identifies a number of actions chiefs took to mitigate the impact of AIDS in their villages. These included outlawing funerary vigils at the height of the epidemic as a way of alleviating the burdens of families who were experiencing multiple deaths (Heald, 2006, 38).

Lesotho

There is not much published on Lesotho chiefs responding to AIDS, but there have been policy documents and academic articles suggestive of chiefs' potential as agents of AIDS intervention. For example, in a study seeking strategies to increase HIV testing among men, villager participants suggested the village chief should call a *pitso* – a village meeting – of all men to advise them to be HIV-tested (DiCarlo et al., 2014, 876–7). Another example comes from an assessment of OVC programs in Lesotho and Swaziland that has profiles of two beneficiaries, one of which demonstrates the village chief as a conduit of information. One beneficiary of the OVC program in Lesotho reported that he learned of the program through a village meeting of children called and led by the local chief (Open Society Initiative for Southern Africa and Open Society Foundations Education Support Program, 2012, 48).

Chiefs feature prominently in an HIV/AIDS strategy document that emerged from a partnership between the Lesotho government and the UN-supported Expanded Theme Group on HIV/AIDS Lesotho (Kimaryo et al., 2004). The document, *Turning a Crisis into an Opportunity: Strategies for Scaling Up the National Response to the HIV/AIDS Pandemic in Lesotho*, takes stock of Lesotho's AIDS response to date and makes specific recommendations for the response going forward. Principal Chiefs[43] committed to helping disseminate information about HIV/AIDS through the large network of chiefs and traditional leaders under their jurisdiction (Kimaryo et al., 2004, xxix). Prior to the Lesotho government adopting *Turning Crisis into an Opportunity* as an official working/reference document in late 2003, however, chiefs were excluded in Lesotho's national AIDS strategic plan (Makoa, 2004, 72).

Zambia

Most portrayals of headmen's response to AIDS in Zambia suggest they are part of the problem. For example, a study on preventing mother-to-child transmission of HIV reported how a senior headman who was also a traditional healer thought babies should be exclusively breastfed, at a time when leaders in the global AIDS intervention community were promoting formula feeding (Bond, Chase and Aggleton, 2002, 351). This headman was being called out for advising women in ways that were inconsistent with the global intervention community's recommendations.

Another study of AIDS orphans is similarly suggestive of headmen as problematic. Like in Malawi, in Zambia, NGOs often go to village headmen for help with identifying beneficiaries of programs. Yamba (2005) shares a cautionary example of a headman's influence: a household of orphans were originally excluded from a beneficiary list provided by their village headman because one of the children had "disrespected" him (210). Although the situation was ultimately rectified, the example portrays headmen as making harmful, arbitrary judgments that have a negative impact on the HIV/AIDS-affected.

There is some faith in the potential of Zambian headmen as important and influential in AIDS intervention. Support to the HIV/AIDS Response (SHARe) is a USAID-funded program that works with Zambian chiefs and headmen in its HIV prevention efforts. Headmen and other local cultural leaders trained by SHARe conducted HIV awareness programs targeted at adolescent youth, which was followed by significant increases in demand for HIV and reproductive health-related services (John Snow, Inc., 2015, 8). Additionally, recent

---

[43] Principal Chiefs are akin to Malawi's Paramount Chiefs in that they are perched at the top of Lesotho's chieftaincy hierarchy.

evidence shows formal decrees and HIV/AIDS policies written and adopted by chiefs in Zambia has led to changes in behavior among their subjects, including increases in women seeking HIV tests during antenatal care and declines in early marriage (Chanda et al., 2014).

* * *

A shallow dive into secondary literature capturing headmen and chiefs' anti-AIDS activities in Botswana, Lesotho, and Zambia shows similarities to the Malawian case studied in-depth in this chapter. Like village headmen in Malawi, chiefs in Botswana and Lesotho and village headmen in Zambia act – or have the potential to act – as influential conduits of information. Chiefs and headmen in these other countries also help external organizations identify program beneficiaries. Finally, while some have recognized the potential for chiefs and headmen to act as agents in the international intervention against AIDS in Africa, there has not been meaningful incorporation of these locally informative, influential leaders in a coordinated response to AIDS.

6.6 Alternative Village-Level Agents

Village headmen are not the only local agents through which organizations can implement AIDS interventions. Religious congregations, community-based organizations, and community health workers are also active in the fight against AIDS. Their coverage areas often cover more than one village, however. Are there other village-level actors who could be agents of AIDS interventions?

Instead of working with headmen, external actors could work through village committees. Village committees are usually made up of volunteers living in the village who meet occasionally to discuss and organize efforts around an issue. Some of these include village development committees and village AIDS committees. Many Malawian villages have village committees, but the activities committees engage in and the regularity with which they operate is less well understood. A few headmen we interviewed were suspicious of the motivations of village committee members. A recently installed headman accused his village health committee of benefitting from donations received on behalf of HIV-positive villagers.[44] It is, of course, to the headman's

---

[44] Headman Interview #153, Balaka District, August 24, 2009.

advantage to paint himself as the most reliable agent and we have no way of corroborating his story nor can we judge him in the same way he has judged the committee. However, evidence from this chapter has shown that there are constraints or "checks" on headmen's power. It is not clear that there are similar mechanisms checking the power of village committees.

An additional drawback of working through village committees is that they are not uniformly distributed across villages. Less than a third of the villages in our study had AIDS committees. In villages that had them, AIDS committees met only once a month on average. In Malawi, the National AIDS Commission tried to promote creation of village AIDS committees across the country, but top-down efforts to generate grass-roots organization is about as successful as you would expect. Villages with active AIDS committees often created them in response to local needs. For example, in one village in Mchinji District, the headman reported that the village started an AIDS committee because there were so many orphans.[45] While a donor agency seeking a village committee to act as a local agent may be lucky in that Mchinji village, in most other villages, they would struggle to identify such a group.

Finally, committees also introduce more veto players; whereas headmen can make unilateral decisions – albeit in consultation with influential villagers – committees require consensus or majority agreement. Relatedly, locating multiple committee members – typically active, mobile people – would be more challenging than finding the headman, whose authority and residence is known village-wide. Even when tracking down committee members, external actors rely on headmen's help in locating them, thus not divorcing headmen from the process.

6.7 Conclusion

Village headmen are informed, influential actors in the global AIDS intervention, and regional actors recognize the value of engaging headmen in implementing interventions. Yet national and global policymakers often overlook the role headmen play. While essential in their role as gatekeepers to rural populations, headmen remain external to the policymaking process. Chieftaincy runs counter to Western notions of democracy, particularly regarding free elections and rotation of

---

[45] Headman Interview #49, Mchinji District, July 10, 2008.

power. However, the data presented here suggest that headmen: (1) operate in a system with informal checks on their power; (2) have priorities aligned with their villagers; and (3) are active in the fight against AIDS in Africa – often absent external prodding. The aligned priorities of villagers and their headmen in my study provide the first evidence suggesting headmen can represent the interests of their villagers. Data matching headmen and villagers' opinions challenge earlier studies' assertions that traditional authorities are unrepresentative (Ribot, 1999; Chiweza, 2007a; Ntsebeza, 2008).

However representative headmen can be of their villagers' interests, the local-level data clearly demonstrate low prioritization of AIDS. Some headmen in the open-ended interviews said that AIDS programs were important and that the people who are sick with AIDS in their villages need more. But when pressed to choose between assisting the HIV-affected and others, they asked why not provide something that will benefit everyone? This response fits with the idea that one of the headman's central responsibilities is maintaining village harmony and suppressing or resolving conflict. When resources go only to some people (e.g., HIV-positive villagers or AIDS orphans), these resources could become the source of envy or ill will. While an external principal might question a headman redistributing externally sourced goods more broadly to villagers as inconsistent with a targeted intervention's goal, the headman sees their role as caretaker of the *whole* village, not just of those affected by AIDS.

My survey data also show, however, that headmen in villages more affected by AIDS will give higher priority to AIDS. Data from Malawi estimates that only 10% of Malawians know their HIV status, suggesting a policy implication for the findings here: by increasing the number of people tested for HIV and making more people aware of their HIV status, headmen might give higher priority to AIDS as they will likely be more knowledgeable of more villagers' HIV serostatus. This chapter promotes the idea that to understand what shapes a headman's priorities, we have to see the village from his point of view. Were he to know that a sizeable number of his villagers were HIV-positive, he may be even more active in responding to AIDS. Because headmen have great influence in rural areas, where most Malawians reside, and because they are active in the global intervention against AIDS – often absent tangible rewards – a promising initiative for garnering their support would be increasing testing of rural villagers.

Given concerns about the nondemocratic nature of headmen selection, international NGOs sometimes seek alternative agents to implement AIDS interventions, e.g., village committees or CBOs. However, Schou (2009) shows how decentralized HIV/AIDS service delivery through CBOs fails to achieve local accountability (Schou, 2009). We should expect elite capture to be more likely for these organizations because they develop privileged access to outside resources but without the responsibility for the welfare of the village as a whole, as that falls to the headman. Calling organizations community-based is misleading given findings that organizations were typically formed "from above" and "their downward accountability [to villagers] was weak or absent" (Schou, 2009, 162). While I cannot judge the accountability of headmen compared to CBOs, the survey data suggest headmen would be representative of their villagers' interests and qualitative data suggest headmen have healthy concern about responsibly carrying out their duties or facing potential dethronement, or in the case of venue-shopping for divorces discussed earlier in this chapter, losing legitimacy and power.

There are certainly some headmen and chiefs in Malawi and elsewhere in Africa who abuse their power and position, but this study suggests such abuse is rare. In Malawi, effective norms against inequality and corruption for individual gain limit chiefs from such abuses (Eggen, 2011, 320). Although there was noise in local media about corrupt headmen,[46] so few resources make it to the village level that even if corruption were rampant at this level in the global hierarchy of AIDS intervention, the relative impact would be small (Swidler and Watkins, 2009).

This chapter's findings that headmen can be effective agents of AIDS intervention constrained by their villagers' priorities and interests challenge the conventional perspective of chieftaincy – in both published scholarship and popular media portrayals. Although chieftaincy is not a democratic institution as we in the West imagine – e.g., involving free and fair elections in which all citizens can participate in leadership selection – in some contexts, chiefs and headmen may be the best representatives of citizens' priorities and interests. Returning to the hierarchy of the global AIDS intervention in Africa, my findings of priority alignment at the local level – between villagers and

---

[46] For example, see James Chimpweya, "Stop Using, Dumping Us, NAPHAM Says," *The Nation*, May 25, 2008.

headmen – suggest problems implementing AIDS interventions are occurring higher up the chain. Put another way, key stakeholders in national government and the global community are out of sync with citizens and their local leaders. While donor agencies may wonder how to change the opinions of citizens and local leaders, an alternative question may be what does it take to change the priorities of people in corridors of power?

7 | *Conclusion*

The government is never wrong. It does what it wants.
Headman Interview #70, Mchinji District, July 8, 2008

I also must thank you because for the government to know that we have problems it's through these kinds of interviews. So I thank those who sent you to continue this that you will come again to ask us because in so doing you will know the thoughts of all the chiefs.
Headman Interview #122, Rumphi District, October 16, 2008

My Fulbright fellowship ended with a dissemination of preliminary findings to "key stakeholders" in Lilongwe, Malawi's capital city, where most government offices are located and many international NGOs base their country headquarters. The people shaping Malawi's national response to AIDS – technocrats from government ministries and program officers representing bilateral partners (e.g., the US Department of State) or major international NGOs (e.g., Save The Children) – gathered in a conference room at the US Embassy in late 2008. I went through slides with interview quotes and histograms of survey data documenting what I learned during my fellowship. The bulk of that presentation drew from early analysis of what now makes up Chapters 5 and 6 – results showing that among Malawian villagers and their headmen, AIDS is a relatively low priority. The participants were surprised at my findings. I was, in turn, surprised at their surprise: I expected these highly educated, locally posted specialists to have already known AIDS was a low priority among citizens and to be annoyed to have sat through another dull powerpoint presentation by an academic only in Malawi for a few months.[1] Instead, after registering their surprise, they asked questions akin to "Now what?" With

---

[1] I should note the Malawians in the room reacted differently than their North American and European counterparts. My read of their reactions was that they found the presentation unsurprising and perhaps even dull.

160

that, my cynical view of the bureaucratic world of AIDS intervention in Africa shifted.

Powerful decision-makers – at least in one African capital – wanted to reconfigure their response to reflect the priorities of their intended beneficiaries. Questions they asked reflected an intuition that matching interventions to local policy priorities would increase the likelihood that an intervention would succeed. One program officer asked my opinion on whether an AIDS program "bundled" with a water well initiative would increase the AIDS program's potential for success. Their questions demonstrated how they were constrained: the higher-ups in their North American and European headquarters would continue to prioritize AIDS programs and the locally posted expatriates were not seeking strategies to change those minds. Rather, the decision-makers in that embassy conference room were trying to see how they could spend their budgets allocated to AIDS in a way that would make their AIDS interventions more successful by also providing a good or service intended beneficiaries think is more greatly needed.

My dissemination exercise in Malawi in 2008 exemplifies the misalignment of priorities in AIDS-stricken African countries I have described in detail in this book. One could be discouraged by the fact that many decision-makers "on the ground" were essentially unaware of local priorities. Readers could also be discouraged by the continued prioritization of AIDS in corridors of power in the wake of learning intended beneficiaries of AIDS interventions prioritized other pressing issues. But there is also reason to be optimistic. The specialists posted to Malawi by their international agencies to carry out AIDS interventions recognized their efforts would face challenges if they did not align with beneficiaries' priorities. They wanted to redesign their interventions to follow the constraints set by their bosses back home but also serve the interests of those to whom interventions were targeted. The hard work being done in global interventions to improve the human condition is by these interstitial actors navigating the competing interests of "dueling principals."

7.1 Summary of Findings

The challenges of aligning priorities in a global hierarchy of actors was the focus point I offered in this book for understanding humanitarian interventions in Africa. I drew a stylized model of the many actors fighting AIDS in Africa. I used that stylized model to illustrate how: (1) the nested principal–agent relationships inherent in the multi-tiered intervention produce multiple opportunities for mismanagement or misalignment and (2) local agents actually implementing interventions on the ground will likely favor the priorities of the citizens with whom they interact with frequently (their "local principals") over the priorities of stakeholders funding and designing interventions (their "external principals").

I studied original survey data from Malawi and cross-national survey data from more than 20 African countries to document the priorities of African citizens to whom AIDS interventions are targeted. I showed in Chapter 5 that HIV/AIDS was a low priority when compared to other pressing issues like access to clean water or agricultural development. While people living with HIV/AIDS were more likely to rank AIDS interventions higher on their policy priority list than their HIV-negative counterparts, AIDS interventions remained a relatively low priority. I showed in Chapter 6 that like the villagers under their care, village headmen in rural Malawi gave lower priority to AIDS interventions. Nevertheless, headmen faced with more serious AIDS epidemics in their villages gave AIDS interventions higher priority. Unfortunately, villagers and their headmen are typically overlooked but critically important to the intervention's success. As international donors fund governments to pursue programs out of sync with local priorities, citizens are unlikely to act as monitors of government progress on those programs, leaving accountability to faraway donors.

The policy priorities of citizens and their local leaders stand in stark contrast with those in the international community deciding how to prioritize the many issues ailing the world. The data on official development assistance from rich to poor countries analyzed in Chapter 5 showed AIDS was a top priority for donors, who spent lavish sums on AIDS, especially considering the higher death tolls from other diseases. However, the vast sums of money supporting AIDS interventions is susceptible to corruption, whether by the head of Kenya's National AIDS Control Committee lining her own pockets or the fabrication of a "briefcase NGO" to siphon funds for community-based activities in Gambia. The vast amounts of aid for AIDS led some to see AIDS less as a serious health epidemic and more as a "growth industry and career opportunity" (Epstein, 2007, 206).

Malawian citizens and their counterparts elsewhere in Africa did not rank AIDS a relatively low priority out of ignorance. Unfortunately, the headmen and Malawian villagers interviewed in the course of my research know all too well the tragedy of the AIDS epidemic. More than three decades since its scientific discovery, AIDS continues to claim a million lives globally each year. In 2014 alone, 48,000 Malawians were estimated to have died of AIDS (Government of Malawi, 2015, 24). Chapter 2 documented the scale of AIDS in Africa and the response to it by governments, organizations, and most importantly, the people who are themselves navigating the epidemic. Likewise, Chapter 4 showed that in Malawi, citizens were aware of the disease and were responding to AIDS, including taking care of ill family and advising youth on HIV prevention – before the government or donors undertook any serious initiative against AIDS.

7.2 Implications

Scholars and activists have enumerated a list of necessary conditions for successful AIDS response. It requires scientifically sound approaches (Green, 2011), political will from governments (Campbell, 2003; de Waal, 2006), and significant financial resources (Attaran and Sachs, 2001; Stover et al., 2002). Scholars imagine that through these, individuals and societies navigating the AIDS epidemic will be compelled to change their behavior to avoid HIV infection, and those already infected will be cared for. Would we witness progress in the fight against AIDS in places where political will and significant financial resources supported scientifically sound interventions? Perhaps. But so many of the interventions against AIDS in Africa are designed from afar and these "well-intentioned and technically well-informed" HIV interventions fail to fit the reality of local conditions (Campbell, 2003).[2]

Since late in the second decade of AIDS, governments have been measured on how they are responding to HIV/AIDS (USAID et al., 2003; Desmond et al., 2009; Lieberman, 2009). For example, since 2006, UNAIDS has published in its biannual Global Report on AIDS some measures against which countries can be judged on their commitment to fighting AIDS. In 2006, UNAIDS referred to these as

---

[2] Take one exchange writer Helen Epstein had with a USAID official charged with assisting AIDS response in Uganda. The USAID official said that she had invited a Brazilian consultant to lecture Ugandans about Brazil's AIDS programs and was considering "importing programs from the United States" (Epstein, 2007, 209). Even if these AIDS programs in Brazil and the United States were successful, it does not necessarily follow that they will be successful in Uganda.

"country progress indicators."[3] By 2013, the specific measures of a country's progress in the fight against AIDS had shifted and expanded, to now taking up 42 pages of the 198-page report. Despite reasonable questions a decade earlier about whether government interventions were having as strong an impact on the epidemic as the individual-level behavior changes initiated by the people navigating the epidemic (Green, 2003), UNAIDS spends considerable resources to collect this information about government response. This data collection suggests governments *should* be responding to AIDS, however, findings from this book beg the question: are African governments responding with great fervor out of touch with citizens who prioritize other pressing issues?

Why have some African governments acted out of sync with their citizens in responding to AIDS? A simple answer is resources. Many poor countries heavily dependent on foreign aid accept the earmarks dictated by donor preferences, even as they might reappropriate the funds to other purposes. In her book on the AIDS epidemic in Africa, Helen Epstein describes a number of AIDS corruption scandals in a chapter titled, "When Foreign Aid Is an ATM." As political scientist Nicolas van de Walle (2001) points out, officials have come to view donor resources as a series of free excludable benefits to be appropriated. AIDS earmarks, then, are a source of revenue for cash-strapped governments. The funds are often grants (rather than loans) and typically come without strings attached. The primary constraint, however, is that AIDS funds be spent on AIDS programming, but significant sums of AIDS funds have been siphoned through corruption, with little consequence for those in power. As one of the village headmen quoted at the start of the chapter said, the government will do what it wants.

A closer look at the policy priorities of ordinary Africans teaches us something about self-interest influencing policy preferences. In the

---

[3] These included: the amount of expenditures devoted to anti-AIDS efforts; percent of teachers trained in and teaching life skills-based HIV curriculum; percent of public and private enterprises that have HIV workplace policies; percent of STD patients appropriately diagnosed, counseled, and treated; percent of HIV-positive pregnant women receiving prophylaxis to prevent mother-to-child transmission; percent of people with advanced AIDS receiving ARVs; percent of orphans and vulnerable children whose households received support; percent of donated blood screened for HIV; percent of youth with comprehensive knowledge about HIV/AIDS; percent of youth engaging in casual sex; percent of youth reporting condom use; and ratio of orphans attending school.

face of an incurable disease, self-interest can predict one's preferences for allocation of public resources. Given only a small minority population of individuals is infected with HIV, in aggregating individual preferences to the population level, we will see weak prioritization of AIDS as a problem government should be addressing. Even at the individual level, however, while my analysis shows self-interest matters, many HIV-positive Malawians still gave relatively low priority to HIV/AIDS.

One potential policy solution from this book's analysis is to increase awareness among HIV-affected populations about the scope of the AIDS pandemic. In Chapter 5, I found that rural Malawians who knew themselves to be HIV-positive were more likely to give higher priority to HIV/AIDS interventions. Similarly, in Chapter 6, survey data showed headmen of villages with more pronounced experiences with AIDS – measured as the number of villagers who tested positive for HIV by our study – gave relatively higher priority to HIV/AIDS interventions. Because many people in the countries most heavily affected by AIDS are unaware of their HIV status, key decision-makers who prioritize HIV/AIDS interventions could increase the number of people tested for HIV, thus making more people aware of their HIV status. As Chapter 6 showed, a promising conduit through which an organization can encourage villagers to participate in such a campaign would be their village headmen.

Another policy approach one could draw from this book's findings is that HIV/AIDS programming could benefit from integration with interventions focused on those other issues that ordinary Africans give higher priority. In fact, the dissemination event with stakeholders in Malawi in 2008 described earlier suggests some implementers are keen to do so. To my knowledge, there exists no research that explicitly compares singularly focused HIV/AIDS interventions and integrated HIV/AIDS interventions that would allow us to distinguish whether HIV/AIDS interventions are more effective when they are bundled with those issues of higher priority to ordinary Africans. Despite this lack of evidence, there have been interventions that bundle HIV/AIDS and livelihoods programming that merit study. For example, CARE Malawi designed and implemented a series of livelihood security programs that recognize HIV/AIDS as a major feature of the risk and vulnerability environment. One such program was the Consortium for Southern Africa Food Security Emergency, which targeted food aid to at-risk women and girls to help avoid survival sex (Drimie and Mullins,

2006). Future research could test explicitly the comparative impact of integrated versus focused HIV/AIDS interventions.

Going beyond HIV policy implications, I argue that this book raises an even more important question: does AIDS intervention in Africa simply demonstrate the power of donors and the weakness of citizens? Given the findings here that other development issues have higher priority among ordinary Malawians, taken together with the findings from Morfit (2011) that AIDS efforts may have hindered attempts to address other, non-AIDS development issues, the normative question we should ask: When there is a misalignment of priorities, whose preferences should take precedence? Those of international donors or those of citizens?

Relatedly, what are the implications for democracy in African countries experiencing a generalized epidemic? The disconnect between the supply of and demand for HIV/AIDS services in sub-Saharan Africa provides an insight into two competing pressures African policymakers face in the democratic era: the preferences of international donors and the preferences of citizens. Donors provide essential resources for development and health interventions, whereas citizens are relevant for electoral purposes. More than a decade ago, scholars debated the potential impact on state capacity of AIDS disease (Ostergard, 2002; Price-Smith, 2002; de Waal, 2003), but the intervention against the disease also has potential political costs. As young democracies in Southern Africa – where AIDS has hit hardest – grapple with their many development challenges, the external push for prioritization of HIV/AIDS may provide short-term benefits to power brokers in the form of earmarked aid, but leaders risk future dissatisfaction from citizens by overlooking matters more important to them.

Another related implication of the study is to examine how citizens can be empowered to engage with government and donors to have their priorities reflected in policies and interventions. The two quotes in this chapter's epigraph reflect different views of how policies or interventions can reflect Malawian needs. The first quote suggests the government will do what it wants, regardless of citizen needs. The second quote is optimistic that the kind of research employed in this study – simply asking villagers and their headmen the problems they face and the priorities they have – can inform government response. In response to an open-ended question about what interventions could improve village conditions, another headman we interviewed suggested no specific policy or intervention, but instead a process for identifying one:

The government asks people what they want. If the government is convinced and satisfied with that thing, the thing progresses. If the government is not satisfied with that thing, the thing can't go on.[4]

The growing body of public opinion data – especially the multinational efforts by Afrobarometer – have generated a wealth of information about citizens' priorities. However, mobilization of citizens (perhaps by civil society) will also be critical in turning that information into action. With the exception of South Africa, the AIDS epidemic has largely failed to spur a response from civil society (Patterson, 2006). Perhaps "failure" of civil society to mobilize citizens to demand more from their governments in response to AIDS is actually a "democratic success" given the relatively weak prioritization of HIV/AIDS issues among ordinary Africans. A recent wave of popular protests in some African countries shows mass mobilization is not just possible but powerful when issues of great priority to citizens are at stake (Branch and Mampilly, 2015).

* * *

This book used the specific case of AIDS intervention in Africa to contribute more generally to our understanding of the principal–agent problem. In particular, it adds complexity to a simple principal–agent model by highlighting both the multiple opportunities for negative outcomes associated with nested principal–agent problems and the potential for policy priority misalignment across a global hierarchy of intervention. Though the study focuses on a specific intervention (against HIV and AIDS) and most of the analysis draws from one country's experience (Malawi), the principal–agent framework and analysis of policy priorities across the global supply chain of intervention should push scholars, policymakers, and practitioners to consider both the policy preferences of intervention agents and those of the intended beneficiaries to whom agents can be held accountable. The framework is applicable to health and development initiatives in the developing world more broadly. The insights generated from this study contribute to our understanding of why aid fails – a rich debate that is still searching for solutions.

---

[4] Headman Interview #37, Mchinji District, June 23, 2008.

7.3 Going Forward

As we confront health epidemics and development challenges, it is important we document and scrutinize our earlier attempts to improve the human condition. As my study of the response to the AIDS epidemic shows, there are broader lessons to be learned from the nature of a global intervention to address a problem in Africa. Advocates urge the world to focus attention on affected regions and to make substantial resources available but seek little insight from the populations most at risk – the people to whom such interventions are targeted. These interventions from afar fail to match local priorities and lack understanding of local constraints. As billions of dollars pour in to support an intervention from afar, a disinterested or disengaged population is unlikely to act as a monitor of its government's handling of the intervention or its related responsibilities in acting as a good steward of the intervention's finances.

This book suggests a democratic approach to improving the human condition – one that learns about the issues citizens prioritize. In many African countries, this has become increasingly easy to do since the late 1990s as the African-led public opinion survey Afrobarometer has asked nationally representative samples of people in more than 30 countries their opinions on what issues are important to them. The current approach of most interventions to improve the human condition – interventions designed from afar usually providing financial support to African governments to intervene – is decidedly undemocratic as it often ignores the opinions of citizens and also provides governments a source of revenue unattached to its citizens' assessments of government performance. Relatedly, interventions from afar that bypass African governments can reshape citizens' expectations about what goods and services government is responsible for providing – effectively reducing those expectations. The conventional approach in interventions to improve the human condition runs counter to stated goals in the West of supporting democratic development in Africa. Even if these interventions were having a positive impact on the measurable outcomes donors care about – e.g., declining HIV incidence – it is important to ask at what cost for the future of accountability and representation in Africa.

Bibliography

Acemoglu, Daron, Tristan Reed and James Robinson. 2014. "Chiefs: economic development and elite control of civil society in Sierra Leone." *The Journal of Political Economy* 122(2):319–68.

ACHAP. 2014. "ACHAP Website." Accessed 10/20/14 from www.achap .org/.

Afrobarometer. 2004. "Public Opinion and HIV/AIDS: Facing Up to the Future?" Afrobarometer Briefing Paper No. 12.

Agadjanian, Victor and Soma Sen. 2007. "Promises and challenges of faith-based AIDS care and support in Mozambique." *American Journal of Public Health* 97(2):362–6.

Ainsworth, Martha and Waranya Teokul. 2000. "Breaking the silence: setting realistic priorities for AIDS control in less-developed countries." *The Lancet* 356(9223):55–60.

Alcázar, Lorena, F Hasley Rogers, Nazmul Chaudhury, et al. 2006. "Why are teachers absent? Probing service delivery in Peruvian primary schools." *International Journal of Educational Research* 45(3):117–36.

Allen, Tim and Suzette Heald. 2004. "HIV/AIDS policy in Africa: what has worked in Uganda and what has failed in Botswana?" *Journal of International Development* 16(8):1141–54.

Anderson, Emma-Louise and Amy S Patterson. 2017. *Dependent Agency in the Global Health Regime: Local African Responses to Donor AIDS Efforts.* Palgrave MacMillan US.

Anglewicz, Philip and Hans-Peter Kohler. 2009. "Overestimating HIV infection: the construction and accuracy of subjective probabilities of HIV infection in rural Malawi." *Demographic Research* 20(6):65–96.

Angotti, Nicole, Kim Yi Dionne and Lauren Gaydosh. 2011. "An offer you can't refuse: provider-initiated HIV testing at antenatal clinics in rural Malawi." *Health Policy and Planning* 26(4):307–15.

Attaran, Amir and Jeffrey Sachs. 2001. "Defining and refining international donor support for combating the AIDS pandemic." *The Lancet* 357(9249):57–61.

Autesserre, Séverine. 2010. *The Trouble with the Congo: Local Violence and the Failure of International Peacebuilding.* New York: Cambridge University Press.

Auvert, Bertran, Dirk Taljaard, Emmanuel Lagarde, et al. 2005. "Randomized, controlled intervention trial of male circumcision for reduction of HIV infection risk: The ANRS 1265 Trial." *PLoS Medicine* 2(11):e298.

Bailey, Robert C, Stephen Moses, Corette B Parker, et al. 2007. "Male circumcision for HIV prevention in young men in Kisumu, Kenya: a randomised controlled trial." *The Lancet* 369(9562):643–56.

Baird, Sarah J, Richard S Garfein, Craig T McIntosh and Berk Özler. 2012. "Effect of a cash transfer programme for schooling on prevalence of HIV and herpes simplex type 2 in Malawi: a cluster randomised trial." *The Lancet* 379(9823):1320–29.

Baker, Colin. 1975. *The Evolution of Local Government in Malawi*. University of Ife Press for the Institute of Administration.

Baldwin, Kate. 2013. "Why vote with the chief? Political connections and public goods provision in Zambia." *American Journal of Political Science* 57(4):794–809.

Baldwin, Kate. 2015. *The Paradox of Traditional Chiefs in Democratic Africa*. New York: Cambridge University Press.

Banerjee, Abhijit, Angus Deaton and Esther Duflo. 2004. "Health, health care, and economic development: wealth, health, and health services in rural Rajasthan." *The American Economic Review* 94(2):326–30.

Banerjee, Abhijit and Esther Duflo. 2006. "Addressing absence." *The Journal of Economic Perspectives* 20(1):117–32.

Banerjee, Abhijit, Esther Duflo and Rachel Glennerster. 2008. "Putting a band-aid on a corpse: incentives for nurses in the Indian public health care system." *Journal of the European Economic Association* 6(2–3):487–500.

Banerjee, Abhijit, Raghabendra Chattopadhyay, Esther Duflo, Daniel Keniston and Nina Singh. 2014. "Improving police performance in Rajasthan, India: experimental evidence on incentives, managerial autonomy and training." No. w17912. National Bureau of Economic Research.

Baral, Stefan, Gift Trapence, Felistus Motimedi, et al. 2009. "HIV prevalence, risks for HIV infection, and human rights among men who have sex with men (MSM) in Malawi, Namibia, and Botswana." *PLoS One* 4(3):e4997.

Beall, Jo. 2005. "Exit, voice and tradition: loyalty to chieftainship and democracy in metropolitan Durban, South Africa." Crisis States Programme Working Papers Series, Working Paper No. 59.

Beall, Jo, Sibongiseni Mkhize and Shahid Vawda. 2005. "Emergent democracy and 'resurgent' tradition: institutions, chieftaincy and transition in KwaZulu-Natal." *Journal of Southern African Studies* 31(4):755–71.

Benton, Adia. 2015. *HIV Exceptionalism: Development through Disease in Sierra Leone*. Minneapolis: University of Minnesota Press.

Berelson, Bernard, Paul Lazarsfeld and William McPhee. 1954. *Voting: A Study of Opinion Formation in a Presidential Campaign*. Chicago: University of Chicago Press.

Biruk, Crystal. 2014. "'Aid for gays': the moral and the material in 'African homophobia' in post-2009 Malawi." *The Journal of Modern African Studies* 52(3):447–73.

Björkman, Martina and Jakob Svensson. 2009. "Power to the people: evidence from a randomized field experiment on community-based monitoring in uganda." *Quarterly Journal of Economics* 124(2):735–69.

Bloom, Gerald, Wycliffe Chilowa, Henry Lucas Ephraim Chirwa, et al. 2005. *Poverty Reduction during Democratic Transition: The Malawi Social Action Fund 1996–2001*. Institute of Development Studies.

Bond, Virginia, Elaine Chase and Peter Aggleton. 2002. "Stigma, HIV/AIDS and prevention of mother-to-child transmission in Zambia." *Evaluation and Program Planning* 25(4):347–56.

Bor, Jacob. 2007. "The political economy of AIDS leadership in developing countries: an exploratory analysis." *Social Science & Medicine* 64(8):1585–99.

Boyd, Lydia. 2015. *Preaching Prevention: Born-again Christianity and the Moral Politics of AIDS in Uganda*. Athens, Ohio: Ohio University Press.

Braitstein, Paula, Martin Brinkhof, Francois Dabis, et al. 2006. "Mortality of HIV-1-infected patients in the first year of antiretroviral therapy: comparison between low-income and high-income countries." *The Lancet* 367(9513):817–24.

Branch, Adam and Zachariah Cherian Mampilly. 2015. *Africa Uprising: Popular Protest and Political Change*. London: Zed Books.

Bratton, Michael. 2009. Are you being served? Public satisfaction with health and education services in Africa. In *Democratic Deficits*, ed. Cynthia Arnson and Gary Bland. Washington, DC: Woodrow Wilson Center.

Bratton, Michael. 2012. "Citizen perceptions of local government responsiveness in sub-Saharan Africa." *World Development* 40(3):516–27.

Bratton, Michael, Robert Mattes and E. Gyimah-Boadi. 2005. *Public Opinion, Democracy, and Market Reform in Africa*. New York: Cambridge University Press.

Briggs, Ryan C. 2015. "The influence of aid changes on African election outcomes." *International Interactions* 41:201–25.

Buxton, Jean C. 1963. *Chiefs and Strangers*. New York: Oxford University Press.

Caldwell, John C and Pat Caldwell. 1996. "The African AIDS epidemic." *Scientific American* 274(3):62–8.

Cammack, Diana. 2012. "Malawi in crisis, 2011–12." *Review of African Political Economy* 39(132):375–88.

Cammack, Diana, Edge Kanyangolo and Tam O'Neill. 2009. "'Town Chiefs' in Malawi." *Africa Power and Politics Working Paper* (3).

Campbell, Angus, Philip Converse, Warren Miller and Donald Stokes. 1960. *The American Voter*. New York: Wiley.

Campbell, Catherine. 2003. *'Letting Them Die': Why HIV/AIDS Prevention Programmes Fail*. Bloomington, IN: Indiana University Press.

Carr, Stephen J. 1997. "A green revolution frustrated: lessons from the Malawi experience." *African Crop Science Journal* 5(1):93–8.

Cassidy, Rebecca and Melissa Leach. 2009a. "AIDS, citizenship and global funding: a Gambian case study." *IDS Working Papers* (325): 1–31.

Cassidy, Rebecca and Melissa Leach. 2009b. "Science, politics, and the presidential AIDS 'cure.'" *African Affairs* 108(433):559–80.

Chanda, Michael Mulimansenga, Muka Chikuba-McLeod, et al. 2014. "Traditional leaders in selected chiefdoms in Zambia take the lead in HIV/AIDS fight through development of decrees to improve local policy and regulatory environment." Poster presented at the *20th International AIDS Conference*, Melbourne, Australia, July 20–25, 2014.

Chatora, Rufaro. 2003. "An overview of the traditional medicine situation in the African region." *African Health Monitor* 4(1):4–7.

Chaudhury, Nazmul, Jeffrey Hammer, Michael Kremer, Karthik Muralidharan and F. Hasley Rogers. 2006. "Missing in action: teacher and health worker absence in developing countries." *Journal of Economic Perspectives* 20(1):91–116.

Cheesbrough, JS 1986. "Acquired immunedeficiency syndrome in Malawi." *Malawi Medical Journal* 3(1):5–13.

Chimwaza, Angela and Susan Watkins. 2004. "Giving care to people with symptoms of AIDS in rural sub-Saharan Africa." *AIDS Care* 16(7): 795–807.

Chinsinga, Blessings. 2002. The politics of poverty alleviation in Malawi: a critical review. In *A Democracy of Chameleons: Politics and Culture in the New Malawi*, ed. Harri Englund. Uppsala: Nordic Africa Institute.

Chirwa, Wiseman Chijere. 1998. "Aliens and AIDS in southern Africa: the Malawi–South Africa debate." *African Affairs* 97(386):53–79.

Chirwa, Wiseman, Nandini Patel and Fidelis Edge Kanyongolo. 2013. "Democracy Report for Malawi." International Institute for Democracy and Electoral Assistance.

Chiweza, Asiyati L. 2007a. The ambivalent role of chiefs: rural decentralization initiatives in Malawi. In *State Recognition and Democratization in Sub-Saharan Africa: A New Dawn for Traditional Authorities?*, ed. L Buur and HM Kyed. New York: Palgrave MacMillan, pp. 53–78.

Chiweza, Asiyati L. 2007b. Local government. In *Government and Politics in Malawi*, ed. Nandini Patel and Lars Svåsand. Zomba, Malawi: Kachere Books, pp. 137–74.

Cilliers, Jacobus, Ibrahim Kasirye, Claire Leaver, Pieter Serneels and Andrew Zeitlin. 2014. "Pay for locally monitored teacher attendance?" NEUDC Conference Paper.

Clinton Health Access Initiative. 2015. "Case Study: Improving Efficiency and Effectiveness of HIV Spending through Resource Mapping in Malawi." Accessed 7/13/2016 from www.clintonhealthaccess.org/content/uploads/2015/08/Case-Study_HF-Resource-Mapping.pdf.

Cohen, Cathy. 1999. *The Boundaries of Blackness: AIDS and the Breakdown of Black Politics*. Chicago: University of Chicago Press.

Cohen, Jon. 1997. "The rise and fall of Projet SIDA." *Science* 278(5343):1565–68.

Comaroff, John. 1978. "Rules and rulers: political processes in a Tswana Chiefdom." *Man* 13(1):1–20.

Crane, Johanna Tayloe. 2013. *Scrambling for Africa: AIDS, Expertise, and the Rise of American Global Health Science*. Ithaca, NY: Cornell University Press.

de Kadt, Daniel and Horacio Larreguy. Forthcoming. "Agents of the regime? Traditional leaders and electoral behavior in South Africa." *Journal of Politics*.

de Waal, Alex. 1997. *Famine Crimes: Politics and the Disaster Relief Industry in Africa*. Bloomington, IN: Indiana University Press.

de Waal, Alex. 2003. "How will HIV/AIDS transform African governance?" *African Affairs* 102(406):1–23.

de Waal, Alex. 2006. *AIDS and Power: Why There is No Political Crisis – Yet*. New York: Zed Books.

Deaton, Angus, Jane Fortson and Robert Tortora. 2010. Life (evaluation), HIV/AIDS, and death in Africa. In *International Differences in Well-Being*, ed. Ed Diener, Daniel Kahneman and John Helliwell. New York: Oxford University Press, pp. 105–36.

Department of Institutional Integrity. 2007. "Kenya Detailed Implementation Review Report (As Supplemented)." online.wsj.com/public/resources/documents/WSJ20080304-opinion-worldbank1kenya.pdf. The World Bank.

Desmond, Chris, Evan Lieberman, Anita Alban and Anna-Mia Ekström. 2009. "Relative response: ranking country responses to HIV and AIDS." *Health and Human Rights: An International Journal* 10(2): 105–19.

DiCarlo, Abby L, Joanne E Mantell, Robert H Remien, et al. 2014. "'Men usually say that HIV testing is for women': gender dynamics and perceptions of HIV testing in Lesotho." *Culture, Health & Sexuality* 16(8):867–82.

Dieleman, Marjolein, Jurrien Toonen, Hamadassalia Touré and Tim Martineau. 2006. "The match between motivation and performance management of health sector workers in Mali." *Human Resources for Health* 4(2).

Dionne, Kim Yi. 2011. "The role of executive time horizons in state response to AIDS in Africa." *Comparative Political Studies* 44(1): 55–77.

Dionne, Kim Yi. 2012. "Local demand for a global intervention: policy priorities in the time of AIDS." *World Development* 40(12): 2468–77.

Dionne, Kim Yi, Amanda Robinson and John Kadzandira. 2013. "Risk of political violence and protest participation: evidence from contemporary Malawi." Unpublished manuscript.

Dionne, Kim Yi and Boniface Dulani. 2013. "Constitutional provisions and executive succession: Malawi's 2012 transition in comparative perspective." *African Affairs* 112(446):111–37.

Dionne, Kim Yi and Jeremy Horowitz. 2016. "The political effects of agricultural subsidies in Africa: evidence from Malawi." *World Development* 87:215–26.

Dionne, Kim Yi and Michelle Poulin. 2013. "Ethnic identity, region and attitudes towards male circumcision in a high HIV-prevalence country." *Global Public Health* 8(5):607–18.

Dionne, Kim Yi, Patrick Gerland and Susan Cotts Watkins. 2013. "AIDS exceptionalism: another constituency heard from." *AIDS and Behavior* 17(3):825–31.

Doctor, Henry and Alexander Weinreb. 2003. "Estimation of AIDS adult mortality by verbal autopsy in rural Malawi." *AIDS* 17:2509–13.

Doran, Marissa CM. 2007. "Reconstructing Mchape '95: AIDS, Billy Chisupe, and the politics of persuasion." *Journal of Eastern African Studies* 1(3):397–416.

Dow, Unity and Max Essex. 2010. *Saturday is for Funerals*. Cambridge, MA: Harvard University Press.

Drimie, Scott and Dan Mullins. 2006. "Mainstreaming HIV and AIDS into livelihoods and food security programs: the experience of CARE Malawi." In *AIDS, Poverty and Hunger: Challenges and Responses*. Washington, DC: IFPRI.

Duflo, Esther, Rema Hanna and Stephen Ryan. 2012. "Incentives work: getting teachers to come to school." *The American Economic Review* 102(4):1241–78.

Dulani, Boniface, Gift Sambo and Kim Yi Dionne. 2016. "Good Neighbours? Africans Express High Levels of Tolerance for Many, But Not for All." Afrobarometer Dispatch No. 74.

Dulani, Boniface and Jan Kees van Donge. 2005. A Decade of Legislature-Executive Squabble in Malawi, 1994–2004. In *African Parliaments: Between Governance and Government*, ed. MA Mohamed Salih. New York: Palgrave Macmillan, pp. 201–24.

Dulani, Boniface and Kim Yi Dionne. 2014. "Presidential, parliamentary, and local government elections in Malawi, May 2014." *Electoral Studies* 36:218–25.

Dunkle, Kristin L, Rob Stephenson, Etienne Karita, et al. 2008. "New heterosexually transmitted HIV infections in married or cohabiting couples in urban Zambia and Rwanda: an analysis of survey and clinical data." *The Lancet* 371(9631):2183–91.

Easterly, William. 2006. *The White Man's Burden: Why the West's Efforts to Aid the Rest Have Done So Much Ill and So Little Good*. New York: The Penguin Press.

Ebrahim, Alnoor. 2003. "Accountability in practice: mechanisms for NGOs." *World Development* 31(5):813–29.

Education Policy and Data Center. 2014. "Malawi National Education Profile 2014 Update." Washington, DC: fhi360 Education Policy and Data Center. Accessed 9/14/16 from www.epdc.org/sites/default/files/documents/EPDC%20NEP_Malawi.pdf.

Eggen, Øyvind. 2011. "Chiefs and everyday governance: parallel state organisations in Malawi." *Journal of Southern African Studies* 37(2): 313–31.

Elbe, Stefan. 2002. "HIV/AIDS and the changing landscape of war in Africa." *International Security* 27(2):159–77.

Eng, Eugenia, Deborah Glik and Kathleen Parker. 1990. "Focus-group methods: effects on village-agency collaboration for child survival." *Health Policy and Planning* 5(1):67–76.

England, Roger. 2007. "Are we spending too much on HIV?" *British Medical Journal* 334(7589):344.

Englebert, Pierre. 2002. "Patterns and theories of traditional resurgence in tropical Africa." *Mondes en Développement* 30(118):51–64.

Englund, Harri. 2006. *Prisoners of Freedom: Human Rights and the African Poor*. Berkeley, CA: University of California Press.

Epstein, Helen. 2007. *The Invisible Cure: Why We Are Losing the Fight against AIDS in Africa*. New York: Picador.

Epstein, Steven. 1996. *Impure Science: AIDS, Activism, and the Politics of Knowledge*. Berkeley, CA: University of California Press.

Erickson, Bonnie H. 1988. The relational basis of attitudes. In *Social Structures: A Network Approach*, ed. Barry Wellman and SD Berkowitz. New York: Cambridge University Press, pp. 99–122.

Fallers, Lloyd. 1955. "The predicament of the modern African chief: an instance from Uganda." *American Anthropologist* 57(2):290–305.

Fanthorpe, Richard. 2005. "On the limits of liberal peace: chiefs and democratic decentralization in post-war Sierra Leone." *African Affairs* 105(418):27–49.

Farmer, Paul. 1992. *AIDS and Accusation: Haiti and the Geography of Blame*. Berkeley, CA: University of California Press.

Feldbaum, Harley, Kelley Lee and Preeti Patel. 2006. "The national security implications of HIV/AIDS." *PLoS Medicine* 3(6):171–5.

Ferguson, James. 1990. *The Anti-politics Machine: "Development," Depoliticization, and Bureaucratic Power in Lesotho*. New York: Cambridge University Press.

Fisher, Robert J. 1993. "Social desirability bias and the validity of indirect questioning." *Journal of Consumer Research* 20(2): 303–15.

Fleming, Peter and Sara Yeatman. 2008. "Demographic Determinants and Utilization of Voluntary Counseling and Testing (VCT) in Rural Malawi." Paper presented at the Mellon Summer School Meeting.

Franco, Lynne Miller, Sara Bennett and Ruth Kanfer. 2002. "Health sector reform and public sector health worker motivation: a conceptual framework." *Social Science & Medicine* 54(8):1255–66.

Freedom House. 2015. "Freedom of the Press Country Report: Malawi." Accessed 9/18/16 from https://freedomhouse.org/report/freedom-press/2015/malawi.

Freedom House. 2016. "Freedom in the World: Malawi." Accessed 7/28/16 from: https://freedomhouse.org/report/freedom-world/2016/malawi.

Funders Concerned about AIDS. 2014. "Philanthropic Support to Address HIV/AIDS in 2013." Washington, DC: Funders Concerned about AIDS.

Garbus, Lisa. 2003. "HIV/AIDS in Malawi." University of California San Francisco Country AIDS Policy Analysis Project.

Garmaise, David. 2009. *A Beginner's Guide to the Global Fund*. Nairobi: Aidspan.

Garrett, Laurie. 2007. "The Challenge of Global Health." *Foreign Affairs* 86(1):14–38.

Gibson, Clark, Krister Andersson, Elinor Ostrom and Sujai Shivakumar. 2005. *The Samaritan's Dilemma: The Political Economy of Development Aid*. New York: Cambridge University Press.

Gloppen, Siri and Fidelis Edge Kanyongolo. 2007. The judiciary. In *Government and Politics in Malawi*, ed. Nandini Patel and Lars Svåsand. Zomba, Malawi: Kachere Books, pp. 109–35.

Gluckman, Max, J Clyde Mitchell and JA Barnes. 1949. "The Village Headman in British Central Africa." *Africa: Journal of the International African Institute* 19(2):89–106.

Glynn, Judith R, Jörg Pönnighaus, Amelia C Crampin, et al. 2001. "The development of the HIV epidemic in Karonga District, Malawi." *AIDS* 15(15):2025–9.

Government of Malawi. 2015. "Malawi AIDS Response Progress Report." Accessed 3/28/16 from www.unaids.org/sites/default/files/country/documents/MWI_narrative_report_2015.pdf.

Granich, Reuben M, Charles F Gilks, Christopher Dye, Kevin M De Cock and Brian G Williams. 2009. "Universal voluntary HIV testing with immediate antiretroviral therapy as a strategy for elimination of HIV transmission: a mathematical model." *The Lancet* 373(9657): 48–57.

Gray, Ronald H, Godfrey Kigozi, David Serwadda, et al. 2007. "Male circumcision for HIV prevention in men in Rakai, Uganda: a randomised trial." *The Lancet* 369(9562):657–66.

Green, Edward C. 2011. *Broken Promises: How the AIDS Establishment Has Betrayed the Developing World*. Sausalito, CA: PoliPointPress.

Green, Edward C, Annemarie Jurg and Armando Dgedge. 1993. "Sexually-transmitted diseases, AIDS and traditional healers in Mozambique." *Medical Anthropology* 15(3):261–81.

Green, Edward Crocker. 2003. *Rethinking AIDS Prevention: Learning from Successes in Developing Countries*. Westport, CT: Praeger Publishers.

Grépin, Karen A. 2012. "HIV donor funding has both boosted and curbed the delivery of different non-HIV health services in sub-Saharan Africa." *Health Affairs* 31(7):1406–14.

Hanson, Holly. 2010. "Privatized Public Healing?: Women's Narratives of Escaping Violation in Kampala's Violent Times." Paper presented at Social Health: A Conference in Honor of Steven Feierman, Philadelphia, PA.

Hargrove, John. 2008. "Migration, mines and mores: the HIV epidemic in southern Africa." *South African Journal of Science* 104(1–2): 53–61.

Heald, Suzette. 2006. "Abstain or die: the development of HIV/AIDS policy in Botswana." *Journal of Biosocial Science* 38(1):29–41.

Herbst, Jeffrey I. 2000. *States and Power in Africa*. Princeton, NJ: Princeton University Press.

Herek, Gregory M. 1999. "AIDS and stigma." *American Behavioral Scientist* 42(7):1106–16.

Hermann, Katharina, Wim Van Damme, George W Pariyo, et al. 2009. "Community health workers for ART in sub-Saharan Africa: learning from experience-capitalizing on new opportunities." *Human Resources for Health* 7(31).

Hogan, Daniel R and Joshua A Salomon. 2005. "Prevention and treatment of human immunodeficiency virus/acquired immunodeficiency syndrome in resource-limited settings." *Bulletin of the World Health Organization* 83(2):135–43.

Human Sciences Research Council. 2014. "South African National HIV Prevalence, Incidence and Behaviour Survey, 2012." Cape Town, South Africa: HSRC Press.

Iliffe, John. 2006. *A History of the African AIDS Epidemic*. Athens, OH: Ohio University Press.

Independent Evaluation Group. 2009. "Improving Effectiveness and Outcomes for the Poor in Health, Nutrition, and Population." Washington, DC: World Bank.

Institute for Health Metrics and Evaluation. 2015. "GBD Compare." Seattle, WA: IHME, University of Washington. Accessed 7/25/16 from http://vizhub.healthdata.org/gbd-compare/.

Institute for Health Metrics and Evaluation. 2016. "Country Profile: Malawi." Seattle, WA: IHME, University of Washington. Accessed 9/17/16 from www.healthdata.org/malawi.

Jackson, Robert H and Carl G Rosberg. 1984. "Personal rule: theory and practice in Africa." *Comparative Politics* 16(4):421–42.

Jacobs, Bart and Neil Price. 2006. "Improving access for the poorest to public sector health services: insights from Kirivong Operational Health District in Cambodia." *Health Policy and Planning* 21(1):27–39.

Jochelson, Karen, Monyaola Mothibeli and Jean-Patrick Leger. 1991. "Human immunodeficiency virus and migrant labor in South Africa." *International Journal of Health Services* 21(1):157–73.

John Snow, Inc. 2015. "Support to the HIV/AIDS Response in Zambia (SHARe II) Quarterly Report January to March 2015." Accessed 11/2/16 from http://pdf.usaid.gov/pdf_docs/PA00KW7V .pdf.

Justesen, Mogens. 2015. "Too poor to care? The salience of AIDS in Africa." *Political Research Quarterly* 68(1):89–103.

Kaiser Family Foundation. 2009. "2009 Survey of Americans on HIV/AIDS: Summary of Findings on the Domestic Epidemic." Number 7889. Menlo Park, CA: The Henry J. Kaiser Family Foundation.

Kaiser Family Foundation and Pew Global Attitudes Project. 2007. "A Global Look at Public Perceptions of Health Problems, Priorities, and Donors: The Kaiser/Pew Global Health Survey." Menlo Park, CA: The Henry J. Kaiser Family Foundation.

Kaleeba, Noerine. 2004. Excerpt from "We Miss You All: AIDS in the Family." In *HIV & AIDS in Africa: Beyond Epidemiology*, ed. Ezekiel Kalipeni, Susan Craddock, Joseph R Oppong and Jayati Ghosh. Malden, MA: Blackwell Publishing.

Kaler, Amy. 2004a. "AIDS-talk in everyday life: the presence of HIV/AIDS in men's informal conversation in Southern Malawi." *Social Science & Medicine* 59(2):285–97.

Kaler, Amy. 2004b. "The moral lens of population control: condoms and controversies in southern Malawi." *Studies in Family Planning* 35(2):105–15.

Kalibala, Samuel and Noerine Kaleeba. 1989. "AIDS and community-based care in Uganda: the AIDS support organization, TASO." *AIDS Care* 1(2):173–5.

Kalibala, Samuel, Ruranga Rubaramira and Noerine Kaleeba. 1997. "Non-governmental organizations and community responses to HIV/AIDS and the role of HIV-positive persons in prevention and care." *AIDS* 11(Supplement B):S151–7.

Kalipeni, Ezekiel. 2000. "Health and disease in southern Africa: a comparative and vulnerability perspective." *Social Science & Medicine* 50(7):965–83.

Kapstein, Ethan B and Joshua W Busby. 2013. *AIDS Drugs for All: Social Movements and Market Transformations*. New York: Cambridge University Press.

Kates, Jennifer, Eric Lief and Jonathan Pearson. 2009. *U.S. Global Health Policy: Donor Funding in Low- and Middle-Income Countries, 2001–2007*. Menlo Park, CA: Henry J. Kaiser Family Foundation.

Kates, Jennifer, Adam Wexler and Eric Lief. 2015. *Financing the Response to HIV in Low- and Middle-Income Countries: International Assistance from Donor Governments in 2014*. Menlo Park, CA: Henry J. Kaiser Family Foundation.

Kates, Jennifer, Josh Michaud, Adam Wexler and Allison Valentine. 2013. *Mapping the Donor Landscape in Global Health: HIV/AIDS*. Menlo Park, CA: Henry J. Kaiser Family Foundation.

Kengeya-Kayondo, Jane F, Lucy M Carpenter, Peter M Kintu, et al. 1999. "Risk perception and HIV-1 prevalence in 15,000 adults in rural south-west Uganda." *AIDS* 13(16):2295–302.

Kim, Jim Yong and Paul Farmer. 2006. "AIDS in 2006 – moving toward one world, one hope?" *New England Journal of Medicine* 355(7): 645–7.

Kimaryo, Scholastica Sylvan, Joseph O. Okpaku, Sr, Anne Githuku-Shongwe and Joseph Feeney. 2004. *Turning a Crisis into an Opportunity: Strategies for Scaling Up the National Response to the HIV/AIDS Pandemic in Lesotho*. New Rochelle, NY: Third Press Publishers.

Klaits, Frederick. 2010. *Death in a Church of Life: Moral Passion during Botswana's Time of AIDS*. Berkeley, CA: University of California Press.

Kohler, Hans-Peter, Susan C Watkins, Jere R Behrman, et al. 2015. "Cohort Profile: The Malawi Longitudinal Study of Families and Health (MLSFH)." *International Journal of Epidemiology* 44(2):394–404.

Koter, Dominika. 2013. "King makers: local leaders and ethnic politics in Africa." *World Politics* 65(2):187–232.

Kyed, Helene Maria and Lars Buur. 2007. Introduction: traditional authority and democratization in Africa. In *State Recognition and Democratization in Sub-Saharan Africa: A New Dawn for Traditional Authorities?*, ed. Helene Maria Kyed and Lars Buur. Palgrave MacMillan, pp. 1–28.

Lee, Melissa M and Melina Platas Izama. 2015. "Aid externalities: evidence from PEPFAR in Africa." *World Development* 67:281–94.

Li, Tania Murray. 2007. *The Will to Improve: Governmentality, Development, and the Practice of Politics*. Durham, NC: Duke University Press.

Lieberman, Evan. 2007. "Ethnic politics, risk, and policy-making: a cross-national statistical analysis of government responses to HIV/AIDS." *Comparative Political Studies* 40(12):1420–37.

Lieberman, Evan. 2009. *Boundaries of Contagion: How Ethnic Politics Have Shaped Government Responses to AIDS*. Princeton, NJ: Princeton University Press.

Logan, Carolyn. 2009. "Selected chiefs, elected councillors and hybrid democrats: popular perspectives on the co-existence of democracy and traditional authority." *The Journal of Modern African Studies* 47(01):101–28.

Logan, Carolyn. 2013. "The roots of resilience: exploring popular support for African traditional authorities." *African Affairs* 112(448):353–76.

Lordan, Grace, Kam Ki Tang and Fabrizio Carmignani. 2011. "Has HIV/AIDS displaced other health funding priorities? Evidence from a new dataset of development aid for health." *Social Science & Medicine* 73(3):351–5.

Lupia, Arthur. 1992. "Busy voters, agenda control, and the power of information." *American Political Science Review* 86(02):390–403.

Lupia, Arthur. 2003. Delegation and its perils. In *Delegation and Accountability in Parliamentary Democracies*, ed. Kaare Strøm, Wolfgang C Müller and Torbjörn Bergman. New York: Oxford University Press, pp. 33–54.

Lwanda, John Lloyd. 2002. Tikutha: the political culture of the HIV/AIDS epidemic in Malawi. In *A Democracy of Chameleons: Politics and Culture in the New Malawi*, ed. Harri Englund. Uppsala: Nordic Africa Institute.

Lwanda, John Lloyd. 2004. Politics culture and medicine: an unholy trinity? Historical continuities and ruptures in the HIV/AIDS story in Malawi. In *HIV & AIDS in Africa: Beyond Epidemiology*, ed. Ezekiel Kalipeni, Susan Craddock, Joseph R Oppong and Jayati Ghosh. Malden, MA: Blackwell Publishing.

Maccoby, Eleanor E and Nathan Maccoby. 1954. "The interview: a tool of social science." *Handbook of Social Psychology* 1:449–87.

MacKellar, Landis. 2005. "Priorities in global assistance for health, AIDS, and population." *Population and Development Review* 31(2):293–312.

Maes, Kenneth and Ippolytos Kalofonos. 2013. "Becoming and remaining community health workers: perspectives from Ethiopia and Mozambique." *Social Science & Medicine* 87:52–9.

Makoa, Francis K. 2004. "AIDS policy in Lesotho: implementation challenges." *African Security Studies* 13(1):71–7.

Makuwira, Jonathan. 2004. "Non-governmental organizations (NGOs) and participatory development in basic education in Malawi." *Current Issues in Comparative Education* 6(2):1–11.

Malamba, Samuel S, Jonathan H Mermin, Rebecca Bunnell, et al. 2005. "Couples at risk: HIV-1 concordance and discordance among sexual partners receiving voluntary counseling and testing in Uganda." *JAIDS Journal of Acquired Immune Deficiency Syndromes* 39(5): 576–80.

Mamdani, Mahmood. 1996. *Citizen and Subject: Contemporary Africa and the Legacy of Late Colonialism*. Princeton, NJ: Princeton University Press.

Manongi, Rachel, Tanya C Marchant and Ib Christian Bygbjerg. 2006. "Improving motivation among primary health care workers in Tanzania: a health worker perspective." *Human Resources for Health* 4(1):6.

Mansfield, Edward D and Diana C. Mutz. 2009. "Support for free trade: self-interest, sociotropic politics, and out-group anxiety." *International Organization* 63:425–57.

Mapanje, Jack. 2011. *And Crocodiles are Hungry at Night*. Oxfordshire: Ayebia Clarke Publishing Limited.

Mathauer, Inke and Ingo Imhoff. 2006. "Health worker motivation in Africa: the role of non-financial incentives and human resource management tools." *Human Resources for Health* 4(1):24.

McCoy, David, Sara Bennett, Sophie Witter, et al. 2008. "Salaries and incomes of health workers in sub-Saharan Africa." *The Lancet* 371(9613):675–81.

Miller, Gary. 1992. *Managerial Dilemmas*. Cambridge University Press.

Ministry of Finance [Malawi]. 2011. "Malawi Aid Atlas 2010/11FY." Lilongwe, Malawi: Ministry of Finance.

Ministry of Health HIV Unit [Malawi]. 2010. "Malawi Antiretroviral Treatment Programme Quarterly Report." Lilongwe, Malawi: Ministry of Health.

Ministry of Health [Malawi]. 2005. "Treatment of AIDS: A Five-Year Plan for the Provision of Antiretroviral Therapy and Good Management of HIV-Related Diseases to HIV-Infected Patients in Malawi 2006–2010." Lilongwe, Malawi: Ministry of Health.

Ministry of Health [Malawi]. 2010. "Quarterly HIV Programme Report, April–June 2010." Lilongwe, Malawi: Ministry of Health.

Mitchell, J. Clyde. 1949. "The political organization of the Yao of Southern Nyasaland." *African Studies* 8(3):141–59.

Mkandawire, Paul, Isaac N Luginaah and Rachel Bezner-Kerr. 2011. "Deadly divide: Malawi's policy debate on HIV/AIDS and condoms." *Policy Sciences* 44(1):81–102.

Mocroft, Amanda, Stefano Vella, Thomas Benfield, et al. 1998. "Changing patterns of mortality across Europe in patients infected with HIV-1." *The Lancet* 352(9142):1725–30.

Mocroft, Amanda, Bruno Ledergerber, Christine Katlama, et al. 2003. "Decline in the AIDS and death rates in the EuroSIDA study: an observational study." *The Lancet* 362(9377):22–9.

Moe, Terry M. 1984. "The new economics of organization." *American Journal of Political Science* 28(4):739–7.

Morfit, Simon. 2011. "'AIDS is money': how donor preferences reconfigure local realities." *World Development* 39(1):64–76.

Morris, Martina and Mirjam Kretzschmar. 1997. "Concurrent partnerships and the spread of HIV." *AIDS* 11(5):641–8.

Moyo, Dambisa. 2009. *Dead Aid: Why Aid Is Not Working and How There Is a Better Way for Africa.* New York: Farrar, Straus and Giroux.

Mshana, Gerry, Mary L Plummer, Joyce Wamoyi, et al. 2006. "She was bewitched and caught an illness similar to AIDS: AIDS and sexually transmitted infection causation beliefs in rural northern Tanzania." *Culture, Health & Sexuality* 8(1):45–58.

Mtika, Mike Mathambo. 2001. "The AIDS epidemic in Malawi and its threat to household food security." *Human Organization* 60(2): 178–88.

Mukherjee, Joia S, Paul Farmer, D Niyizonkiza, et al. 2003. "Tackling HIV in resource poor countries." *British Medical Journal* 327(7423): 1104–6.

Müller, Wolfgang C, Torbjörn Bergman and Kaare Strøm. 2003. Parliamentary democracy: promise and problems. In *Delegation and Accountability in Parliamentary Democracies*, ed. Kaare Strøm, Wolfgang C Müller and Torbjörn Bergman. New York: Oxford University Press, pp. 3–32.

Muralidharan, Karthik and Venkatesh Sundararaman. 2011. "Teacher performance pay: experimental evidence from India." *The Journal of Political Economy* 119(1):39–77.

Muriaas, Raghnild. 2009. "Local perspectives on the 'neutrality' of traditional authorities in Malawi, South Africa and Uganda." *Commonwealth and Comparative Politics* 47(1):28–51.

Murray, Christopher JL, Theo Vos, Rafael Lozano, et al. 2013. "Disability-adjusted life years (DALYs) for 291 diseases and injuries in 21 regions, 1990–2010: a systematic analysis for the Global Burden of Disease Study 2010." *The Lancet* 380(9859):2197–223.

Muula, Adamson S and Fresier C. Maseko. 2006. "How are health professionals earning their living in Malawi?" *BMC Health Services Research* 6(1):97.

Muula, Adamson S and Joseph M Mfutso-Bengo. 2005. "When is public disclosure of HIV seropositivity acceptable?" *Nursing Ethics* 12(3): 288–95.

Mwai, Grace W, Gitau Mburu, Kwasi Torpey, et al. 2013. "Role and outcomes of community health workers in HIV care in sub-Saharan Africa: a systematic review." *Journal of the International AIDS Society* 16(1).

Nahmias, AJ, J Weiss, X Yao, et al. 1986. "Evidence for human infection with an HTLV III/LAV-like virus in Central Africa, 1959." *The Lancet* 327(8492):1279–80.

National AIDS Commission [Malawi]. 2010. "Malawi HIV and AIDS Monitoring and Evaluation Report: 2008–2009 UNGASS Country Progress Report." Lilongwe, Malawi: Government of Malawi.

National AIDS Commission [Malawi]. 2014. "Global AIDS Response Progress Report (GARPR): Malawi Progress Report for 2013." Lilongwe, Malawi: Government of Malawi.

National Democratic Institute for International Affairs. 1995. "Traditional Authority and Democratic Governance in Malawi." Washington, DC: NDI.

National Statistical Office [Malawi]. 2008. "2008 Population and Housing Census Main Report." Zomba, Malawi: NSO.

National Statistical Office [Malawi] and ICF Macro. 2011. "Malawi Demographic and Health Survey 2010." Zomba, Malawi and Calverton, MD: NSO and ICF Macro.

National Statistical Office [Malawi] and Macro International Inc. 1997. "Malawi Knowledge, Attitudes and Practices in Health Survey 1996." Zomba, Malawi and Calverton, MD: NSO and Macro International Inc.

National Statistical Office [Malawi] and ORC Macro. 2001. "Malawi Demographic and Health Survey 2000." Zomba, Malawi and Calverton, MD: NSO and ORC Macro.

National Statistical Office [Malawi] and ORC Macro. 2005. "Malawi Demographic and Health Survey 2004." Zomba, Malawi and Calverton, MD: NSO and ORC Macro.

National Statistical Office [Malawi] and The DHS Program. 2016. "Malawi Demographic and Health Survey 2015–16 Key Indicators." Zomba, Malawi and Rockville, MD: NSO and ICF International.

National Statistical Office [Malawi] and United Nations Children's Fund. 2008. "Malawi Multiple Indicator Cluster Survey 2006." Zomba, Malawi: NSO.

Nattrass, Nicoli. 2009. "Poverty, sex and HIV." *AIDS and Behavior* 13(5):833–40.

Ntsebeza, Lungisile. 2006. *Democracy Compromised: Chiefs and the Politics of Land in South Africa*. Cape Town, South Africa: HSRC Press.

Ntsebeza, Lungisile. 2008. The resurgence of chiefs: retribalization and modernity in post-1994 South Africa. In *Readings in Modernity in Africa*, ed. Peter Geschiere, Birgit Meyer and Peter Pels. Bloomington, IN: Indiana University Press, pp. 71–9.

Oomman, Nandini, Michael Bernstein and Steven Rosenzweig. 2008. "Seizing the opportunity on AIDS and health systems." HIV/AIDS Monitor. Washington, DC: Center for Global Development.

Open Society Initiative for Southern Africa and Open Society Foundations Education Support Program. 2012. "The Role of the Education Sector in Providing Care & Support for Orphans & Vulnerable Children in Lesotho & Swaziland." Accessed 11/2/16 from www.opensocietyfoundations.org/sites/default/files/lesotho-and-swaziland-orphans-20130327.pdf.

Organisation for Economic Co-operation and Development. 2015. "DAC Statistics: Query Wizard for International Development Statistics (QWIDS)." Accessed 6/2/15 from: http://stats.oecd.org/qwids.

Ostergard, Robert L. 2002. "Politics in the hot zone: AIDS and national security in Africa." *Third World Quarterly* 23(2):333–50.

Paas, Steven. 2005. *Chichewa–Chinyanja English Dictionary*, Second Edition. Vol. Buku la Mvunguti No. 20 Zomba, Malawi: Kachere Series.

Painter, Thomas M. 2001. "Voluntary counseling and testing for couples: a high-leverage intervention for HIV/AIDS prevention in sub-Saharan Africa." *Social Science & Medicine* 53(11):1397–1411.

Parkhurst, Justin O, David Chilongozi and Eleanor Hutchinson. 2015. "Doubt, defiance, and identity: understanding resistance to male circumcision for HIV prevention in Malawi." *Social Science & Medicine* 135:15–22.

Parkhurst, Justin O and Louisiana Lush. 2004. "The political environment of HIV: lessons from a comparison of Uganda and South Africa." *Social Science & Medicine* 59(9):1913–24.

Patel, Nandini, Richard Tambulasi, Bright Molande and Andrew Mpesi. 2007. "Consolidating Democratic Governance in Southern Africa: Malawi." Technical Report Research Report No. 33 EISA.

Patterson, Amy S. 2006. *The Politics of AIDS in Africa*. Boulder, CO: Lynne Rienner Publishers.

Patterson, Amy S. 2011. *The Church and AIDS in Africa: The Politics of Ambiguity*. Boulder, CO: Lynne Rienner Publishers

Patterson, Amy S. 2018. *Africa and Global Health Governance: Domestic Politics and International Structures*. Baltimore, MD: Johns Hopkins University Press.

PEPFAR. 2013. "Malawi Operational Plan Report FY 2013." PEPFAR Website. Accessed 7/27/16 from www.pepfar.gov/documents/organization/228344.rtf.

Pepin, Jacques. 2011. *The Origins of AIDS*. New York: Cambridge University Press.

Peratsakis, Christian, Joshua Powell, Michael Findley, Justin Baker and Catherine Weaver. 2012. "Climate Coded and Geocoded Activity-Level Data from the Government of Malawi's Aid Management Platform." Washington, DC: AidData and the Robert S. Strauss Center for International Security and Law.

Peters, Pauline E. 1997. "Against the odds: matriliny, land and gender in the Shire Highlands of Malawi." *Critique of Anthropology* 17(2):189–210.

Peters, Pauline E, Peter A Walker and Daimon Kambewa. 2008. "Striving for normality in a time of AIDS in Malawi." *Journal of Modern African Studies* 46(4):659–87.

Pew Research Center. 2014. "Public Health a Major Priority in African Nations." Accessed 5/27/2015 from www.pewglobal.org/files/2014/04/Pew-Research-Center-Public-Health-in-Africa-Report-FINAL-MAY-1-2014.pdf.

Pfeiffer, James. 2004a. "Civil society, NGOs, and the holy spirit in Mozambique." *Human Organization* 63(3):359–72.

Pfeiffer, James. 2004b. "Condom social marketing, Pentecostalism, and structural adjustment in Mozambique: a clash of AIDS prevention messages." *Medical Anthropology Quarterly* 18(1):77–103.

Piot, Peter and Awa Marie Coll Seck. 2001. "International response to the HIV/AIDS epidemic: planning for success." *Bulletin of the World Health Organization* 79(12):1106–12.

Piot, Peter, Joan K Kreiss, Jeckoniah O Ndinya-Achola, et al. 1987. "Heterosexual transmission of HIV. Editorial review." *AIDS* 1(4):199–206.

Population Reference Bureau. 2016. *2016 World Population Data Sheet*. Washington, DC: PRB.

Posner, Daniel. 2004. "The political salience of cultural difference: why Chewas and Tumbukas are allies in Zambia and Adversaries in Malawi." *American Political Science Review* 98(04):529–45.

Posner, Daniel N. 1995. "Malawi's new dawn." *Journal of Democracy* 6(1):131–45.

Posner, Daniel N. 2005. *Institutions and Ethnic Politics in Africa*. New York: Cambridge University Press.

Poulin, Michelle and Adamson S Muula. 2011. "An inquiry into the uneven distribution of women's HIV infection in rural Malawi." *Demographic Research* 25(28):869–902.

Poulin, Michelle, Kathryn Dovel and Susan Cotts Watkins. 2016. "Men with money and the 'vulnerable women' client category in an AIDS epidemic." *World Development* 85:16–30.

Powers, Kimberly A, Azra C Ghani, William C Miller, et al. 2011. "The role of acute and early HIV infection in the spread of HIV and implications for transmission prevention strategies in Lilongwe, Malawi: a modelling study." *The Lancet* 378(9787):256–68.

Price-Smith, Andrew T. 2002. *The Health of Nations: Infectious Disease, Environmental Change, and Their Effects on National Security and Development.* Cambridge, MA: MIT Press.

Przeworski, Adam. 2003. *States and Markets: A Primer in Political Economy.* New York: Cambridge University Press.

Quinlan, Tim and Malcolm Wallis. 2003. Local governance in Lesotho: the central role of chiefs. In *Grassroots Governance? Chiefs in Africa and the Afro-Caribbean,* ed. Donald I Ray and PS Reddy. Calgary: University of Calgary Press, pp. 145–72.

Ramiah, Ilavenil and Michael R Reich. 2006. "Building effective public–private partnerships: experiences and lessons from the African Comprehensive HIV/AIDS Partnerships (ACHAP)." *Social Science & Medicine* 63(2):397–408.

Ray, Donald I. 2003. Rural local governance and traditional leadership in Africa and the Afro-Caribbean: policy and research implications from Africa to the Americas and Australasia. In *Grassroots Governance? Chiefs in Africa and the Afro-Caribbean,* ed. Donald I Ray and PS Reddy. Calgary: University of Calgary Press, pp. 1–30.

Reeve, Paul Anthony. 1989. "HIV infection in patients admitted to a general hospital in Malawi." *British Medical Journal* 298(6687):1567–8.

Reniers, Georges. 2008. "Marital strategies for regulating exposure to HIV." *Demography* 45(2):417–38.

Reniers, Georges and Jeffrey Eaton. 2009. "Refusal bias in HIV prevalence estimates from nationally representative seroprevalence surveys." *AIDS* 23(5):621–9.

Republic of Malawi. 2005. "Malawi HIV and AIDS Monitoring and Evaluation Report 2005: Follow-up to the Declaration of Commitment on HIV and AIDS (UNGASS)." Lilongwe, Malawi: Office of the President and Cabinet.

Republic of Malawi and National AIDS Commission [Malawi]. 2008. "HIV and Syphillis Sero-Survey and National HIV Prevalence and AIDS Estimates Report for 2007." Lilongwe, Malawi: National AIDS Commission.

Resnick, Danielle. 2013. Two steps forward, one step back: the limits of foreign aid on Malawi's democratic consolidation. In *Democratic Trajectories in Africa: Unraveling the Impact of Foreign Aid*, ed. Danielle Resnick and Nicolas van de Walle. New York: Oxford University Press, pp. 110–38.

Ribot, Jesse C. 1999. "Decentralisation, participation and accountability in Sahelian forestry: legal instruments of political-administrative control." *Africa* 69(1):23–65.

Robinson, Rachel Sullivan. 2017. *Intimate Interventions in Global Health: Family Planning and HIV Prevention in Sub-Saharan Africa*. New York: Cambridge University Press.

Romer, Thomas and Howard Rosenthal. 1978. "Political resource allocation, controlled agendas, and the status quo." *Public Choice* 33(4): 27–43.

Ryder, Robert W, Wato Nsa, Susan E Hassig, et al. 1989. "Perinatal transmission of the human immunodeficiency virus type 1 to infants of seropositive women in Zaire." *New England Journal of Medicine* 320(25):1637–42.

Sachs, Jeffrey D. 2005. *The End of Poverty*. New York: The Penguin Press.

Salehyan, Idean, Cullen S. Hendrix, Jesse Hamner, et al. 2012. "Social conflict in Africa: a new database." *International Interactions* 38(4): 503–11.

Schatz, Enid. 2005. " 'Take your mat and go!': rural Malawian women's strategies in the HIV/AIDS era." *Culture, Health & Sexuality* 7(5): 479–92.

Schneider, Helen, Hlengiwe Hlophe and Dingie van Rensburg. 2008. "Community health workers and the response to HIV/AIDS in South Africa: tensions and prospects." *Health Policy and Planning* 23(3):179–87.

Schocken, Celina. 2006. *Overview of the Global Fund to Fight AIDS, Tuberculosis and Malaria*. Washington, DC: Center for Global Development.

Schoepf, Brooke Grundfest. 1991. "Ethical, methodological and political issues of AIDS research in Central Africa." *Social Science & Medicine* 33(7):749–63.

Schoepf, Brooke Grundfest. 1992. "AIDS, sex and condoms: African healers and the reinvention of tradition in Zaire." *Medical Anthropology* 14:225–42.

Schou, Arild. 2009. "Who benefits from demand-driven distribution of HIV/AIDS services? An analysis of the emerging CBO sector in Malawi." *Public Administration and Development* 29:155–66.

Schou, Arild and Maxton Tsoka. 2012. "Governing the geographies of the nongovernmental organization sector: analyzing coverage challenges in the HIV/AIDS campaign in Malawi." *Journal of HIV/AIDS & Social Services* 11(3):305–21.

Schwartländer, Bernhard, John Stover, Neff Walker, et al. 2001. "Resource needs for HIV/AIDS." *Science* 292(5526):2434–36.

Scott, James C. 1998. *Seeing Like a State: How Certain Schemes to Improve the Human Condition Have Failed*. New Haven, CT: Yale University Press.

Sears, David O, Carl P Hensler and Leslie K Speer. 1979. "Whites' opposition to 'busing': self-interest or symbolic politics?" *American Political Science Review* 73(2):369–84.

Sears, David O and Carolyn L Funk. 1990. Self-interest in Americans' political opinions. In *Beyond Self-Interest*, ed. Jane J Mansbridge. Chicago: The University of Chicago Press, pp. 147–70.

Serwadda, David, Nelson Sewankambo, J. Wilson Carswell, et al. 1985. "Slim disease: a new disease in Uganda and its association with HTLV-III infection." *The Lancet* 326(8460):849–52.

Shiffman, Jeremy. 2006a. "Donor funding priorities for communicable disease control in the developing world." *Health Policy and Planning* 21(6):411–20.

Shiffman, Jeremy. 2006b. "HIV/AIDS and the rest of the global health agenda." *Bulletin of the World Health Organization* 84(12):923.

Shiffman, Jeremy. 2008. "Has donor prioritization of HIV/AIDS displaced aid for other health issues?" *Health Policy and Planning* 23(2):95–100.

Shiffman, Jeremy. 2009. "A social explanation for the rise and fall of global health issues." *Bulletin of the World Health Organization* 87(8):608–13.

Shilts, Randy. 1987. *And the Band Played On: Politics, People, and the AIDS Epidemic*. New York: St. Martin's Press.

Short, Philip. 1974. *Banda*. London: Routledge & Kegan Paul.

Smiddy, Kimberly and Daniel J Young. 2009. "Presidential and parliamentary elections in Malawi, May 2009." *Electoral Studies* 28(4):662–6.

Smith, Adrian D, Placide Tapsoba, Norbert Peshu, Eduard J Sanders and Harold W Jaffe. 2009. "Men who have sex with men and HIV/AIDS in sub-Saharan Africa." *The Lancet* 374(9687):416–22.

Smith, Kirsten P and Susan Cotts Watkins. 2005. "Perceptions of risk and strategies for prevention: responses to HIV/AIDS in rural Malawi." *Social Science & Medicine* 60(3):649–60.

Stover, John, Stefano Bertozzi, Juan-Pablo Gutierrez, et al. 2006. "The global impact of scaling up HIV/AIDS prevention programs in low-and middle-income countries." *Science* 311(5766):1474–6.

Stover, John, Neff Walker, Geoff P Garnett, et al. 2002. "Can we reverse the HIV/AIDS pandemic with an expanded response?" *The Lancet* 360(9326):73–7.

Sturges, Paul and George Chimseu. 1996. "The chain of information provision in the villages of Malawi: a rapid rural appraisal." *International Information and Library Review* 28(2):135–56.

Swidler, Ann. 2013. Cultural sources of institutional resilience: lessons from chieftaincy in rural Malawi. In *Social Resilience in the Neoliberal Era*, ed. Peter A Hall and Michéle Lamont. New York: Cambridge University Press, pp. 319–45.

Swidler, Ann and Susan Cotts Watkins. 2009. " 'Teach a man to fish': the sustainability doctrine and its social consequences." *World Development* 37(7):1182–96.

Swidler, Ann and Susan Cotts Watkins. 2017. *A Fraught Embrace: The Romance and Reality of AIDS Altruism in Africa*. Princeton, NJ: Princeton University Press.

Tanui, Kipkoech and Nixon Ng'ang'a. 2006. "Corruption in Kenya's National AIDS Control Council." Transparency Watch, Transparency International Kenya.

The Economist Intelligence Unit. 1999. "Malawi: Country Profile 1998–99." London: The Economist Intelligence Unit.

The Economist Intelligence Unit. 2006. "Malawi: Country Profile 2006." London: The Economist Intelligence Unit.

The Global Fund to Fight AIDS, Tuberculosis and Malaria. 2016. "Financials." Global Fund Website. Accessed 7/27/16 from www .theglobalfund.org/en/financials/.

Thornton, Rebecca L. 2008. "The demand for, and impact of, learning HIV status." *American Economic Review* 98(5):1829–63.

Timberg, Craig and Daniel Halperin. 2012. *Tinderbox: How the West Sparked the AIDS Epidemic and How the World can Finally Overcome It*. New York: The Penguin Press.

Trinitapoli, Jenny. 2006. "Religious responses to AIDS in sub-Saharan Africa: an examination of religious congregations in rural Malawi." *Review of Religious Research* 253–70.

Trinitapoli, Jenny and Alexander Weinreb. 2012. *Religion and AIDS in Africa*. New York: Oxford University Press.

UNAIDS. 2002. "Ancient Remedies, New Disease: Involving Traditional Healers in Increasing Access to AIDS Care and Prevention in East Africa." Geneva, Switzerland: UNAIDS.

UNAIDS. 2004. "2004 Report on the Global AIDS Epidemic." Geneva, Switzerland: UNAIDS.

UNAIDS. 2005. "The 'Three Ones' in Action: Where We Are and Where We Go from Here." Geneva, Switzerland: UNAIDS.

UNAIDS. 2007. "2006 UNAIDS Annual Report: Making the Money Work." Geneva, Switzerland: UNAIDS.

UNAIDS. 2008. "2008 Report on the Global AIDS Epidemic." Geneva, Switzerland: UNAIDS.

UNAIDS. 2013. "Global Report: UNAIDS Report on the Global AIDS Epidemic 2013." Geneva, Switzerland: UNAIDS.

UNAIDS. 2015. "How AIDS Changed Everything." Geneva, Switzerland: UNAIDS.

UNAIDS. 2016. "AIDSinfo Online Database." Accessed 12/28/16 from http://aidsinfo.unaids.org/.

UNAIDS. 2017. "AIDSinfo Online Database." Accessed 8/2/17 from http://aidsinfo.unaids.org/.

U.S. President's Emergency Plan for AIDS Relief. 2015. "PEPFAR Dashboard." Accessed 2/14/16 from https://data.pepfar.net.

USAID, UNAIDS, WHO and The POLICY Project. 2003. *The Level of Effort in the National Response to HIV/AIDS: The AIDS Program Effort Index (API) 2003 Round*. Washington, DC: POLICY Project, Futures Group International.

van de Walle, Nicolas. 2001. *African Economies and the Politics of Permanent Crisis, 1979–1999*. New York: Cambridge University Press.

van Griensven, Frits. 2007. "Men who have sex with men and their HIV epidemics in Africa." *AIDS* 21(10):1361–2.

Verheijen, Janneke. 2013. *Balancing Men, Morals and Money: Women's Agency between HIV and Security in a Malawi Village*. Vol. 53. Leiden, the Netherlands: African Studies Centre.

Vidal, Nicole, Martine Peeters, Claire Mulanga-Kabeya, et al. 2000. "Unprecedented degree of human immunodeficiency virus type 1 (HIV-1) group M genetic diversity in the Democratic Republic of Congo suggests that the HIV-1 pandemic originated in Central Africa." *Journal of Virology* 74(22):10498–507.

VonDoepp, Peter. 2005. "The problem of judicial control in Africa's neopatrimonial democracies: Malawi and Zambia." *Political Science Quarterly* 120(2):275–301.

VonDoepp, Peter. 2006. "Politics and judicial assertiveness in emerging democracies: High Court behavior in Malawi and Zambia." *Political Research Quarterly* 59(3):389–99.

VonDoepp, Peter and Daniel J Young. 2013. "Assaults on the fourth estate: explaining media harassment in Africa." *Journal of Politics* 75(1): 36–51.

Walton, David, Paul Farmer, Wesler Lambert, et al. 2004. "Integrated HIV prevention and care strengthens primary health care: lessons from rural Haiti." *Journal of Public Health Policy* 25(2):137–58.

Watkins, Susan Cotts. 2004. "Navigating the AIDS epidemic in rural Malawi." *Population and Development Review* 30(4): 673–705.

Watkins, Susan Cotts and Ann Swidler. 2009. "Hearsay ethnography: conversational journals as a method for studying culture in action." *Poetics* 37(2):162–84.

Watkins, Susan Cotts, Eliya M. Zulu, Hans-Peter Kohler and Jere R. Behrman. 2003. "Introduction to: social interactions and HIV/AIDS in rural Africa." *Demographic Research* 1:1–30.

West, Harry G and Scott Kloeck-Jenson. 1999. "Betwixt and between: traditional authority and democratic decentralization in post-war Mozambique." *African Affairs* 98(393):455–84.

Whiteside, Alan, Robert Mattes, Samantha Willan and Ryann Manning. 2004. What people really believe about HIV/AIDS in Southern Africa. In *The Political Economy of AIDS in Africa*, ed. Nana Poku and Alan Whiteside. Burlington, VT: Ashgate Publishing Company, pp. 127–50.

Whiteside, Alan. 2009. "Is AIDS Exceptional?" AIDS 2031 Working Paper No. 25.

Whitford, Andrew B. 2005. "The pursuit of political control by multiple principals." *Journal of Politics* 67(1):28–49.

Williams, J. Michael. 2010. *Chieftaincy, the State, and Democracy: Political Legitimacy in Post-Apartheid South Africa.* Bloomington, IN: Indiana University Press.

Wilson, Anika. 2013. *Folklore, Gender, and AIDS in Malawi.* New York: Palgrave MacMillan.

Wirtz, Andrea L, Vincent Jumbe, Gift Trapence et al. 2013. "HIV among men who have sex with men in Malawi: elucidating HIV prevalence and correlates of infection to inform HIV prevention." *Journal of the International AIDS Society* 16(4).

World Bank. 2007. "Implementation Completion Report (IDA-34150) on a Credit in the Amount of US$50 Million to the National AIDS Control Council Government of Kenya for a HIV/AIDS Disaster Response Project." www-wds.worldbank.org/external/default/WDSContentServer/WDSP/IB/2007/05/09/000020953_20070509095903/Rendered/INDEX/36852.txt.

World Bank. 2014. "PovcalNet: The On-line Tool for Poverty Measurement Developed by the Development Research Group of the World Bank." http://iresearch.worldbank.org/PovcalNet/.

World Health Organization. 2007. "Male Circumcision and HIV Prevention: Operations Research Implications." Nairobi, Kenya: World Health Organization Report of an International Consultation.

World Health Organization. 2009. "Rapid Advice: Antiretroviral Therapy for HIV Infection in Adults and Adolescents." Geneva, Switzerland: World Health Organization.

World Health Organization. 2012. "Guidance on Couples HIV Testing and Counselling Including Antiretroviral Therapy for Treatment and

Prevention in Serodiscordant Couples: Recommendations for a Public
Health Approach." Geneva, Switzerland: World Health Organization.

World Health Organization Regional Office for Africa. 2013. *Progress in
Scaling Up Voluntary Medical Male Circumcision for HIV Prevention
in East and Southern Africa, January–December 2012*. Brazzaville:
WHO Regional Office for Africa.

Worobey, Michael, Marlea Gemmel, Dirk E Teuwen, et al. 2008. "Direct
evidence of extensive diversity of HIV-1 in Kinshasa by 1960." *Nature*
455(7213):661–4.

Wroe, Daniel. 2012. "Donors, dependency, and political crisis in Malawi."
African Affairs 111(442):135–44.

Yamba, Christian Bawa. 2005. "Loveness and her brothers: trajectories of
life for children orphaned by HIV/AIDS in Zambia." *African Journal
of AIDS Research* 4(3):205–10.

Youde, Jeremy. 2007. "Ideology's role in AIDS policies in Uganda and
South Africa." *Global Health Governance* 1(1).

Youde, Jeremy. 2012. "Public opinion and support for government AIDS
policies in sub-Saharan Africa." *Social Science & Medicine* 74(1):52–7.

Young, Daniel J. 2014. "An initial look into party switching in Africa:
evidence from Malawi." *Party Politics* 20(1):105–15.

Zachariah, Rony, Anthony David Harries, Marcel Manzi, et al. 2006.
"Acceptance of anti-retroviral therapy among patients infected with
HIV and tuberculosis in rural Malawi is low and associated with cost
of transport." *PloS one* 1(1):e121.

Index

Action Aid, 84–85
African Comprehensive HIV/AIDS Partnership (ACHAP), 33
Afrobarometer, 9, 65, 66, 107–110, 117, 120, 137–138, 151, 167, 168
AidData, 82
AIDS
  orphans, 128, 142–145, 154
  stigma, 19, 21–22, 73, 74–75, 100, 118–122
AIDS Program Effort Index (API), 24, 80
Annan, Kofi, 27, 124
Anti-Corruption Bureau (ACB), 64
anti-retroviral (ARV) therapy, 6–8, 14–15, 23, 36, 69, 73–74, 95, 124, 146
Apartheid, 129, 131

bakgatla, 152
Balaka, 90, 94, 100, 135, 139–141, 143–144
Banda, Hastings Kamuzu, 63, 66, 79–80, 134
Banda, Joyce, 64–65, 84
Beautify Malawi (BEAM) Trust, 83–84
Benin, 42, 130
Blantyre, 70, 73, 139
Bor, Jacob, 24
Botswana, 32–33, 107, 109–110, 151–152
Briggs, Ryan, 64
budget, 24–25, 28–29, 62, 64, 68, 84, 85, 87, 104

CARE Malawi, 165
Chewa (people), 72, 94, 96–97, 100, 138
Chichewa, 90–93, 135

chiefs, 1–2, 47–50, 57–59, 91–93, 98–100, 126–159, 160–162, 166–167
Chimbalanga, Tiwonge, 68–69
Chisupe, Billy, 77–78
Chitumbuka, 90–91
Chiyao, 90–91
circumcision (male), 16, 23, 73, 83, 85–89, 152–153
civil society, 25, 28, 32, 51, 76, 78, 81, 83–85, 167
Clinton Foundation, 48, 82. *See also* philanthropy
community based organizations (CBOs), 47, 49, 53, 78, 81–82, 124–125, 126–127, 158
Congo, Democratic Republic of, 19, 22, 31
Constituency AIDS Control Committees (CACCs), 52–54
corruption, 4, 11, 52, 53, 63–64, 83–85, 124, 158, 162, 164

decentralization, 52–53, 129, 136–137, 158
Democratic Progressive Party (DPP), 64–65, 67
Demographic and Health Surveys (DHS), 10, 72, 94, 98, 120–121
Department of Defense (U.S.), 28, 85–88
disconnect, 31–38, 85–89, 161
donors. *See* foreign aid.

East Africa, 2, 24, 80, 87
England, Roger, 35
Europe, 29, 31, 48, 82, 93, 161

Ford Foundation, 30
foreign aid, 9, 26–30, 36–37, 40, 64, 68–69, 74, 80, 82–88, 92–93,